Becoming
Two in Love

Becoming
Two in Love

*Kierkegaard, Irigaray, and
the Ethics of Sexual Difference*

ROLAND J. DE VRIES

⌒PICKWICK *Publications* • Eugene, Oregon

BECOMING TWO IN LOVE
Kierkegaard, Irigaray, and the Ethics of Sexual Difference

Copyright © 2013 Roland J. De Vries. All rights reserved. Except for brief quotations in critical publications or reviews, no part of this book may be reproduced in any manner without prior written permission from the publisher. Write: Permissions, Wipf and Stock Publishers, 199 W. 8th Ave., Suite 3, Eugene, OR 97401.

Pickwick Publications
An Imprint of Wipf and Stock Publishers
199 W. 8th Ave., Suite 3
Eugene, OR 97401

www.wipfandstock.com

ISBN 13: 978-1-61097-517-9

Cataloguing-in-Publication data:

De Vries, Roland J.

Becoming two in love : Kierkegaard, Irigaray, and the ethics of sexual difference / Roland J. De Vries.

xx + 236 pp. ; 23 cm. Includes bibliographical references and index.

ISBN 13: 978-1-61097-517-9

1. Kierkegaard, Søren, 1813–1855. 2. Irigaray, Luce. 3. Sex role—Religious aspects—Christianity. 4. Sex—Religious aspects—Christianity. I. Title.

BT708 D297 2013

Manufactured in the U.S.A.

The poem "Roofing" published in *Poems* 1975–1995 by Micheal O'Siadhail Copyright © 1999 by Bloodaxe Books Ltd. (www.bloodaxebooks.com). Used by permission of the publisher.

For my parents

Roofing

A livelong day, a night's secrecies:
Only the rafters themselves must know
The beams' strains and stresses, slow
Givings and takings, the touch and go
Of our attunements and compromise, how
We raise the roof or make our peace.

A timber's head nestles in another's,
A mitred joint, this bevelled match,
Two beams and their collar-beam which
Shape a triangle, the tie and apex
Of togetherness. So easily one forgets
Couples are a liaison of two rafters.

And always under us or in between
That dangerous breach we never close,
A zone for household gods we choose
Or need. Here, then, allow some room
For unlike memories, dreams to dream,
A living space for a separate passion.

A roof is framing our slanted intimacy.
Unless each of these matching couples
Beds snugly down into opposite walls,
The timbers sag. Somehow we're stronger
In separateness; this slopping encounter
Our braced ridge, our tie of ecstasy.

Micheal O'Siadhail
Poems 1975–1995

Contents

Illustrations   viii

Acknowledgments   ix

Introduction   xi

PART ONE: Irigaray and Love's Possibility

1. The Negative: Toward a Culture of Sexual Difference   3
2. Mind the Gap: The Ethics of Sexual Difference   37

PART TWO: Kierkegaard and Love's Promise

3. Søren Kierkegaard: God as the Middle Term   69
4. Judge William: Human Becoming and Sexual Difference   108

PART THREE: Between Irigaray and Kierkegaard

5. Sexual Difference   149
6. Intersubjectivity   181
7. Communication   203

Bibliography   221

Index   233

Illustrations

Figure 1	Kierkegaard's view of intersubjectivity	72
Figure 2	Judge William on human becoming	125, 156
Figure 3	A Kierkegaardian theory of sexual difference	164
Figure 4	An augmented Kierkegaardian theory of sexual difference	166
Figure 5	A Kierkegaardian ethics of sexual difference	182
Figure 6	Self Love in Irigaray	190
Figure 7	Self Love in a Kierkegaardian ethics of sexual difference	193

Acknowledgments

As this volume goes to print, I want to extend heartfelt thanks to my wife Becky for her encouragement, support, and presence in my life and work—not least in the tasks of writing, editing, and revising. And along with Becky, my joyful thanks to our children Tabea and Reuben and Esther for being constant and delightful distractions from the quotidian. Their energy and life have been energy and life for me through writing and revisions.

Two communities of faith have provided a spiritual home to me and to my family over the past years (as well as freedom to pursue academic endeavors) and I extend my thanks to Westminster Presbyterian Church and Kensington Presbyterian Church for their gracious hospitality, and for the path we have shared on the way with Christ together.

For their friendship in life and faith along the way, I also express my gratitude to Cameron and Kerry, John and Lynn, Clyde, Dan, Steve and Sandy, and Harry and Marianne, and many others who are not mentioned here.

In the task of writing and revising, there have been various individuals who offered support by reading and offering critical comment on sections of this volume. First among these is Douglas Farrow, my thesis supervisor, who offered invaluable insight along the way, from the first development of my thesis proposal all the way to the publication of this revised version of my doctoral thesis. To him I offer a heartfelt thank you. I am also grateful to Alison Stone, Patricia Kirkpatrick, Daniel Shute, Francis Watson, and Luce Irigaray, each of whom has offered comment on some portion of what follows. My appreciation is also extended to those who engaged meaningfully with my work in the context of the Doktorklub meeting of the McGill Faculty of Religious Studies and the 2006 Irigaray Seminar at the University of Nottingham.

My thanks also to Robin Parry and all of the staff at Wipf and Stock for their professionalism and care in bringing this project to completion.

Acknowledgments

I would not have made it this far without significant financial support, and I express my gratitude to those organizations that have supported my work in a monetary way: McGill University; The Faculty of Religious Studies, McGill University; The Cameron Doctoral Bursary Committee of the Presbyterian Church in Canada; and The Priscilla and Stanford Reid Trust. The generosity of these has surpassed expectations.

This volume is dedicated to my parents, Frank De Vries and Aartje De Vries (née Baak). The thanks I owe them are beyond what can be expressed here.

Introduction

From start to finish, the present volume is a profoundly personal work. This is so not only because its subject matter is decidedly personal (it deals with the relationship between man and woman, and the difference between them) but for other reasons also. Without denying that serious and rigorous analysis unfolds within these pages, at the outset we can and should also acknowledge the profoundly personal nature of the work. Of course almost every piece of academic research or scholarly writing has some personal dimension to it—thus it could fairly be asked whether the personal nature of this particular work requires illumination. The only response I will offer to this question or objection, however, is the substance of this introduction, within which I will outline two salient, personal dimensions of this work. I leave it to the reader to assess whether I have made the case that these personal realities are both vital to the work and an apt subject for its introduction.

Discovering Irigaray: A Parable

In his *Nicomachean Ethics*, Aristotle insists that political science, or ethics, is not an exact science and therefore does not admit of precise conclusions. Rather, since the subject matter of ethics is the conventions of a given culture (and not nature itself), the truths of political science, or ethics, can be described only roughly and in outline. Without offering any kind of analysis of Aristotle's argument, it is likely that his methodological assumptions will resonate with us, since in our own ethical reflection we are often led to conclusions that are less than precise.

Going a step beyond Aristotle, while continuing in the broad trajectory of his thought, it is perhaps uncontroversial to insist that in the realm of ethical reflection we are also often shaped by experiences and intuitions that are not entirely transparent to us—we are often attracted to certain ethical principles, or convinced of specific injunctions, without fully

Introduction

comprehending the basis of these principles or injunctions, or our attraction to them. There is invariably something "intuitive" about ethical reflection and action. Otherwise put, we are shaped by cultural, philosophical, and theological presuppositions that we hold in a habitual way and may not have subjected to critical analysis. This is not necessarily cause for embarrassment (intellectual or otherwise) since to some extent it simply reflects the nature of the human and the nature of ethical reflection.

This particular work began its life as a doctoral dissertation and, before that, as a series of vague notions about how something constructive might arise out of a conversation between Luce Irigaray and Søren Kierkegaard on the question of sexual difference. Taking a step even further back, there is also the question of how I was first introduced to the thought of Irigaray. In fact, my introduction to the thought and writings of Irigaray is, in important ways, illustrative of the assumption we have been describing—namely, that our ethical commitments often originate in somewhat vague or amorphous notions of what is good, true, and beautiful. It is worth sharing the story of my introduction to Irigaray in order to demonstrate how this is so, at the same time demonstrating the decidedly personal nature of this work and of the ethical enterprise generally.

While attending an academic conference in 2005, I entered into an informal discussion with one of the speakers, with the conversation eventually coming around to the subject of possible dissertation topics. The person in question was aware of my general interests and suggested that I look at the writings of a French feminist who had written on the subject of sexual difference. Some weeks later, taking him up on the suggestion, I began to do some preliminary research on this possibility—though I was immediately confronted with the problem that I couldn't remember the name of the French feminist he had mentioned. A few internet searches later I had hit upon the name of Luce Irigaray and had generated a list of various works by Irigaray held in the McGill University library system. I began my reading with three volumes I would later come to understand belong to the third phrase of Irigaray's oeuvre: namely, *Je, Tu, Nous: Toward a Culture of Difference*; *I Love to You: Sketch of a Possible Felicity in History*; and *To Be Two*.

As I began reading, I was immediately intrigued by, and enamored with, both the style and content of Irigaray's works. Her account of the relationship of woman and man in difference was imaginative and refreshing, opening up possibilities for both distance and encounter that struck me as compelling and hopeful. The reasons for this initial interest

Introduction

in Irigaray's work were, to some extent, not transparent to me—though it is fair to suggest that my own personal experiences as well as my cultural and religious formation played an important part in the formation of these initial impressions. In any case, this initial interest and these initial intuitions were sufficient to lead me deeper into her work, the assumption being that there was something on offer that might make a difference both to my own relationships and self-understanding and to the wider life of western societies. Whether or not Irigaray's thought could ultimately be reconciled with the basic theological framework that I hold both personally and intentionally was a question that remained open for me—as was the question of whether I would find her thought ultimately coherent and compelling. However, without having reached a clear or final answer on either of these questions, the exploration of Irigaray's writings continued.

The present volume, then, represents a deeper engagement with the writings of Luce Irigaray as I seek to demonstrate that my initial impression of (the promise of) her writings was not misplaced or mistaken. Indeed, my conclusion will be that Irigaray's account of the relationship of man and woman in difference—her ethics of sexual difference—is indeed coherent, and can be embraced within a specifically theological framework. Otherwise put: her writings have a contribution to make in the development of a specifically *theological* ethics of sexual difference. On the way to this conclusion, and to this theological ethics of sexual difference, the first two chapters of this work will explore (i) Irigaray's theory of sexual difference as it is expressed in her reformulation of the Hegelian negative, and (ii) Irigaray's description of an ethical intersubjectivity between man and woman as it is expressed through wonder, through the caress, and through particular patterns of speech/silence. Having provided this outline and analysis of her thought, I will proceed to draw Irigaray into conversation with Kierkegaard—who becomes a representative, here, of the broad, Christian theological tradition within which I would locate myself.

Before turning to a second and important personal dimension of the present work, it is worth pointing out that there was some degree of serendipity or providence at play in my discovery of, and initial engagement with, the writings of Luce Irigaray. Several months after that encounter with Professor Daniel Cere (the speaker I encountered at that conference in 2005) I encountered him again in another context. He picked up the conversation where we had left off by asking: "So, did you ever get around to looking at the work of Sylviane Agacinski." [Pregnant pause.] My internal reply was, "Who?" Of course it quickly became apparent that, following

xiii

Introduction

our previous conversation, I had gone looking for a French feminist of difference named Sylviane Agacinski (whose name had escaped me) but had discovered a French feminist of difference named Luce Irigaray.[1] In any case, at that point I sufficiently engaged with, and interested in the writings of Irigaray that there would be no turning back.

In telling this story there is perhaps some feeling of awkwardness—either at my forgetfulness or at my initial ignorance of the names and writings of these two French intellectuals and authors. Yet any such awkwardness is finally misplaced since this story clearly illustrates the necessarily personal dimension of every academic or intellectual endeavor. The story of my initial encounter and engagement with Irigaray reflects an approach to theological ethics (we could go as far as to call it a "methodology") in which it is assumed that great clarity and precision are not always granted or achieved, particularly at the outset of any such ethical inquiry. We often begin with intuitions, hopes, and aspirations (in this case, regarding the relationship between man and woman), and then discover where they lead us. The present work represents a venturing down that path of discovery.

A similar, personal story could of course be told with reference to my introduction to the thought of Kierkegaard, and to his *Works of Love* more specifically, a text that takes centre stage in the pages that follow. In fact, there has been a more general rediscovery of that non-pseudonymous and specifically religious text over the past decade, particularly with the publication of M. Jamie Ferreira's *Love's Grateful Striving: A Commentary on Kierkegaard's Works of Love*, in 2001. Having been relegated to the sidelines of Kierkegaard scholarship over many decades, Kierkegaard's imaginative and theological approach to the ethics of intersubjectivity (in *Works of Love*) now finds an appropriate place of prominence within Kierkegaard scholarship generally and within my development of a theological ethics of sexual difference.

Where Do You Stand?

We have already alluded to a further personal question that is important to this exploration of sexual difference—namely, the question of where one stands within the broad scope of the western tradition, theologically

---

1. Among other of her writings, of course, Sylviane Agacinski is known for her *Parity of the Sexes,* in which she insists on sexual difference as a universal trait that cannot be ignored.

Introduction

speaking. It is a question of where I stand, of where the reader stands, and of where Luce Irigaray stands. In her Introduction to the section on religion and spirituality in *Key Writings*, Irigaray writes as follows: "As many people in Europe, I was born and educated in a Christian context. Also, as many people, upon becoming an adult, I left my own tradition, at least the conscious part of it. Later, I came to understand that a religious dimension is an important aspect of our culture and that it is crucial in considering both how we have been determined by this dimension and how we can, in the present, situate ourselves with respect to it."[2] While the religious dimension is an important feature of Western culture, and one that Irigaray remains profoundly and personally aware of, the Christian tradition is nevertheless not Irigaray's in a determinative or normative sense. Indeed, her reference to "becoming an adult," should be read as a (not so gentle, perhaps) judgment of those who remain uncritically situated within the Christian tradition—of those who fail to mature and to achieve a "critical distance" from the tradition. That is, in referring to her "becoming an adult," Irigaray is moving beyond mere description into prescription. She goes on to argue: "I also have understood that we have to become adult and responsible towards our tradition and that which it has produced in ourselves: that is, neither to remain children nor to become iconoclasts."[3]

Irigaray's posture toward the Christian tradition, however, is neither one of complete repudiation nor of mere acquiescence. Rather, she seeks a middle ground between these two possible responses.[4] In continuing to speak of a mature and adult engagement with Christianity, Irigaray describes the intention of her work as follows: "Thus, I tried to make apparent the main spiritual aspects of my tradition, and to render them fruitful for a becoming divine of my feminine subjectivity. I think that such work was necessary for my own liberation, but also for a human liberation in which the Christian tradition represents a crucial historical step and has still a decisive function to secure when it is faithful to its spiritual message."[5] Again, the language employed by Irigaray suggests that she is at a significant remove from the classical Christian tradition, since most within that tradition would be hesitant to write of the "becoming divine

---

2. Irigaray, *Key Writings*, 145.

3. Ibid.

4. To suggest that Irigaray seeks a middle ground between acquiescence and repudiation, of course, is not to say much at all. However, these are the terms within which Irigaray articulates her own sense of how one must relate to the tradition.

5. Irigaray, *Key Writings*, 145.

of my feminine subjectivity" (and not only because the majority of those writers have been men). Indeed, in her essay entitled "The Redemption of Women," Irigaray assumes a decidedly more critical tone with respect to the teachings of Christianity as she explores what she refers to as the incarnation of Jesus Christ, in the body of a woman, at the behest of God the Father. She writes: "For years I have tried to navigate on the raft of such truths, such dogmas. I trusted them, was wounded by them, and then distanced myself from them." Importantly, however, she adds: "I have come back to them, but to question and no longer to submit blindly. To me, this task seemed a necessary one, but also for all women and all men in search of their liberation."[6] Thus she concludes: "I have . . . returned to my tradition in a more enlightened manner, more autonomous as a woman, and with a little Far Eastern culture which has given me some perspective on my own beliefs and taught me much about the figure of Jesus."[7]

For Irigaray, the Christian tradition is significant because of the mutual implication of the Western tradition and Christianity with each other. Since we are shaped, in profound ways, by the social, historical, and philosophical context into which we are born and within which we live, and cannot simply step outside of it or repudiate it, Irigaray argues that we must both recognize our tradition and seek to distance ourselves from it in the process of human becoming. To the extent that the tradition contributes to human becoming it is to be embraced (or its narratives and doctrines reinterpreted, accordingly), and to the extent that it prevents such a becoming it is to be repudiated.

Importantly, then, Irigaray does not construe human becoming according to the vision of fulfilled humanity expressed in the theological commitments of the classical Christian tradition. Rather, for Irigaray the maturing and becoming of the human must be understood in terms of the philosophy and culture of sexual difference that she herself articulates. However, this creates certain methodological difficulties for anyone who wishes to learn from Irigaray while remaining rooted, both methodologically and substantively, within the Christian tradition. For example, according to the theological presuppositions that shape my own engagement with Irigaray, human becoming can only be understood and experienced with reference to Jesus Christ, the one in whom God creates the world and through whom creation comes to fulfillment. The tension between these theological commitments and the thought of Irigaray is sufficient that our

6. Ibid., 150.
7. Ibid., 150–51.

Introduction

engagement with Irigaray will require a simple refusal of various aspects of her thought, even as her own thought has required a refusal of various aspects of the Christian tradition. And yet, as I will argue, this does not prevent us from engaging profitably with Irigaray—it does not mean that we cannot learn from her.

We can turn briefly, and helpfully, to Bruce Marshall's *Trinity and Truth*, and to his concept of "epistemic primacy," to clarify the nature of our engagement with Irigaray. Marshall points out that the classical Christian tradition has always included beliefs and truth claims that are not central or vital to the identity of the Christian community. That is, as we proceed outward from the central and identity-constituting truth claims of the tradition, we arrive at beliefs and truth claims that are not vital to the identity of the church. These tertiary beliefs and truth claims are such that the church can amend or even reject them in the face of *novel* truth claims that call these tertiary beliefs into question. Novel truth claims, according to Marshall, are "claims which the Christian community and its members have encountered as live options for belief, but about whose epistemic status the community has on the whole not yet come to a decision." Such novel claims come with reasons attached—reasons that might make these claims persuasive—and will at times impinge closely enough on the identity-forming beliefs of the community that it is worth the trouble for the church to expend time, energy, and prayer in deciding about their truth.[8] Although Marshall is dealing with specifically theological questions (and not with broader ethical questions), it is no stretch to extend his analysis to our knowledge of the created order and of human nature and identity as central to that order.

The classical Christian tradition, in the light of God's self-revelation in Jesus Christ, makes certain claims about the nature of the human and of the created order. But others outside of that tradition also make claims about the nature of the created order. And the claims of those outside of the tradition may confront the Christian community in such a way that it finds itself compelled to either refuse or accommodate or embrace these novel claims. With respect to Irigaray's thought, while we must refuse various of her theological commitments, we are not necessarily compelled to reject everything she has to say about sexual difference or about intersubjectivity between woman and man. Indeed, Irigaray's insistence on the human as two (and not as one)—as both woman and man—resonates with the insistence of the classical Christian tradition that God created the

---

8. Marshall, *Trinity and Truth*, 140.

Introduction

human as male and female, together. It is a question, then, of whether the novel claims of Irigaray, concerning the nature of sexual difference and of mediation between the sexes, are consistent with the epistemic primacy of Jesus Christ, and might be incorporated within the church's wider convictions and beliefs about the nature of human being in the world.[9]

This volume is not offered as a final answer to that question, but is a step along the way of engagement with the novel and (from my point of view) compelling ethical and philosophical arguments of Luce Irigaray. The conversation about sexual difference, gender identity, and an ethical intersubjectivity is a conversation that has long been under way within western culture, and will no doubt continue long into the future. In a very personal sense, one can only be glad but to play some part in the discussion, and glad to explore these questions with Luce Irigaray.

A (Very) Brief Word on Content and Structure

At first glance, the possibility of a conversation between Irigaray and Kierkegaard might raise suspicions among those who are familiar with the thought of each. The question will be asked whether these two share enough in common to profitably pursue a conversation between them. For her part, Irigaray is a feminist and continental philosopher of sexual difference whose decisive criticisms of Western philosophy have exposed its inability to take woman seriously as a subject in her own right. For his part, Kierkegaard is known as the philosopher-theologian whose pseudonymous and non-pseudonymous writings paint a portrait of the existentially engaged individual—writings, we should add, that do little to address the concerns of feminist critics. It will be asked, then, whether these two have anything meaningful or constructive to say to one another. Yet this is precisely the assumption and contention of the present work. Our goal, in fact, is nothing less than the development of a constructive, Kierkegaardian ethics of sexual difference—an account of intersubjectivity

---

9. Francis Watson approaches these questions in a slightly different, but highly instructive way. He argues: "To regard the church as a self-sufficient sphere closed off from the world is ecclesiological docetism.... The Spirit is, according to Genesis 1, the creative matrix out of which all living beings proceed." Watson continues: "It is true that in the New Testament the presence of the Spirit is largely confined to the Christian community.... Yet the broader canonical context suggests that the Spirit dwells within the created and human world as well as within the church, in which case truth may proceed from the world to the church as well as from the church to the world...." See his *Text, Church, and World*, 237.

between man and woman that is informed by both Irigaray's account of sexual difference and Kierkegaard's theological and ethical vision.

The opening two chapters of this work will take up the thought of Luce Irigaray as this is expressed in the third phase of her writings. These chapters will outline her theory and her ethics of sexual difference, respectively. The second two chapters will take up the thought of Kierkegaard—the first dealing with his account of love (his ethical thought) as this is expressed in *Works of Love*, and the second dealing with his theory of human becoming as this is developed in his pseudonymous *Either/Or*, Volume 2. In the third section of the book (the final three chapters) we will bring Irigaray and Kierkegaard into conversation on the theory and ethics of sexual difference, demonstrating a sufficient confluence between them for the articulation of a constructive Kierkegaardian or theological ethics of sexual difference.

PART ONE

Irigaray and Love's Possibility

1

The Negative

Toward a Culture of Sexual Difference

> Man is willing to accept woman as an equal, as a man in skirts, as an angel, a devil, a baby-face, a machine, an instrument, a bosom, a womb, a pair of legs, a servant, an encyclopedia, an ideal or an obscenity; the one thing he won't accept her as is a human being, a real human being of the feminine sex.[1]
>
> —D. H. Lawrence, *Assorted Articles*

Luce Irigaray has developed an ethics of sexual difference that we have described in our introduction as compelling and promising, and what follows here is an attempt to confirm that these initial impressions are warranted.[2] Right at the outset of our engagement with Irigaray's writings, however, a fundamental question arises since the reader is at times left with the impression that Irigaray has spun her ethical vision out of thin air. That is, it is not immediately apparent that she has established an adequate foundation upon which to construct her ethics of sexual difference. Of course, if it turns out that Irigaray either has not, or cannot establish such a foundation—cannot provide a *theory* of sexual different to support her

---

1. Quoted in Sayers, *Are Women Human?* 45.

2. My thanks to Professor Alison Stone, Lancaster University, for comments offered on a previous draft of this chapter.

ethics—then her ethical framework must finally collapse under its own weight. And so the question that must preoccupy us at the outset, and in advance of the development of any theological ethics of sexual difference, concerns the nature and adequacy of the foundation upon which Irigaray's ethical framework is constructed.

In exploring these theoretical foundations, we will begin by considering Irigaray's new elaboration of "the negative." The negative, traditionally associated with the dialectical thought and method of Hegel, is reformulated and put to work by Irigaray in such a way that it becomes central and vital to her philosophy and ethics of sexual difference. Indeed, Irigaray argues that her new elaboration of the negative might open a new era of human becoming.[3] In tracing the outlines of a foundation for Irigaray's ethics, then, we cannot fail to consider what she takes to be the cornerstone of her whole philosophy and ethics.

Having dug into Irigaray's account of the negative it will become evident that while this concept is vital to (understanding) her thought, it does not by itself suffice as a foundation for her ethics of sexual difference. Thus we must push deeper, posing the following rather straightforward question: What is the difference between man and woman? Or, perhaps: On what basis do we insist on a difference between man and woman? While these questions do not admit of a straightforward answer, from the perspective of Irigaray's writings, we will begin to answer them by considering two over-lapping "Irigarayan" accounts of the difference between man and woman.

Having gone as far as we can with Irigaray in positing a foundation for her ethics of sexual difference, we will turn finally in this chapter to an initial consideration of her ethical thought. This will lead, naturally enough, to a fuller examination of the ethics of sexual difference in subsequent chapters.

THE NEGATIVE: RECOVERING NATURE

In *The Way of Love* Irigaray introduces her discussion of the negative as follows: "If the negative in speculative dialectic had for its function to reduce difference by integrating it into a more accomplished level of the Absolute, here it has the role of safeguarding difference."[4] If the negative in the Hegelian dialectic is a moment in which the opposition between two

---

3. Irigaray, *I Love to You*, 13–14.
4. Irigaray, *The Way of Love*, 101.

terms is overcome in a synthetic move, Irigaray's negative represents a refusal of that synthesis. Rather than defining the two terms of the dialectic in terms of an opposition that can be sublated in a more universal concept or pattern of life, Irigaray will insist on the persistence and preservation of difference. The negative, then, is a way of conceptualizing the gap or interval that persists between the two terms of the dialectic—woman and man—and a way of articulating Irigaray's insistence that the difference between these two terms prevents a movement beyond two to one. Accordingly, Irigaray insists that there are two universals. There are two terms that endure, neither of which can be sublated in favor of *the* universal. The human, here, is two and not one, and the negative is a theoretical conceptualization which guarantees that neither man nor woman will be construed as "the human"—also, that "the human" will not be construed as an abstract identity in which both man and woman can be said to "participate" in some way. Irigaray's new elaboration is nothing less than a refusal of the Hegelian negative, of the Hegelian insistence on a movement beyond two to one.

To highlight, briefly, the ethical implications of this account of the negative, Irigaray's new elaboration of the negative implies that man and woman must each acknowledge that they are only half of the human. As Irigaray puts it, "difference demands . . . the relinquishing of the whole."[5] This means, more to the point, that man, who has traditionally been identified as "the human," and as representative of the whole, must relinquish the claim that he is or can represent the whole. That woman and man each represent only half of the human also implies that woman may rightfully accede to full subjectivity. Irigaray warns: "not accepting and respecting this permanent duality between the two human subjects, the feminine one and the masculine one, amounts to preventing one of the two—historically the feminine—from attaining its own Being, and thus from taking charge of the becoming of what it already is and of the world to which it belongs, including as made up of other humans, similar or different."[6] As should already be apparent, this reformulation of the negative is expected to bear the weight of nothing less than a new human culture, a human becoming as two. While Western culture has always functioned according to the phallocentric logic of the *one*, according to which woman has been

---

5. Irigaray, *The Way of Love*, 157. Similarly, in *This Sex Which Is Not One*, Irigaray argues for a new approach to language that would mean that the masculine would no longer be "everything." See Irigaray, *This Sex*, 80.

6. Irigaray, *The Way of Love*, 110.

PART ONE—Irigaray and Love's Possibility

defined in relation to man and has been prevented from acceding to her own identity and subjectivity, Irigaray advances an account of the negative that insists on the twoness of the human and on the necessity that both woman and man accede to a subjectivity and identity particular to them as sexuate beings.

With this sketch of Irigaray's reformulated negative in mind, we move toward a fuller elaboration by identifying several criticisms Irigaray brings against the Hegel's definition of man and woman (and their relationship) in terms of dialectical logic.[7] Irigaray's criticism of Hegel is threefold. In the first instance she suggests that the Hegelian negative entails a dramatic devaluing of the natural; second, she insists that Hegel's account of the negative leaves woman in a state of natural immediacy; and third, she argues that Hegel's insistence on the unity of the couple in the child reflects a failure to spiritualize the relationship between man and woman.

Irigaray argues that the Hegelian negative entails a devaluing of the natural in favor of the cultural/spiritual and "is still the mastery of consciousness (historically male), over nature ..."[8] In the Western tradition and in Hegel's thought, the natural is overcome and sublated in the work of spirit, in the development of culture. As Cheah and Grosz put it: "Hegel defines spirit as the process of rational-purposive work or the labor of the concept, understood as a movement of negation. For Hegel, nature is finite, immediate, and devoid of universal life. However, rational consciousness can invest nature with universal life by negating what is immediate in nature. It does this by imbuing brute matter with rational-purposive form. Spiritual work is ... the activity by which the rational subject negates, sublates, and transcends natural facticity ..."[9] Indeed, in affirming that the becoming of consciousness consists in the passage from nature to spirit, Hegel goes so far as to call nature the *refuse* of spirit.[10] The negative, here, represents a decisive movement beyond that which is inadequate for the universalizing life of spirit, so that if the dialectic is conceived in terms of a three-fold movement, the negative expresses the inadequacy of the first and second moments, and the necessity of moving beyond them.[11]

7. Miller, "Freedom," 136–37. We return to this question, below.
8. Irigaray, *I Love to You*, 13.
9. Cheah and Grosz, "Of Being-Two," 8.
10. Miller, "Freedom," 134.

11. Stewart, we should note, argues that the Hegelian concept of *aufheben* includes both the negative and the positive. So that while the first and second moments are themselves inadequate, something of each is preserved in the higher truth to which the dialectician accedes. See Stewart, "Hegel's Doctrine," 57–78. See, also, Stewart, *Unity*, 41–45.

Irigaray argues, then, that Hegel's dialectical logic implies a denial of the natural, or at least a dramatic *disjunction* between the natural and the rational/spiritual. The harmful ramifications of this privileging of culture over nature are multiple, according to Irigaray, including the destruction of the natural environment and man's denial of woman as subject.[12] Overagainst this account of the negative as a movement beyond nature, Irigaray will insist precisely that culture is a movement *within* nature, a movement in which nature and culture are in continuity with each other.

The second criticism that Irigaray brings against Hegel's negative relates closely to the first since it addresses Hegel's interpretation of the identity and roles of man and woman in terms of the dialectical logic. His is an interpretation that results in a social and political order in which the first term (woman–nature) is sublated in favor of the second (man–culture). As Elaine Miller puts it: "The problem with Hegel's ethical life, according to Irigaray, is that he conceives of the couple dialectically, of the man and woman as opposites, thus mandating the sublation of one of the terms in the opposition."[13] Inevitably it is woman who is identified with the sublated term, which produces precisely the social and political order that Hegel outlines in the *Philosophy of Right*, where man is associated with the overcoming of the natural and the attainment of the universal. While the movement of negation begins in the family, to which woman accedes, it is fulfilled only in the public realm, to which only man accedes. Even if we express hesitation over Irigaray's use of the language of "natural immediacy" when applied to woman's place in the Hegelian account of society (since the family, for Hegel, represents a first move beyond mere nature), it is apparent that woman is not capable of a full accession to culture. Man, as subject and citizen, attains to a universal human identity in the public realm, while woman remains in a state of natural immediacy within the home.[14]

12. Cheah and Grosz: "Irigaray argues that any spiritual world, that is to say, any culture, society, or political community built on the negation/disavowal of nature, inevitably becomes totalitarian and sacrificial. It leads to totalitarianism because any project of the subject that denies its debt to nature also denies the fact that existence is necessarily two. The subject thereby sets himself up as an exhaustive whole or totality, repressing all that is different from himself." See Cheah and Grosz, "Of Being-Two," 9.

13. Miller, "Freedom," 136–37.

14. As Tina Chanter argues, Hegel's association of woman with the natural is also implied in his interpretation of the physiology of women and men. "Women's sexual anatomy, compared to men's is inactive, undifferentiated, and inferior according to Hegel's account. This supposedly natural state of affairs is used as a basis on which to ground women's inability to develop ethical consciousness, despite the fact that the

PART ONE—Irigaray and Love's Possibility

We might helpfully say more about the implications of this social and political order for woman who must live "on behalf of" the universal, on behalf of the man who attains to the fully human status of citizen. Irigaray writes: "As far as [woman] is concerned, she is wife and mother inasmuch as these roles represent a task vis-à-vis the universal which she discharges by renouncing her singular desires."[15] For Irigaray, this means that woman does not achieve singularity or subjectivity but lives out the role of wife and mother as an abstract duty—thus making possible her husband's life as subject and citizen. While he is permitted both a singular existence in the home (loving *this* woman and *these* children) as well as a universal existence in the public sphere, she is permitted neither a specific existence in the home (her duty is not toward *this* husband and *these* children, but toward them as a general task on behalf of the universal) nor a universal existence in the public sphere.[16] As Cheah and Grosz put it, "self-effacement in a family-related role is [woman's] civil task."[17]

Contrary to Hegel's denial of full subjectivity to woman, it is Irigaray's intention to provide theoretical resources (an account of the negative) by which woman can attain to subjectivity, to the transcendental and cultural existence that has traditionally been reserved for man. This is not to say that Irigaray will simply insist on the right of woman to a subjective existence on the masculine model propounded by Hegel, since her goal has been to open up the possibility of a subjectivity particular to woman, independent of any identification of/with/by man and independent of the assumptions and values of patriarchal (male) culture.[18] Let it be clear, as well, that this overturning of patriarchal assumptions and culture has implications for man's subjectivity—he cannot remain what he has been since his subjectivity and culture has been bound up with the denial of woman's subjectivity.[19]

The third criticism that Irigaray levels against Hegel revolves around his insistence that the unity of the couple is finally fulfilled in the child

---

anatomical descriptions themselves are already loaded in favor of women's exclusion from the public realm." See Chanter, *Ethics of Eros*, 92.

15. Irigaray, *I Love to You*, 21.

16. Ibid., 21–23. See also, again, Miller, "Freedom," 136–37. On this see White, "Elemental," 43.

17. Cheah and Grosz, "Of Being-Two," 8.

18. Whitford, *Luce Irigaray*, 93.

19. As Irigaray has said of her work: "It's aimed at the male subject too, inviting him to redefine himself as a body with a view to exchanges between sexed subjects." See Irigaray, *Je, Tu, Nous*, 59.

produced by the relationship. Indeed, Miller has argued that Irigaray's *I Love to You* can be read as a commentary on Hegel's fragment, "Love," in which he insists that "love strives to annul even the distinction [between the lover as lover and the lover as physical organism], to annul the possibility [of separation] as mere possibility, to unite even the mortal element, to make it immortal."[20] The love of a man and woman therefore expresses the drive toward an undifferentiated existence, which is achieved only in the child produced by the relationship. In the child, "the spirits [of the lovers] become more united than before, and that which was still separated from determinate consciousness is completely shared; all points at which one had touched the other, or had been touched by the other, in other words that had felt or thought alone, are reconciled, the spirits are exchanged."[21] As Hegel puts it elsewhere: "what in the first instance is most the individual's own is united into the whole in the lovers' touch and contact; consciousness of a separate self disappears, and all distinction between the lovers is annulled. The mortal element, the body, has lost the character of separability, and a living child, a seed of immortality, of the eternally self-developing and self-generating [race], has come into existence."[22] All opposition between woman and man (opposition being appropriate only in the realm of understanding, and not in the context of intersubjectivity[23]) is overcome in unity, expressed and fulfilled in the child.

Irigaray argues, however, that Hegel's insistence on the child as an expression of the couple's unity represents a failure to achieve a genuine and spiritual sharing. To express it differently, Irigaray argues that Hegel's account puts love in the service of genealogy, and therefore in the service of the whole edifice of patriarchal Western culture, which is built on the elision of woman as subject and constructed around woman's status as commodity passed from father to husband.[24] Where love is reduced to

20. G. W. F. Hegel, "Love," 305. Quoted in Miller, "Freedom," 131. Throughout this paragraph I rely on Miller for an account of Hegel's view of the child's role in the man-woman relationship.

21. Quoted in Miller, "Freedom," 131.

22. G. W. F. Hegel, "Love," 307.

23. Ibid., 303–4. Hegel adds: "This genuine love excludes all oppositions. It is not the understanding, whose relations always leave the manifold of related terms as a manifold and whose unity is always a unity of opposites [left as opposites]. It is not reason either, because reason sharply opposes its determining power to what is determined."

24. Miller puts it as follows: "For Hegel, the natural immediacy linked with the family is considered a stage in spiritual sublation, but only by virtue of reproduction, and not by virtue of the difference of the sexes." See Miller, "Freedom," 130.

the production of a child, each member of the family (man, woman, child or children) inevitably loses or alienates "their own identity in a whole cemented by naturalness, but an already abstract and neuter naturalness that erases the physical, psychological, or legal singularity of each person."[25] Here, the family becomes "a more or less unified whole, dominated by procreation, genealogy or filiation, parental authority, particularly paternal authority, and the possession of goods."[26]

What Irigaray envisages, by contrast, is a love relationship between man and woman that does not rule out procreation but which begins with a recognition that the human consists in two distinctive natures/cultures. In this framework, the couple itself is the primary instance of the family; the family is first two and not three. Thus Irigaray argues that if there is ever to be a genuine *one* in love, a genuine unity between a man and woman who love each other, we first have to "discover the two."[27] Thus far in Western society, she says, we have only ever achieved a false kind of unity, a unity "which is incarnated in the child—thus trapping the three terms in an alliance which is no alliance."[28] This relationship is an uncultivated union, a union achieved only at physical/natural level. What Irigaray aspires to, then, is union and sharing at the level of spirit, prior to any question of procreation. She writes: "It is not the reduction of the family to its natural dimension that can assure its future, but a culture of the union between man and woman respecting their differences, which implies that nature becomes conscious."[29]

Having sketched out Irigaray's critique of the limited and restrictive nature of Hegel's negative, we proceed to consider Irigaray's reformulated negative. Doing so, the relationship between nature and culture remains central since Irigaray's new elaboration requires that we begin again with the natural. She argues: "The natural is at least two: male and female. All the speculation about overcoming the natural in the universal forgets that nature is not one. The universal has been thought as *one*, thought on the basis of *one*. But this *one* does not exist."[30] Furthermore, as long as philosophy denies the essential twoness of humanity it will be implicated in a denial of the natural, with all of the destructive and (un)ethical implications

---

25. Irigaray, *Between East and West*, 106.
26. Ibid.
27. Irigaray, *Ethics*, 67.
28. Ibid.
29. Irigaray, *I Love to You*, 156.
30. Ibid., 35.

The Negative

which follow from such a denial: "The natural, aside from the diversity of its incarnations or ways of appearing, is at least two: male and female. This division is not secondary or unique to human kind. It cuts across all realms of the living which, without it, would not exist. Without sexual difference, there would be no life on earth. It is the manifestation of and the condition for the production and reproduction of life. Air and sexual difference may be the two dimensions vital for/to life. *Not taking them into account would be a deadly business.*"[31]

The return to nature, then, requires recognition that the *one* does not exist and that limit is inscribed within nature itself: "Before the question of the need to surpass nature arises, it has to be apparent that it is two. This two inscribes finitude in the natural itself."[32] On the basis of this two, as noted, Irigaray argues that neither the male nor the female can claim to correspond to the whole of human nature and that each must acknowledge that it can only ever represent half of the whole. Here the negative "is not a process of consciousness of which only man is capable"[33] but is an expression of the limitation inscribed in nature. To return to the statement with which we began our discussion of the negative, Irigaray contends that "if the negative in speculative dialectic had for its function to reduce difference by integrating it into a more accomplished level of the Absolute, here it has the role of safeguarding difference."[34]

For Irigaray one of the great ironies of Hegel's account of the negative is that it leaves man in a state of natural immediacy, even as he presumes to have superseded this condition. She argues that man is in fact "determined by a natural naïveté: 'I am the whole.'"[35] In failing to recognize that he is not the whole, man has left unthought the most basic truth of human being and identity—that the human is two and not one—and has therefore remained in a state of natural immediacy:

> Since he has not pulled himself out of his intuitive natural immediacy—I represent humanity—man has not begun to think. He lives in a pseudo-nature, between reality and spirituality; these have been disconnected from one another by a cultural epoch (our own) in which philosophy, as Hegel would say, is still in a state of somnambulism rather than a state of awakening.

31. Irigaray, *I Love to You*, 37. Italics added.
32. Ibid., 35.
33. Ibid.
34. Irigaray, *The Way of Love*, 101.
35. Irigaray, *I Love to You*, 36.

PART ONE—Irigaray and Love's Possibility

> Man has not raised himself above a state of immediate unity with nature, so he dreams of being the whole. He dreams that he alone is nature and that it is up to him to undertake the spiritual task of differentiating himself from (his) nature and from himself.[36]

The beginning of culture, the movement beyond natural immediacy, consists in the recognition of sexual difference as basic to the human, the recognition that neither man nor woman is the whole. For humans to become fully human requires that man and woman acknowledge that each knows only its own genre, and cannot claim to know or represent the other. "If man and woman respect each other as those two halves of the universe that they represent, then by recognizing the other they have overcome their immediate instincts and drives. They are spiritual humans from the fact of recognizing that they do not represent the whole of the person . . ."[37] In this moment of recognition nature is spiritualized, culture commences. As Cheah and Grosz express it: "Sexual difference undoes the binary opposition between nature and spirit because it is nothing other than the internal natural means by which nature becomes spiritualized."[38]

Returning to Irigaray's critique of the Hegelian negative, we note Alison Stone's argument that the whole edifice of Western culture represents nothing less than a failure to spiritualize nature, and nothing less than an existence of nature against itself: "Irigaray believes that male nature has generated a culture which opposes itself to nature, including to female bodies and to male bodies qua natural. There is, then, a part of nature—the male sex—that turns against itself. Western culture arises in this turning of (the male part of) nature against itself, thereby acquiring the enduring form of an anti-natural, ecologically damaging culture."[39] It is the denial of sexual difference that is the defining moment in the anti-natural existence of the masculine subject, since the denial of sexual difference is a denial of what is given in nature. Cheah and Grosz, again, write:

> Irigaray argues that any spiritual world, that is to say, any culture, society, or political community built on the negation/disavowal of nature, inevitably becomes totalitarian and sacrificial. It leads to totalitarianism because any project of the subject that denies its debt to nature also denies the fact that existence is necessarily

36. Ibid., 40.
37. Ibid., 51.
38. Cheah and Grosz, "Of Being-Two," 9.
39. Stone, "Irigaray and Hölderlin," 421.

two. The subject thereby sets himself up as an exhaustive whole or totality, repressing all that is different from himself. . . . But more importantly, such spiritual projects can only establish societies of death because they are cut off from the generativity of nature. Instead of spiritualizing the body and incarnating itself, universal spirit becomes sundered from the earth, corporeality, and flesh.[40]

Throughout her writings Irigaray offers various examples of the antinatural mode of existence that prevails under patriarchy. To cite only one example, she argues that denial of the body (nature) leads to an incapacitation of our physical senses: "A body breathes, smells, tastes, sees, hears and touches or is touched. These bodily attributes are endangered. But how can we live without bodies? What does this extinction mean? It means that men's culture has polluted our air, food, sight, hearing and touch to such an extent that our senses are on the verge of destruction."[41] This assault on the senses is paralleled, according to Irigaray, by an assault on the earth through pollution and environmental degradation, which results from the denial of nature and a supposed privileging of the spiritual and cultural.

According to Irigaray, then, the negative of sexual difference becomes the means by which we might affirm both nature and culture, and her later writings are taken up with how the negative might be introduced into Western culture—how a spiritualization of nature might become possible. However, since the recognition of sexual difference is itself the first moment in the spiritualization of nature, Irigaray situates a renewed intersubjectivity between man and woman (one built on the negative of sexual difference) at the heart of this project. Thus, her theory of sexual difference suggests that "a renewed relationship between the sexes can itself open up a future beyond the destruction we now face because it is the site for the formulation, cultivation, and dissemination of values that respect the generative difference of living nature. As finite beings, we owe our present and continuing existence to this generative principle in nature. Thus, sexual difference is nothing less than the possibility of the future as such. Herein lies its redemptive dimension . . ."[42] Living nature has produced sexual difference, and respect for this difference must be the basis of human culture. The couple is precisely that locus in which respect for the givenness of nature may be expressed and acknowledged. The traditional

---

40. Cheah and Grosz, "Of Being-Two," 10.

41. Irigaray, *Thinking*, 22.

42. Cheah and Grosz, "Of Being-Two," 7.

family has been reduced to a natural immediacy in which reproduction, sexual drives, and questions of property are primary—here woman is in service to male genealogy. The traditional family is incapable of a task necessary to a culture of sexual difference: it cannot re-educate the desires of the male child. The couple, on the other hand, is the context in which woman is set free to be herself (in relation to her genre) and in which man begins to develop "a new kind of 'world in the male,' centering around a specifically male genre."[43] In the context of this relationship, man learns self-control as he respects the becoming of woman, and is therefore able to mitigate the anti-natural mode of existence that is perpetuated under patriarchy.[44]

The Nature of Sexual Difference

We have been attempting to discern a foundation for Irigaray's ethics of sexual difference—and to that end have explored the deconstructive and constructive aspects of Irigaray's new formulation of the negative. In doing so, the accent has been placed on the possibility and desirability of woman becoming a subject in her own right—and on the failure of Western culture to imagine or facilitate such a possibility. In exploring Irigaray's new elaboration of the negative, we are in many respects at the heart of both her theory and her ethics of sexual difference. Even so, the question that preoccupies us has not received an adequate answer. We would express that question as follows: "What is the difference between man and woman?" Or better, perhaps: "On what basis do we insist on a difference between man and woman?" To insist that the human is two is, for some, to insist on the obvious. For others, however, it would be more accurate to describe the human as plural or multiple (are there not many races or ethnicities, many sexualities, many forms of human life in the world?), and Irigaray's insistence on the twoness of the human strikes many of her contemporaries as wrongheaded at best and hopelessly conservative at worst.

---

43. Stone, *Luce Irigaray*, 185.

44. In responding to the question of whether man is capable of this self-control and this quelling of destructive desires, Stone suggests that this self-control is simply another aspect of the male nature's self-opposing tendency. In this she appeals to Freud (and Ricoeur's interpretation of Freud), according to whom culture uses my own self-violence to bring to naught my violence against others. See Stone, *Luce Irigaray*, 186.

Yet it is precisely this difference that Irigaray will insist upon. We will explore this insistence in terms of two over-lapping "Irigarayan" accounts of the difference between man and woman. In the first instance we consider Irigaray's explicit argument that sexual difference is an expression of the boy and girl's distinct experience/identity in relation to the mother. In the second instance we will consider an account of the twoness of the human that Alison Stone (a pre-eminent interpreter of Irigaray) proffers on Irigaray's behalf—specifically, a metaphysical realism that sees man and woman as representatives of the two fundamental rhythms of the cosmos.

Sexual Difference: Relation to the Origin

In *Democracy Begins between Two*, Irigaray argues that the subjectivities of man and woman are differently structured since a boy is born of one who is *different* from him and the girl is born to one who is *like* her. That is, since the mother is the origin of every child, the subjectivity of the child is expressed, or develops, in terms of whether the child is like or unlike the mother. Irigaray argues:

> I cannot avoid the conclusion that woma(e)n and ma(e)n represent two different worlds, two visions of the world which remain irreducibly distinct. Thus the following factors determine a different structuring of subjectivity:
>
> - being born of the same gender or of a different gender from one's own: being the daughter of a mother or the son of a mother;
> - whether or not one can conceive a living being in one's own body;
> - whether one procreates within oneself or outside oneself;
> - whether one can nourish another living being from one's own body or only through one's own labor.
>
> Events of this kind, which are differently organized in the life of a woman or of a man, create two identities, two ways of looking at the world, which cannot be reduced to one.[45]

In this case, Irigaray's negative provides a theoretical conceptualization of the gap or interval that persists between these two distinct identities or subjectivities. These identities or subjectivities, she adds, are both prior to

---

45. Irigaray, *Democracy*, 151.

and more profound than other differences that might exist in the human: "Woma(e)n and ma(e)n are therefore different, more different than Black and White, Catholic and Moslem, European and Oriental. They are different in the constitution of their subjectivity, and in their way of looking at the world."[46] This is to say that among blacks and whites, among Catholics and Moslems, among Europeans and Orientals, the difference between man and woman exists and thus is prior to and more basic than these other differences. Sexual difference is present across human races and cultures and is the first and universal difference from Irigaray's perspective.[47]

Irigaray argues that the distinct subjectivities of boys and girls are revealed in their respective patterns of language use and that empirical studies of language-use affirm this fundamental difference. On the basis of her own research on language-use among schoolchildren in France and Italy, Irigaray concludes:

> Girls and boys, from a very young age, express themselves in different ways, through language and through their behavior in general. ... To maintain that difference is the result of a simple apprenticeship in social stereotypes is to deny that girls and boys come into the world in a different relational context. To be born a girl of a woman, someone belonging to the same gender, and with the ability to engender like her, or to be born a boy of a woman, someone of a different gender, and with whom subjective relations will be complex, notably because it will be impossible for him to engender as she does, entails a different structuring of subjectivity. For a girl, conditions for inter-subjective relations will be favorable, whereas a boy will have to interpose objects and the construction of an own homocultural and homosocial world, in order to protect himself

---

46. Ibid., 152. As Mary Beth Mader argues, "The possibility that other differences or features might obtrude in such a way as to mitigate or displace the centrality of the differences upon which Luce Irigaray focuses, or that the centrality of such differences may vary significantly across cultures or times or other variables is rarely considered and always resisted in her work. In other words, she holds that sexual difference and the relational differences it structures, and that structure it, are human invariants that obtain universally." See Mader, "All Too Familiar," 368.

47. Thus, sexual difference is not a matter of mere biological difference. As Lotringer argues, there are certainly biological and anatomical difference at play here, but it is more significant that biological and anatomical differences "lead to others: in constructing subjectivity, in connecting to the world, in relating." See Lotringer, *Luce Irigaray*, 96. As Irigaray expresses it elsewhere: "context and biology are mixed, and there is no need to raise the issue of essences in this regard." See Irigaray, *Key Writings*, 90.

from the mystery, indeed the abyss, that his origin, his mother, represents for him.[48]

The boy, since he comes from one who is different from him, and since he will never be like her, is in a space of mystery and has to devise a strategy to keep himself from being engulfed by this mysterious origin. Thus, the boy/man invents objects for himself (even transcendental ones—God, Truth), objects that he can control, in order to resolve the difficulty of the relationship between himself and the one who has carried and birthed him.[49]

As might be expected, the development of this sexed identity is correlated with a use of language that prefers subject-object relations over intersubjectivity and relationality. However, "The situation is different for the daughter, who is potentially a mother and can live with her mother without destroying either one of them even prior to the mediation of specific objects. . . . Therefore the daughter's words to the mother may represent the most highly evolved and most ethical models of language, in the sense that they respect the intersubjective relationship between two women, express reality, make correct use of linguistic codes that are qualitatively rich."[50] Girls tend toward a language of intersubjectivity and sharing, while the language of boys reveals a more impoverished relational life, particularly with respect to those of the other sex.[51]

Irigaray concludes that, as a result of differences in the constitution of female and male subjectivity, and as a result of the dominance of the logic of the *one* in Western culture, a genuine sharing between man and woman has become impossible. She writes: "What is lacking is a culture

---

48. Irigaray, *Key Writings*, 90.
49. Irigaray, *Thinking*, 110.
50. Ibid., 110–11.
51. Irigaray, *Key Writings*, 87. On account of this, Irigaray argues that "women and men rely, then, on different subjective configurations and ways of speaking. These cannot be attributed solely to socio-historical determinations, nor to an alienation of the feminine which is to be overcome by making it equal to the masculine. Women's language does, of course, give signs of a degree of alienation and inertia, but it also demonstrates a richness of its own which has nothing to envy in men's language; and, particularly, a taste for intersubjectivity which is definitely not to be abandoned in favor of the subject-object relation dear to men." Irigaray, *Democracy*, 137. We should, however, note Deutscher's objection that Irigaray "reinforces her claim that men and women manifest different structures of language use, by avoiding the discussion of exceptions or ambiguities in the patterns of discourse she analyzes." See Deutscher, "Love Discourses," 113.

PART ONE—Irigaray and Love's Possibility

of horizontal relations between different subjects."[52] Irigaray suggests that the girl's innate tendency toward intersubjectivity and sharing, in the context of Western culture's elision of woman's subjectivity, produces a situation in which the girl "projects all her love, all of her ideals, all of what she herself is, onto him." This "him," however, "inhabits another world, and . . . cannot respond to such feelings, desires, or needs." For the boy, "there is no place for a girl or a woman. Sometimes very young boys refer to Mommy or to a witch, and the older ones to a female mythological character, enemy of the hero, who seeks to kill him, aided by his wife. When the female world is not completely absent, it is represented very negatively."[53] The girl, therefore, imagines that the boy doesn't love her, or that she cannot please him. But the truth of the matter is that he is simply incapable of loving her. As Irigaray says, "He does not have the luxury of a choice in the matter."[54] All of this is to say that the difference in the girl and boy's relation to their origin, and the concomitant difference in their subjectivity, when expressed in a cultural context which denies subjectivity to woman, results in a situation where genuine communication between woman and man becomes impossible.[55]

This insistence on the present impossibility of an ethical intersubjectivity between man and woman brings us back to the question of the anti-natural life of man. In failing to recognize that he is not the whole, man fails to achieve a cultural or spiritual existence, and therefore lives an anti-natural existence. But this raises the question of whether or not Irigaray's thought implies inevitability with respect to male violence toward nature (and toward woman, who is assimilated to nature); the possibility that communication between man and woman is, finally, impossible. A full consideration of this question remains beyond the scope of the present work, yet we note Alison Stone's argument that the anti-natural tendency of man is precisely a *tendency*, which is to say that it will not always, in every circumstance, come to fruition.[56] Culture has an effect in either

52. Irigaray, *Key Writings*, 87.
53. Ibid., 89.
54. Ibid., 87.
55. Elsewhere Irigaray expands on this idea that communication between man and woman has been impossible under patriarchy. She suggests that typical masculine language is self-reflexive, curving back on the masculine subject. Typical feminine language, on the other hand, is invariably interrogative and the woman is not conceived as subject in her utterances. Communication between two is impossible. See Irigaray, *Ethics*, 135.
56. Stone, "Irigaray and Hölderlin," 415–32.

suppressing or enabling this anti-natural tendency. Irigaray argues: "The fact that [man's] impulses, inclinations and desires are violent does not necessarily mean that this is an inherent part of masculine being, but that violence can come from an historical construction."[57] Thus Stone, again, argues:

> Irigaray need not envisage a linear causal relationship between masculine violence and a destructive culture. Rather, men's violent tendencies will become activated in the absence of a sexuate culture, an absence which leaves men without resources to comprehend and acclimatize to sexual difference. The little boy finds himself in a space of unfathomable mystery only because his culture, which is non-sexuate, deprives him of ways to make sense of his mother's difference from him. If femininity were instead recognized as an independent identity, and masculinity were recognized as a correspondingly specific identity . . . then the difficulty would become negotiable.[58]

In effect, humans need to intervene to reorientate nature's self-destructive tendency and to provide cultural resources by which man would be able to resist the anti-natural tendency of his own being. Patriarchal culture, then, has not left humans *utterly* lacking in the cultural resources that would allow for change.[59] Thus Irigaray suggests that "if a woman constitutes her feminine identity, she can help man exit from a simple or a difficult relation with his mother by means of a horizontal rapport between the man and the woman."[60] From out of the midst of the cultural failure that is patriarchy, Irigaray would have us envision a culture of sexual difference in which man and woman communicate for the first time.

Sexual Difference: Stone's "Metaphysical Realism"

Before turning to consider the *ethics* of sexual difference, we take a moment to outline an alternative "Irigarayan" perspective on the difference between man and woman. We do so by turning to the work of Alison Stone, who offers an account of what she refers to as Irigaray's metaphysical

---

57. Irigaray, *To Be Two*, 71. Quoted in Stone, "Irigaray and Hölderlin," 428

58. Stone, "Irigaray and Hölderlin," 428.

59. It is for this reason that Irigaray can argue that her new elaboration of the negative, and the culture of sexual difference she envisages, will build upon what we "scarcely perceive of difference." See Irigaray, *The Way of Love*, 101.

60. Irigaray, "Je-Luce Irigaray," 108.

PART ONE—Irigaray and Loves Possibility

realism. Although this account of Irigaray's deeper presuppositions is nowhere presented by Irigaray in a formal manner, Stone offers a compelling argument that something along these lines almost necessarily lies in the background of Irigaray's thought. This discussion of Irigaray's metaphysical realism overlaps considerably with our discussion of the relation between nature and culture, above, which is to say that we are caught up here with a long debate within feminism (and within Irigaray interpretation) concerning the relation between nature and culture, between sex and gender. Given that, as Stone indicates, Irigaray has only offered a number of non-systematic comments on what "nature" consists in, there is a tentativeness that attaches to Stone's account of Irigaray's wider theory of difference.[61]

Irigaray has argued that any movement beyond the limited and destructive culture of patriarchy requires beginning again with nature, which is two. By this she means, in the first instance, that *human* nature is two. According to Stone, however, Irigaray is also arguing that *all natural processes and phenomena* are sexuate, inasmuch as they "all contain two 'poles' between which a continuous 'alternation' takes place."[62] The climatic process, for example, contains cycles of humidity and dryness and the two poles of this process are interdependent, cyclically supplanting one another."[63] According to Stone, Irigaray is suggesting that there is a rhythmic bipolarity in natural processes or phenomena and that this makes them *sexuate*, since "their bipolarity is structurally isomorphic with human sexual difference."[64] Stone continues: "The way each pole depends upon its other and yet follows its own unique rhythm parallels the situation of the two sexes, who differ fundamentally yet also depend upon one another within the overall regenerative process of human life. The analogy between the bipolarity of natural phenomena and the sexual differentiation of the human species suggest, in turn, a distinctive understanding of

---

61. Stone, "The Sex of Nature," 60–84.

62. Ibid., 62.

63. Ibid., 63. Stone appeals to Irigaray's comments in *Democracy Begins between Two*: "So there is a rhythmic pulse which beats between going out toward the other and returning to the self, between extending oneself as far as the other and returning to dwell within the self, between coming out into the light and going back into the darkness, into the invisibility of interiority, into the mystery of alterity. This movement resembles that of the heart, of the circulation of blood, but also that of the cosmos itself which exists between expansion and concentration. It is true of the entire universe . . ." See Irigaray, *Democracy*, 111.

64. Stone, "The Sex of Nature," 63.

human sexuation as consisting essentially in a difference between the rhythms characteristic of each sex."⁶⁵ The entire cosmos, then, displays a rhythmic bipolarity, and humans themselves are an expression of it. According to Irigaray, humans express or achieve this rhythmic bipolarity in unique ways since they can become (self-)aware of these different rhythms and can express the bipolarity of the cosmos through culture. As Stone puts it: "[Humans] realize nature's drive to dimorphism by progressively *becoming* more and more sexually differentiated. It is in the activity of cultural self-development that humans can fulfill the goal of the universe."⁶⁶

Within this framework, sexual difference is first an ontological difference between man and woman (a difference in rhythm), a difference that is expressed only secondarily in ontic differences.⁶⁷ The rhythmic difference between the sexes leads to their "acquiring distinct physical properties, which arise through the partial consolidation of their fluids."⁶⁸ This is to say that hormonal, physiological, and anatomical differences between men and women are not primary for Irigaray, since these physical differences express a prior rhythmic difference and are themselves an expression of the rhythmic bipolarity of the cosmos.

Stone points out that Irigaray is offering a specifically *non-scientific* account of the human body—an account within which the body is conceived of as fundamentally fluid, as constituted in mucous.⁶⁹ Further, she argues that since the body is essentially fluid "we can expect that . . . the sexes will be distinguished by the rhythms at which they circulate their mucous fluids."⁷⁰ This is also to say that the anatomical, hormonal, and physiological differences between the sexes arise through the partial consolidation of their fluids, and that sexual difference is not in the first instance (or even in a determinative way) biological.⁷¹ An important implication of this

---

65. Ibid., 63–64. In offering this interpretation of Irigaray, in terms of rhythmic bipolarity, Stone appeals to Elaine Miller's account of rhythm. See Miller, *Vegetative Soul*, 47–48.

66. Stone, "The Sex of Nature," 65.

67. For an account of Irigaray's indebtedness to Heidegger, here, see Stone, *Luce Irigaray*, 87–113. See, also, Fielding, "Questioning Nature."

68. Stone, "The Sex of Nature," 67.

69. Ibid.

70. Ibid.

71. In a parallel comment, Irigaray argues that "although one's sex is naturally given, apart from the minimal natural determination that sex is two, sexual identity is paradoxically without content because it is also formed by the spiritual work that occurs through one's respect for the other sex and the collective nurturing of cultural

approach to sexual difference, for Stone, is the conviction that "the two sexes regenerate one another aside from any question of reproduction."[72] Thus: "Through encountering one another as different, the sexes arouse particularly strong passions in one another and correlatively pronounced changes in one another's bodily rhythms. Biological reproduction is one possible outcome of this change, but the capacity to reproduce does not itself define the sexes, arising only in the context of a regenerative process that itself emerges from the essential difference between their temporal rhythms."[73] This is to say, in part, that the relationship between man and woman is an engagement between two distinct rhythms and fluidities that interact with one another and influence one another, thereby contributing to the becoming of the human. That men and women are capable of culture furthermore implies that this engagement between man and woman will be more than an unconscious engagement of rhythms, since women and men are capable of recognizing, respecting, and exploring their rhythmic engagement with each other. Through various cultural practices, and through the symbolic structures we develop, women and men are capable of both recognizing and developing the ways in which their respective rhythms and fluidities interact and are expressed.[74]

The Negative and Mediation

At the outset of *An Ethics of Sexual Difference*, Luce Irigaray argues that "sexual difference is one of the major philosophical issues, if not *the* issue of our age. According to Heidegger, each age has one issue to think through, and one only. Sexual difference is probably the issue in our time

---

values that are faithful to one's own sex." See Cheah and Grosz, "Of Being-Two," 13, where they refer to Irigaray's *I Love to You*.

72. Irigaray, *Je, Tu, Nous*, 15. Quoted in Stone, "The Sex of Nature," 68.

73. Stone, "The Sex of Nature," 69.

74. As mentioned, Irigaray is offering a non-scientific analysis of the body and of sexual difference. In this she refuses what she refers to as the metaphysics of the solid, according to which, as Stone says, "all reality consists in finite entities that have firm boundaries and are intrinsically static or inert. Empirical methodology is only meaningful on the presupposition of this metaphysics, because only finite, static, entities can be taken in through observation." See Stone, "The Sex of Nature," 69. Irigaray employs phenomenological description which remains attentive to the human person's own experience of nature. Most important however, we note that Irigaray's ultimate defence of her theory of sexual difference is ethical (not epistemological), since Irigaray argues that respect for difference will lead to happiness and fecundity. See Stone, "The Sex of Nature."

The Negative

which could be our 'salvation' if we thought it through."[75] Picking up this theme again in *The Way of Love*, Irigaray argues that human becoming beyond the limited and destructive culture of patriarchy requires that we turn to the unthought: that the human is two and not one.[76] For Irigaray, importantly, a return to the unthought entails a transformation of intersubjectivity between man and woman—a return to the unthought is in the first instance an ethical matter.

We have been exploring this question: What is the difference between man and woman? Differently expressed: On what basis do we insist on a difference between man and woman? In reply to these questions we have considered Irigaray's own answer and have looked at the Irigarayan answer put forward by Alison Stone. Certainly the question of the nature of the difference between woman and man remains an important one—for Irigaray and her readers—since without an answer to the question it is difficult to see how an ethics of sexual difference can be sustained. Yet it is important to note Irigaray's insistence that her ethics of sexual difference will result in happiness and fecundity for the human—and that this represents its ultimate defence and vindication. That is, she is at least as interested in the instantiation of an ethical intersubjectivity between the sexes as she is in answering the "how" (or "what") of sexual difference. Otherwise put, while we are seeking a theory of sexual difference to undergird Irigaray's ethics, Irigaray herself will insist that her ethical framework provides its own legitimacy and defense—even as she does not neglect the wider "theoretical" questions.

As observed, Irigaray reformulates the negative in order to affirm the human as irreducibly two, a truth that serves as a check against the solipsistic and anti-natural/woman mode of life that has predominated in Western culture and religion. Indeed, according to Irigaray the culture of the One male subject has produced "social crises, individual illnesses, a schematic and fossilized identity for the two sexes, as well as a general sclerosis of discourse, a hardening, a repetition of instituted sense until it is nonsense, the inflation and devaluation of entrenched signification which refuses to question its own status."[77] It is through the labor of the negative, then, that the failures and limitations of patriarchal culture will be mitigated. As Gail Schwab puts it, the way out of the logic of the same "is through the labor of the negative, conceived . . . as the relation

---

75. Irigaray, *Ethics*, 5.
76. Irigaray, *The Way of Love*, 99.
77. Irigaray, *Éthique*, 129. Quoted in Schwab, "Sexual Difference," 81.

PART ONE—Irigaray and Love's Possibility

between two sexually different subjects. Using one's gender as a reference point, one must inevitably come to recognize that one can only represent at most half of the human experience."[78] Irigaray's ethical thought, therefore, introduces the negative into culture, into relations between man and woman. While Irigaray sees a variety of ways to introduce the negative into culture—for example, through sexuate rights, through civil rights that do not attach to a neuter, universal subject but to women and men as ontologically differentiated beings—we focus on Irigaray's vision of an ethical intersubjectivity. That which is initiated here will be extended in the next chapter, where we consider a number of specific ways in which the "labor of the negative" finds expression.

Each Transcendent to the Other

In *The Way of Love*, Irigaray speaks of the negative in terms of a horizontal transcendence that exists between man and woman, a transcendence that man has generally projected onto the divine. That is, whereas man has construed transcendence primarily in terms of a God whom he posits as ontologically other (to whom man relates and after whom he aspires), Irigaray insists that transcendence must be re-situated between the sexes. Man's projection of transcendence onto God, Irigaray argues, reflects the difficulty of the boy child in coming to grips with the originary transcendence of the maternal You: "The transcendence of this *you* evades any possible knowledge on his part: he cannot make himself the arbiter of her truth. If and when he attempts to do so, she escapes from all of his logical judgments founded upon non-contradiction. She sends the pendulum swinging indefinitely from one pole to the other with no possibility of it stopping on one univocal truth. And he will not be able to decide once and for all if she is this or that. She escapes the mastery of his judgments."[79] In view of the transcendence of the mother, and of the boy/man's inability to come to grips with her difference, she becomes "fused with an undifferentiated nature from which he must emerge and distinguish himself, and that he must deny as a possible partner in any communicative exchange."[80] This produces a solipsistic and autological subject, according to Irigaray, a subject who may finally project transcendence onto God, but does so in order to establish a solid foundation (certainty, truth) for

78. Schwab, "Sexual Difference," 81.
79. Irigaray, "Beyond All Judgment," 68.
80. Ibid.

his own subjectivity—a subjectivity built on the forgetting of the mother.[81] In *Elemental Passions*, Irigaray addresses this question in dialogical form, where woman speaks to man: "The whole is not the same for me as it is for you. For me, it can never be one. Can never be completed, always in-finite. When you talk about Infinity, it seems to me that you are speaking of a closed totality: a solid, empty membrane which would gather and contain all possibilities. The absolute of self-identity—in which you were, will be, could be."[82] While Irigaray seems to acknowledge that the becoming of the man required that he hypostasize the original difference and the originary transcendence onto God, she argues that "this Absolute of justice and goodness prevents him from considering the alterity of the other in its reality . . ."[83]

To speak of a horizontal transcendence between woman and man is, for Irigaray, to speak of an abyss, gap, or interval that persists between them.[84] Irigaray writes: "The rift between the other and me is irreducible. To be sure we can build bridges, join our energies, feast and celebrate encounters, but the union is never definitive, on pain of no longer existing. Union implies returning into oneself, moving away, dissenting, separating."[85] While there is much to unpack in these few words, the notion of the rift is central. The idea of the rift or gap or interval points to the fact that woman and man represent worlds that are utterly distinct from one another. Irigaray argues: "Masculine and feminine subjects belong to *two irreducible worlds*, which are partly pre-given and partly elaborated from an originary identity, which is both corporeal and relational, to take only

---

81. Regarding the originary matricide, Elizabeth Grosz writes: "When, for example, Freud postulates that culture is founded on the patricide of the primal father and the totemic devouring of his body, Irigaray insists that underlying this ancient murder is an earlier, more archaic and unspeakable killing: matricide. The father's death is not the first cultural act; at best, it is the first recognized or recorded act. For the father to occupy this dominant position, in control of all the women and the rivalrous sons, his position must *already* be a consequence of a 'murder' of a kind: the severance of the umbilical link between mother and child." See Grosz, *Sexual Subversions*, 163. For a discussion of the meaning of "originary," see Hodge, "Irigaray Reading," 191–210.

82. Irigaray, *Elemental*, 89.

83. Though it is curious to hear her say so, Irigaray suggests: "It is understandable that man has, for a time, made the working-out of his becoming dependent on a God-the-Father." See Irigaray, "Beyond All Judgment," 70. On this see, also, Irigaray, *Marine Lover*, 173.

84. For this language see Irigaray, *Elemental*, 28.

85. Irigaray, *The Way of Love*, 157.

PART ONE—Irigaray and Love's Possibility

these two most fundamental elements in the construction of identity."[86] Eventually, of course, it will be possible to speak of a meeting of these two worlds, but in the first instance it is necessary to insist on the radical difference between the sexes. "Almost everything has to be reinvented, rebuilt," and the possibility of rebuilding requires that we mark the radical nature of the difference, or other-worldliness, between man and woman. To do otherwise is to leave open the possibility of a drift back toward the logic of the same, where woman is defined in terms of man.[87]

Thus Irigaray employs the concept of transcendence in order to explore the possibility of an ethical intersubjectivity between man and woman. As has been noted, Irigaray's work, throughout, is built upon a refusal of relations of possession, appropriation, or fusion, and she argues that relations of this kind have predominated in Western culture:

> We have been accustomed to reduce the other to ours or to ourselves. On the level of consciousness as on the level of feelings, we have been educated to make our own what we approach or what approaches us. Our manner of reasoning, our manner of loving is often an appropriation, either through a lack of differentiation, a fusion, or through a transformation into an object, an object of knowledge or of love, that we integrate into our world. We act in this way especially towards others who are closest to us, forgetting that they are other, different from us, but also toward the foreigner who is welcomed on the condition that he, or she, agrees to being assimilated to our way of living, our habits our world.[88]

Irigaray's notion of a horizontal transcendence between man and woman is intended to act as a restraint against destructive forms of intersubjectivity and is intended to ground an alternative approach to the other. In this vein Irigaray argues that the concept of the negative is intended to preserve "the transcendence of the other, a 'you' who is not, and will never be mine, remaining irreducible to 'I', to me, to mine. A 'you' whose transcendence will resist any possession, appropriation or fusion, preserving differentiation in this way."[89]

---

86. Irigaray, "Beyond All Judgment," 71. Italics added.

87. For a discussion of Irigaray's philosophy of sexual difference as a movement beyond the limited accomplishments of "equality feminism," see Goux, "Luce Irigaray," 175–90. See also Deutscher, *Politics*, 7–22.

88. Irigaray, *Key Writings*, 5.

89. Ibid., 3.

Irigaray insists that the transcendence between sexuate beings is not modeled on the relation of transcendence between man and his God; it is not a spiritual transcendence beyond, and removed from, the sensible or physical. In *I Love to You* she argues:

> Transcendence is thus no longer ecstasy, leaving the self behind toward an inaccessible total-other, beyond sensibility, beyond the earth. It is respect for the other whom I will never be, who is transcendent to me and to whom I am transcendent. Neither simple nature nor common spirit beyond nature, this transcendence exists in the difference of body and culture that continues to nourish our energy, its movement, its generation and its creation.... The other of sexual difference is he—or she—towards whom it is possible to go as towards a transcendence while remaining in the self, and without turning transcendence on its head in the guise of soul or spirit.[90]

We recall that Irigaray's account of the negative implies continuity between nature and culture, such that culture is construed as a twofold spiritualization of/in nature. The transcendence between man and woman, then, is not a transcendence that associates one pole of the dialectic with nature and the other pole with culture. Since man and woman are ontologically distinct beings (each implicated in a particular nature/culture), the transcendence that persists between them is "neither simple nature nor common spirit beyond nature, this transcendence exists in the difference of body and culture that continues to nourish [the] energy [of man and woman]..."[91] The nature/culture of woman is distinct from that of man, which is to say that their transcendence to one another is a transcendence at both levels—the natural and the cultural.

Irigaray's sensible transcendental is also significant when we consider the *medium* within which the transcendence of man and woman to each other is situated. Irigaray argues that the interval between man and woman "is first of all nature, as it remains left to itself: air, water, earth, and the sun, as fire and light. Being par excellence—matter of the transcendental. And if some other can act as a mediator, it does not seem that this can be to the detriment of the mediation provided by the earthly elemental, as a means of return to oneself and to the other or as building material for the path."[92] Thus, not only are man and woman transcendent to one another

90. Irigaray, *I Love to You*, 104–5.
91. Ibid., 105.
92. Irigaray, *The Way of Love*, 19.

in nature and culture, but their transcendence to one another is expressed in, and mediated by, the elemental. Man and woman each partake in and are shaped by the elements in which the cosmos is constituted, and these elements both mediate and are the medium of their intersubjectivity. For Irigaray, air is the first of the four elements since it is, as she says, "the element that goes hand in hand with Being."[93] She argues, further:

> Air is what is left common between subjects living in different worlds. It is the elemental of the universe, of the life starting from which it is possible to elaborate the transcendental. Air is that in which we dwell and which dwells in us, in varied ways without doubt, but providing for passages between—in ourselves, between us. Air is the medium of our natural and spiritual life, of our relation to ourselves, to speaking, to the other. ... Air can permit us to be in communication if we are going on the way toward each other rather than believing ourselves near because of communion through or immersion in a third.[94]

Air is, and expresses, the possibility of a shared (and individual) spiritual existence for woman and man as they learn to cultivate their breath, as they share air in a communicative pattern that respects their sharing of air and the autonomy of each breathing subject. Within the framework of Irigaray's sensible transcendental, then, man and woman are transcendent to one another in virtue of the fact (i) that each has a share in an independent nature (sensible) and culture (transcendental) and (ii) that the natural element of air (sensible), which they share, represents the possibility of a spiritual (transcendental) existence between them.[95]

With respect to the mutual transcendence of man and woman to each other, we turn finally to the question of truth and knowledge, since Irigaray argues that the interval between two "has to be cleared of *a prioris*, freed from prescribed or solipsistic certitudes . . ."[96] Irigaray argues that the Western tradition, with its closed off (male) subject, has been engaged in a solipsistic debate over God, Truth, Being, and she suggests that "the capital letter with which they have been endowed to designate an absolute reality is to be interpreted as a need for a transcendence in order to close off a world of one's own. In this capital letter, a right to an immunity that

---

93. Irigaray, "From *The Forgetting of Air*," 309.
94. Irigaray, *Thy Way of Love*, 68.
95. These questions will be taken up again at some length in the next chapter.
96. Irigaray, *The Way of Love*, 66.

escapes from every dispute, even from every question, is attested to."[97] This solipsistic search for truth and certitude, however, reflects precisely man's failure to recognize that he is not the whole—man's failure to recognize the one who differs from him in nature and culture.[98] Irigaray writes: "The question of knowing whether living beings exist on other planets is acceptable to traditional science. What the scientist cannot tolerate, without changing logic, is that a living subject near to him, on the same earth, sometimes in the same house, claims to enter into a rational debate starting from a logic that is not his own."[99]

That Irigaray's account of transcendence corresponds to a transformed account of knowledge and truth is confirmed when we refer to her account of female morphology and the feminine imaginary, described in *This Sex Which is Not One*. There Irigaray argues that Freud's account of the oedipal complex defines woman's sexuality in relation to the phallus. In the pre-oedipal phase, for example, woman's sexuality is described as clitoral (which is a small penis) while in the post-oedipal phase her sexuality is described as vaginal (which provides a sheath for the penis), so that in either case her sexuality is conceived only in relation to the penis.[100] Irigaray writes: "Female sexuality has always been conceptualized on the basis of masculine parameters. Thus the opposition between 'masculine' clitoral activity and 'feminine' vaginal passivity, an opposition which Freud—and many others—saw as stages, or alternatives, in the development of a sexually 'normal' woman, seems rather too clearly required by the practice of male sexuality."[101] Over-against this definition of woman's sexuality, "feminine pleasure is not singular, unified, hierarchically subordinated to a single organ, definable or locatable according to the logic of identity."[102] Thus, in *This Sex Which is Not One*, Irigaray suggests that "woman's pleasure does not have to choose between clitoral activity and vaginal passivity, for example. The pleasure of the vaginal caress does not have to be substituted for that of the clitoral caress. . . . [Indeed] woman has sex organs more or less everywhere. She finds pleasure almost everywhere."[103]

---

97. Ibid., 103–4.
98. Ibid., 102.
99. Ibid., 104.
100. Grosz, *Sexual Subversions*, 114.
101. Irigaray, *This Sex*, 23.
102. Grosz, *Sexual Subversions*, 115.
103. Irigaray, *This Sex*, 28.

PART ONE—Irigaray and Love's Possibility

The imagery of the two lips becomes important, here, since the lips are neither one nor two—they cannot be reduced to one or two. Furthermore, the lips represent a self-touching of woman, an auto-affection unrelated to the phallus. Thus: "The *one* of the form, of the individual, of the (male) sexual organ, of the proper name, of the proper meaning . . . supplants, while separating and dividing, that contact of *at least two* (lips) which keeps woman in touch with herself, but without any possibility of distinguishing what is touching from what is touched."[104] This is not to say that insertion of the penis between the lips is an inherently violent act, contrary to the integrity of a woman's self-touching. It is to say, however, that the logic of the one, of the phallus, is incommensurable with the logic of the touching lips, which exceeds any definition as one, or as two. The purpose of the two-lips imagery, as has frequently been pointed out, is not to define woman's sexuality, or to provide a new account of woman. "The 'two lips' is not a truthful image of female anatomy but a new emblem by which female sexuality can be positively represented. For Irigaray, the problem for women is not the experience or recognition of female pleasure, but its representation, which actively constructs women's experience of their corporeality and pleasures. If female sexuality and desire are represented in some relation to male sexuality, they are submerged in a series of male-defined constraints."[105] The point of Irigaray's imagery, then, is to move the definition of woman beyond the masculine economy, so that she may become represented in her own right, according to her truth.[106]

In terms of the logic of the two lips, then, Irigaray argues that *knowledge* in the Western philosophical and cultural tradition always bears the mark of the masculine imaginary, which is to say that "what we take to be universal and objective is in fact male."[107] Furthermore, the search for the universal, objective, and certain is itself a quest particular to a phallic economy. Recognizing this, Irigaray has endeavored, particularly in the first and second phases of her work, to "subvert the functioning of dominant representations and knowledges in their singular, universal claims to truth," and does so "by highlighting the sexualized perspectives from

---

104. Ibid., 26.

105. Grosz, *Sexual Subversions*, 116.

106. As Whitford puts it, the two lips "is an attempt to symbolize auto-affection on the woman's side, the idea that woman is not simply for-men, but that she has an existence of her own." See Whitford, *Luce Irigaray*, 153.

107. Ibid., 56.

which they are produced."[108] Her emphasis on the plural and ambiguous nature of woman's pleasure and sexuality, then, is intended to demonstrate that "there is always a different way of proceeding, other kinds of knowledge possible, and no singular, uncontestable position unapproachable from other directions."[109] As Canters and Janzen point out, Irigaray's point is not that we can utterly do away with categories of thought, but that "when categories are fixed and rigid, when there is no room for fluidity and movement, then the result is impoverishment. In her paradigm, fixed categories have been instrumental in thinking about subjectivity in terms of 'one and not-one,' male and not-male. But this has resulted in the oppression of the not-one, woman."[110] In Irigaray's philosophy of sexual difference, there is "no room for a singular representative of truth, a perspectiveless position, one meaning, hierarchical organization, the normative privilege of the subject-predicate form, the syllogistic structure of arguments, the belief in the translatability of concepts—for these rely on the self-distance, denial of materiality and excess concordant with the privileging of male sexuality."[111]

Toward the Self, Toward the Other

Irigaray's logic of mediation and of the gap/abyss of sexual difference, also introduces motion into her theory and ethics of sexual difference. As observed, Irigaray's negative requires recognition that neither man nor woman is or represents the whole. This limit, she says, "leads each one back to their own self through a coming and going from the outside to the inside, from the inside to the outside of the self. Such a limit helps me to return to myself, in myself. Neither I nor the other corresponds to the absolute: neither I nor you."[112] Or, as she has expressed it in *An Ethics of Sexual Difference*: "It takes two to love. To know how to separate and how to come back together. Each to go, both he and she, in quest of self, faithful to the quest, so that they may greet one another, come close, make merry, or seal a covenant."[113] Since transcendence persists between man and woman, and since an ethical intersubjectivity requires respect

---

108. Grosz, *Sexual Subversions*, 127.
109. Ibid., 128.
110. Canters and Janzen, *Forever fluid*, 83.
111. Grosz, *Sexual Subversions*, 131.
112. Irigaray, "Why Cultivate," 84–85.
113. Irigaray, *Ethics*, 71.

PART ONE—Irigaray and Love's Possibility

for this transcendence, the relationship between the self and the other must be construed in terms of a movement across the gap or interval and of a return to the self. Further, since consummation and unification remain finally impossible, intersubjectivity between man and woman must be thought of in terms of movement, and this movement of the self is to be conceived primarily in terms of self-love or self-affection.[114] We must therefore clarify the question of self-love as it is addressed to man and woman. According to Irigaray, as we should expect by now, the problems that man and woman must overcome in the expression of self-love are unique to each, though not unrelated.

Irigaray argues that male self-love "takes the form or sounds the note of nostalgia for the maternal-feminine that has been forever lost. Insofar as man or men are concerned, it seems that auto-affection is possible only through a search for the first home. Man's self-affection depends on the woman who has given him being and birth, who has born/e him, enveloped him, warmed him, fed him."[115] As Whitford suggests, this longing for the maternal-feminine is expressed in a denial of woman's subjectivity:

> Everyone is born into dereliction through the loss of their original home but men palliate the loss at woman's expense. One will always find in this imaginary a nostalgia for the original home, an attempt to keep it for himself, own it and control it, in order to be able to return to it in phantasy (by keeping women in the home, for example, or ensuring their social dependence). But this phantasy, in symbolic form, prevents woman from acceding to her own separate being; she must always be for-men, available for their transcendence. (This picture is extremely clear in Hegel's account of marriage.)[116]

Man's self-love correlates with a refusal to relate to woman as one who is different from him, as one whose subjectivity and identity cannot be defined in terms of his own.

Man's self-love is also expressed through the creation and production of things external to himself—on account of the fact that "his sex (organ)

---

114. In *Key Writings*, Irigaray discusses this movement in terms of woman's uniting of heaven and earth (the sensible and transcendental) here and now, through her breathing: "This requires one to move but also to remain within oneself, to have exchanges with the outside and then to collect herself, to communicate with the soul of the world, sometimes with the soul of the others, and afterwards to return to the solitude and silence of her own soul." See Irigaray, "Age of Breath," 167.

115. Irigaray, *Ethics*, 60.

116. Whitford, *Luce Irigaray*, 153.

presents itself as something external, through which he can love himself."[117] Although the external nature of his sex means that man is threatened with its loss or fragmentation, "all the same, that organ is on show, on exhibit, presented or represented, even in its movements. . . . Because his sex is on display, man will make an infinite number of substitutes for it; through things that exist, things he creates, objects, women—thereby parceling out his desire. But each time at the expense of one deception or other, he believes he loves, is loved in a virtually definitive way."[118] In a profound sense, then, man is incapable of self-love and relies upon that which is external to himself in order to achieve the sense that he is loved—indeed, he invariably relies upon woman (any woman; 1+1+1+1) to provide an assurance that he is loved. This implies not only that man has not loved himself confidently and appropriately but, correlatively, that man has not taken responsibility for himself and for his own becoming as one half of humanity, since woman is not, and can never be, simply available to hand for him. As it stands, this other (woman) is imprisoned by man's need for a home, dwelling, or space (which she becomes, for him), imprisoned by patriarchy's insistence that she serve his culture and his self-love. Woman's subjectivity and self-love, here, is defined by her need to serve the self-love of man.

Irigaray indicates the relationship of man's self-love to woman's loss of subjectivity (and capacity for self-love) when she writes: "Lost, nostalgic, man entrusts to woman his memory; he makes woman the keeper of his house, his sex (organ), his history. But he is unable to establish a long-lasting love of self. And this puts the maternal-feminine in the position of keeping that love without its loving itself. Woman is meant to assimilate love to herself as her preserve, without any return for her, without any love of her which might offer her access to a space-time 'of her own.'"[119] Woman, according to Irigaray, is enclosed in a space that is in service to man and is in exile "unless she is able, in some other way, to take on the envelope of her 'own' desire, the garb of her 'own' jouissance, of her 'own'

---

117. Irigaray, *Ethics*, 63.

118. Ibid. In her discussion of the caress, also in *An Ethics of Sexual Difference*, Irigaray writes: "But does one who encounters only self in the beloved woman caress himself under the guise of a greater passivity? Adorning and inhabiting her with his own affects? If necessary, endowing her with some sense of touch as impersonal, a tactile *there is* adopted from his own subjectivity. Aporia of a tactility that cannot caress itself but needs the other to touch itself." (Ibid., 204.)

119. Irigaray, *Ethics*, 71.

love."¹²⁰ As Irigaray goes on to say, a whole history separates her from the love of herself. Nevertheless, Irigaray points to modern trends among women in order to affirm that women are taking steps to learn self-love: "Women are no longer willing to be the guardians of love, especially when it is an improbable or even pathological love. Women want to find themselves, discover themselves and their own identity. Which is why they are seeking each other out, loving each other, associating with each other. At least until the world changes. As the historical moment indispensable for women, as the period necessary to achieve love."¹²¹

According to Irigaray there are various mediations required if woman is to achieve the self-love and subjectivity that have been denied her in the culture of patriarchy. Among these necessary mediations is an among-women culture—a culture in which women are able to reestablish relations with their mothers and relations with other women, or sisters, thus overcoming mutual hostility that persisted among women when they competed with each other to take the place as man's other.¹²² Additionally, Irigaray has argued for the establishment of sexuate rights, according to which women would take up their place within society as women and not as neutral citizens (under the guise of which they are again assimilated to the model of the male).¹²³ Irigaray has also argued that women require a divine particular to them as women, in the same way that man has had a divine in his image.¹²⁴ Finally, Irigaray has also argued for the necessity of a transformation in language itself, according to which women would take up a subject position in language in ways that the logic of the one had prevented.¹²⁵

To merely enumerate these various mediations will not do justice to them. In the context of this discussion of the importance of self-love, however, and in view of the importance that self-love takes on in the context

---

120. Ibid., 65.

121. Ibid., 66.

122. Hence Irigaray's insistence—see, for example, *Je, Tu, Nous*, 45–50—on the importance of setting up public images of women together, and of women with their daughters. Elsewhere, Irigaray suggests that "woman must be able to express herself in words, images and symbols in this intersubjective relationship with her mother, then with other women, if she is to enter into a non-destructive relationship with men. This very special economy of women's identity must be permitted, known and defined." See Irigaray, *Thinking*, 20.

123. See, for example, Irigaray, *Je, Tu, Nous*, 75–92.

124. See, for example, Irigaray, "Divine Women."

125. Irigaray, *I Love to You*, 69–78.

The Negative

of intersubjectivity between man and woman, we cannot fail to mention them. If woman is to finally and fully love herself, according to Irigaray, nothing less than a dramatic cultural, religious, linguistic and legal transformation is required. As Deutscher argues, while Irigaray's early writings insisted that woman's identity is in excess of its various representations, more recently Irigaray

> has devised political programs to enable mediated relations between subjects in order to interrupt cultural cannibalism (the tendency to appropriate and interiorize the other). The emphasis is placed on the need for social and political change to interrupt cannibalism. Because the cultural and political problems we face reflect the success of cultural cannibalism, Irigaray argues the need for a series of (linguistic, legal, religious, media, and economic) social reforms that would enable mediated self-other relations and facilitate less appropriative relations between individuals in contemporary life.[126]

Again, we have neither the time nor space to explore the variety of mediations Irigaray suggests for the accomplishment of woman's self-love and for the introduction of the negative into culture. As indicated, however, the full scope of her thought must be kept in mind if we are to rightly situate her account of self-love in the relationship between two.

In concluding this chapter, then, a final word on the nature of self-love, positively construed. In "The Intimate Requires Separate Dwellings," Irigaray writes: "Without a return into oneself, how still to approach the other? To respect the other in their mystery? As invisibility to be sure, but also as proximity with oneself which needs distance in order to touch oneself again, to find oneself again, to restore the integrity of intimacy with oneself."[127] Proximity to the other will only be genuinely realized when each becomes capable of preserving his or her own identity and subjectivity. What is required, then, are places "where each one lives, separated, and where each one restores the weaving of proximity with oneself."[128] Irigaray's concern is that the relationship between two not be reduced again to a circumstance in which the other is apprehended, incorporated, seized or captured. She writes: "To include the other in my universe prevents meeting with the other, whereas safeguarding the obscurity and the silence that

---

126. Deutscher, *Politics*, 133.
127. Irigaray, *The Way of Love*, 150.
128. Ibid., 151.

PART ONE—Irigaray and Love's Possibility

the other remains for me aids in discovering proximity."[129] While Irigaray is certainly open to the transformation of the self on the basis of an encounter with the other, the subject must begin with the self and return to the self. Unless the self can remain with itself, and can make a home with itself, the relation to the other will inevitably become a relationship in which one of the two, man or woman (inevitably woman), is submitted to the logic and intention of the other. *I cannot provide a dwelling for the other, but I can claim a space of dwelling for myself and can control myself in such a way that she too might be free to discover her own dwelling space.*

129. Ibid.

2

Mind the Gap

The Ethics of Sexual Difference

> The other day, in the "Heart-to-Heart" column of one of our popular newspapers, there appeared a letter from a pathetic gentleman about a little disruption threatening his married state: He wrote: "I have been married eleven years and think a great deal of the wedding anniversary. I remind my wife a month in advance and plan to make the evening a success. But she does not share my keenness, and, if I did not remind her, would let the day go by without a thought of its significance. I thought a wedding anniversary meant a lot to a woman. Can you explain this indifference?" Poor little married gentleman, nourished upon generalizations—and convinced that if his wife does not fit into the category of "a woman" there must be something wrong!
>
> —Dorothy L. Sayers, *Are Women Human?*

According to Irigaray, introduction of the negative into culture requires transformations at the deepest levels of society—it requires linguistic, legal, spiritual, and personal transformations.[1] We are particularly concerned with the personal transformations required as the negative is

---

1. My thanks to Professor Alison Stone, Lancaster University, for comments offered on a previous draft of this chapter.

PART ONE—Irigaray and Love's Possibility

introduced into the relationship between man and woman. And in view of the gap or interval that persists between man and woman, and given the logic of movement that has been introduced above, the question of *mediation* inevitably figures prominently in Irigaray's ethics of sexual difference. As a result, the present chapter explores the ways Irigaray conceptualizes mediation and intersubjectivity in difference, the ways she conceives an ethical intersubjectivity between two.

Wonder

In *The Passions of the Soul*, René Descartes argues that wonder is the first of all the passions: "When the first encounter with some object surprises us, and we judge it to be new, or very different from what we knew in the past or what we supposed it was going to be, this makes us wonder and be astonished at it. And since this can happen before we know in the least whether this object is suitable to us or not, it seems to be that Wonder is the first of all the passions"[2] In *An Ethics of Sexual Difference*, Irigaray takes up the notion of wonder arguing that wonder should be returned to its first locus—that of sexual difference. She writes: "To arrive at the constitution of an ethics of sexual difference, we must at least return to what is for Descartes the first passion: *wonder*. This passion has no opposite or contradiction and exists always as though for the first time. Thus man and woman are always meeting as though for the first time because they cannot be substituted one for the other. I will never be in man's place, never will man be in mine. Whatever identifications are possible, one will never exactly occupy the place of the other—they are irreducible one to the other."[3] According to Irigaray, to encounter the sexuate other is to encounter someone who is other than me, who is unlike me, and who resists every attempt to define her/him in terms of my own identity. In every encounter or meeting between a man and a woman, according to Irigaray, the appropriate response is wonder, the first of the passions. Wonder, in Irigaray's thought, is closely related to the idea of the other as an enigma, a theme that appears everywhere in her writings. She suggests: "[T]he other, if s/he is still alive, remains incomprehensible to us since, with every moment, s/he is the source of new gestures whose origin remains a mystery to us. The other is moving within a horizon, and constructing a world, that

2. Descartes, *Passions*, 52.
3. Irigaray, *Ethics*, 13.

38

lie beyond us."⁴ The question is: How could one stand in judgment of that which is a mystery?⁵

While we have identified wonder in terms of a theoretical understanding, it is evident that wonder both points to (theoretically) and instantiates (personally) the becoming of the human as two. In terms of the latter dimension, however, a problem seems to arise. To get clear on this question we are reminded of Descartes' assumption that an object or event will either strike us as new (thus eliciting wonder) or it will not. From Descartes' point of view, wonder seems to be generated spontaneously. Applying this to the relationship between man and woman generates a difficulty since it seems contrary to Descartes' account of wonder to insist that a person could/should generate wonder as an act of the will. To put it differently: If I do not experience wonder before the face of one who differs from me sexually, is that not the end of the story? Isn't wonder simply impossible in this circumstance? It would appear that Irigaray's embrace of wonder functions well in a theoretical sense (in describing sexual difference) but remains problematic as it is introduced into particular relationships between men and women.

To extend this discussion we might consider a related matter discussed by Penelope Deutscher in *A Politics of Impossible Difference*. Deutscher suggests that Irigaray's privileging of the heterosocial and heterosexual as a locus of difference is bound up with the faulty assumption that we have the capacity "to identify and anticipate the site of mystery."⁶ The site of mystery and wonder, according to Deutscher, is, by definition, that which cannot be anticipated ahead of time—indeed, to say that the site of mystery or wonder can be anticipated or identified ahead of time is contradictory. In developing her critique of Irigaray's later writings, Deutscher points out that Irigaray's thought requires that the difference between man and woman be transparent to them, so that each is able to declare "here is difference."⁷ This implies, however, that the site of mystery has been identified ahead of time.

For Deutscher, this contradictory account of mystery in sexual difference is rooted in Irigaray's de-emphasizing of her earlier insistence on the differing/deferring nature of human identity and subjectivity. While

---

4. Ibid., 7.

5. In this single paragraph we have provided a summary of the lengthier treatment offered in De Vries, "Wonder between Two."

6. Deustcher, *Politics*, 141.

7. Ibid., 139.

the earlier writings provide resources for developing an account of sexual difference in which the identity of man or woman remains open, the later writings seem to provide content to sexual difference in a way that denies this earlier impulse.[8] Deutscher writes:

> In her later work, Irigaray would depict a man and woman, understood as foreign to each other, knowing each other as two foreign entities, secure in their recognition of the other as different, the difference lying between them. Difference also lies at the heart of each. This is the very point of Irigaray's concept of belonging to a sexuate genre. This being the case, why are we sometimes presented with images of a peaceful comfortable encounter between a man and a woman, each saying of the other, with confidence: here is difference? Where the encounter is formulated in such terms, some may be reassured that they are in the presence of an identifiable "philosophy of sexual difference." But many critics have noted the risk that difference becomes instead identity and loses its status as à venir. Perhaps the answer to the question "What is sexual difference?" must be left open.[9]

Deutscher suggests that the differing/deferring nature of human identity requires that we locate mystery at the heart of human subjectivity itself. Thus she writes that "it could be counter-argued that it is not the genres that are irreducibly different from each other. Relationship to genre enhances difference between subjects (and difference at the heart of subjects). But the genres are not two radically distinct, different forces. *It is the subjects,* mediated by their relationship to genre, *who are irreducibly different from each other.*"[10] Deutscher adds: "Mystery is the site of that which we cannot predict, and there can be no prior assurance that the homosocial or the homosexual will be less the source of natural or spiritual life than is the heterosocial or heterosexual. Indeed, the definition and locale of life itself must remain as much the locus of unanticipated mystery..."[11] Thus, rather than locating wonder and mystery comfortably between a man and woman, Deutscher would first locate wonder and difference between human subjects themselves. Indeed, she takes this to be the impulse of Irigaray's earlier writings.

8. Ibid., 116.
9. Ibid., 121.
10. Ibid., 140. Italics added.
11. Ibid., 141.

Mind the Gap

Deutscher underscores for us the question whether Irigaray's positive, transparent account of sexual difference (her willingness to answer the question "what is the difference between man and woman") renders the logic of wonder meaningless. Before exploring this question at greater length, however, we should point out that Deutscher's own approach to the question of sexual difference is such that she herself remains indebted to the transparency of sexual difference, even as she undermines the concepts of sexual difference and sexuate genre. In the first instance we consider her undermining of sexual difference and of sexuate genre.

In *A Politics of Impossible Difference*, having insisted that the boundaries between the self and the other can never be secured, Deutscher goes on to write:

> What are the implications [of this] for the relationships between those belonging to different genres? *The boundaries between the sexuate genres to which they belong could similarly never be cordoned from each other.* The series of infinite relations I have with those of my sexuate genre, which sex me as female or male (and as permanently incomplete as such), could not be considered as radically distinct and separable from the infinite series of relations that sex the opposite sex. These series must intertwine in every way, in relations of identification and distinction, of distancing and proximity, and in the relations of identification, love, envy, and aggression one has with those of the same and the other sex.[12]

In the same vein, she earlier suggests that it is plausible that "these two series could not be clearly distinguished from each other."[13] It is evident, then, that Deutscher conceives of the boundaries between the sexuate genres as porous—their boundaries are not fixed and it is possible that they cannot be distinguished from each other. But isn't the concept of sexuate genre very near collapse, here? If the sexuate genres must intertwine in every way, and cannot be clearly distinguished from each other, one is justified in asking whether they don't finally run together into an undifferentiated status, and whether the very concept of sexuate genre is left without meaning.

That the concept of *sexuate* genre is very near collapse in Deutscher's thought becomes apparent when she later asks why we must conceive of

12. Ibid., 137. Italics added.
13. Ibid., 121.

PART ONE—Irigaray and Love's Possibility

two genres.¹⁴ In reply to this question, Deutscher suggests that the logic of two interrupts the logic of one—she is saying that the logic of two can interrupt the destructive logic of sameness that has prevailed in Western culture.¹⁵ But if the sexuate genres ultimately run together into an undifferentiated status, and if the logic of two is simply of strategic value (on the way from the one to the multiple), has the concept of *sexuate* genre not in some sense collapsed? Can the words "man" and "woman" have any content if the sexuate genres are not irreducibly different? Certainly, Deutscher seems to leave us with the concept of something called "genre" (that which might allow for non-identificatory identity structures) but the word "sexuate" is necessarily dropped (thus she ends up with multiple genres). Before turning to the question of Deutscher's own *dependence* on that which she has undermined (namely, *sexuate* genre), we consider briefly a key reason *why* Deutscher has undermined sexuate genre.

As observed, Deutscher insists that a mystery is, by definition, that which cannot be identified ahead of time—one cannot decide ahead of time, therefore, whether mystery will be encountered in the homosocial/homosexual context and/or in the heterosocial/heterosexual context. Deutscher therefore argues as follows: "Irigaray could still situate difference between men and women, so long as she also situated it between women and women, between men and men, and at the heart of every subject, in their differing, deferring identity. But when heterosociality and heterosexuality become the privileged site of difference, and homosociality and homosexuality the privileged site of sameness, then the concept of identity as differing and deferring has collapsed."¹⁶ What is present here in a somewhat opaque manner becomes more obvious when Deutscher goes on to insist, as observed, that "it is *the subjects*, mediated by their relationship to genre, *who are irreducibly different from each other*."¹⁷ According to Deutscher, the subject is by definition in a constant process of becoming, and the boundaries of the subject are porous and flexible (such that his or her identity is always only established in relation to others),

14. Ibid., 186.

15. Thus we find her saying that "the significance of the two should be understood as a critical intervention into a history dominated by one kind of subject. Irigaray emphasizes that there are two sexes because she considers that Western culture has been particularly resistant to the 'two'. Political thought has favored the mode of the 'one' subject (often a subject who is assumed to have a politically invisible domestic helpmate)." See Deutscher, *Politics*, 86.

16. Ibid., 139.

17. Ibid., 40. Italics added.

which is to say that human subjectivity itself is the first locus of difference and mystery. Thus, to insist that the heterosocial is the privileged locus of difference and mystery represents a refusal of the primacy of human identity and subjectivity as differing and deferring. Deutscher undermines *sexuate* genre, then, because a focus on *sexuate* genre distracts from the mystery of human subjectivity itself.[18]

But it is important to note that Deutscher, even as she undermines the significance of *sexuate* genre for human identity, continues to rely on that which she undermines. While she insists that the (sexuate) genres cannot be distinguished from each other, and that they cannot be cordoned off from each other, she nevertheless continues to speak of persons "of the same and the other sex."[19] But if the sexuate genres cannot be cordoned off from each other, what can it mean to speak of persons "of the same and the other sex?" It seems evident that Deutscher's own response to Irigaray is haunted by the transparency of sexual difference. That is, if Deutscher believes that the answer to the question "What is sexual difference?" must be left open, and that the sexuate genres cannot be finally cordoned off from each other, then on what basis does she refer to a person's relation to "those of the same and the other sex?" What can it mean to speak about "man" and "woman" if these are without content, or simply cannot be defined?

It may be Deutscher's contention that present cultural and symbolic configurations require that we think within these categories—that they are all we have. In this case the concepts "man" and "woman" are simply empty placeholders, necessary only so long as a culture of difference (*not* a culture of *sexual* difference) is lacking. At the same time, however, it is worth noting that it is in precisely those passages where Deutscher argues for a new and transformed account of human subjectivity that she invokes the categories of "the same and the other sex." Alternatively, then, perhaps Deutscher conceives of *sexuate* genre (of "man" and "woman") as a merely biological marker utterly at the disposal of culture—thus falling into a familiar pattern of negating the natural in favor of the cultural. Here "man" and "woman" would refer to biological realities that are ultimately insignificant for human identity and subjectivity since (as it would be argued) the essentially human is defined at the level of culture and sociality

---

18. We recall that Deutscher still depends upon the notion of genre, since it is genre, in her framework, that allows for the development of a non-identificatory identity—an identity that remains open, unforeclosed.

19. Deutscher, *Politics*, 137.

PART ONE—Irigaray and Love's Possibility

and spirituality. Thus it is not entirely clear what Deutscher has in mind when she speaks of "the same and the other sex" or when she speaks about "males" and "females." Her account of the impossible sexual difference seems both to require the concepts "man" and "woman" (what is *sexuate* genre without men and women?) and to undermine them (what are men and women when *sexuate* genre is displaced in favor of multiple, intertwining genres?).[20]

In terms of our own engagement with Irigaray, the decisive issue is Deutscher's contention that an insistence on the transparency of sexual difference correlates with an essentialist account of what it is to be man or woman and that the logic of wonder is undermined by insistence on the transparency of sexual difference. However, while Irigaray insists on the transparency of sexual difference, it is not apparent that her account of sexual difference implies knowledge of what man and woman are, essentially. Her account of sexual difference does not, in fact, assume that men and women have utterly distinct, and self-possessed identities. As has been shown, Irigaray conceives of sexual difference in terms of the differing subjectivities of man and woman (which owe to their difference or non-difference in relation to the mother)—a reality that finds expression in the different speech patterns of boys and girls. In view of this, it is surprising to find Deutscher writing as follows: "Irigaray's philosophy of sexual difference *is not* based in claims about the differences between men and women: for example, *how do they use language differently*, or manifest a specific motility and agility. While she does sometimes discuss such data, Irigaray considers them to be illustrative of the absence, not the presence of sexual difference."[21] Similarly, earlier in *A Politics of Impossible Difference* Deutscher argues that the sexedness of discourse, according to Irigaray, "is evidence of the absence of sexual difference. . . . It demonstrates that there is no adequate exchange or communication between sexed subjects."[22]

20. Amy Hollywood suggests that despite Irigaray's explicit antiessentialism, "it is not clear how one can recognize the other as other without some defining characteristics of alterity. If those defining characteristics are to be created and imagined, why reduce them to sexual difference? And why reduce this difference to the difference between only two entities, when we have seen such binaries offer an inadequate account of the multiplicity of sexed bodily experience, and, thus, are potentially exclusionary. If, on the other hand, Irigaray asserts that sexual difference is not created and imagined but ontological (whether as something bodily or psychic), then we return to the charges of essentialism . . ." See Hollywood, *Sensible Ecstasy*, 232.

21. Deutscher, *Politics*, 192. Italics added.

22. Ibid., 112.

In making this argument, however, Deutscher is unjustifiably assimilating Irigaray's later writings to (an interpretation of) her earlier writings—she interprets Irigaray's statements concerning language differences in boys and girls, men and women, in terms of the absence of sexual difference and not in terms of the positive content of difference. While Irigaray will agree that differences in subjectivity contribute to a failure of communication (where a culture of sexual difference is lacking), her explicit statements concerning the different subject positions of men and women, and concerning differences between them in language use and intersubjectivity, rule out Deutscher's interpretation. As Irigaray puts it in *Key Writings*: "Girls and boys, from a very young age, express themselves in different ways, through language and through their behavior in general. . . . *To maintain that difference is the result of a simple apprenticeship in social stereotypes is to deny that girls and boys come into the world in a different relational context.*"[23] Additionally, in *Democracy Begins between Two* Irigaray argues: "Women and men rely, then, on different subjective configurations and ways of speaking. These cannot be attributed solely to socio-historical determinations . . ."[24] Again, while Irigaray accepts that current patterns of language-use point to our lack of a culture of sexual difference, she also argues that differences in language-use allow us to affirm and define (to some extent) sexual difference.

This discussion of Deutscher's response to Irigaray's later writings has not been a pointless digression from our discussion of wonder between two. Indeed, two important questions are now more clearly posed for us:

1. How can we claim both that sexual difference is transparent *and* that man and woman represent a mystery to each other? Or: Is it possible to insist on the transparency of sexual difference and at the same time insist that man and woman cannot be defined?

2. What is the relationship between the mystery at the heart of human subjectivity and identity and the mystery that exists between sexually different being?

The first of these questions is ours more directly in the present chapter. The latter will be taken up in the context of our engagement with Irigaray and Kierkegaard, below.

---

23. Irigaray, *Key Writings*, 87. Italics added. Diane Perpich suggests that while the difference or non-difference of the child in relation to the mother may be significant, it is not necessarily a/the defining difference in the human. See Perpich, "Subjectivity," 407.

24. Irigaray, *Democracy*, 137.

PART ONE—Irigaray and Love's Possibility

Irigaray insists that sexual difference is defined by the differing subjectivities of man and woman and she takes this difference to be transparent—anyone with a tape-recorder can discover it.[25] Yet Irigaray provides only a thin account of what it is to be man or woman. She remains consistently unwilling to describe the identity of man or woman beyond a thin account of their respective subject positions and rhythms. As Diane Perpich argues, Irigaray's is a metaphysics and an ethics of becoming, which is to say that one can never pin down what it means to belong to one sexuate genre or the other.[26] Indeed, as is evident from our exploration thus far, Irigaray's account of the negative, and her ethics of sexual difference, is built precisely on the conviction that man and woman confront, in each other, a mystery beyond naming. Her ethics, then, conforms with the answer she gives to the question "what is sexual difference"—in each case she refuses to say that "*this* is what woman is, essentially" or that "*this* is what man is, essentially."

As a result, in a way that Deutscher would not allow, Irigaray holds together an insistence on the transparency of sexual difference with an insistence that mystery lies at the heart of human subjectivity. Thus we find her saying: "Of course, no one can be reduced to anyone else, but the most fundamental locus of irreducibility is between man and woman."[27] Since each person is in process of becoming, there is no one moment in which we can fully or decisively define that person. On the other hand, the "self-evident" nature of sexual difference implies that we are able to identify each person as either a "woman" or a "man"—thus we are able to insist that the human is composed of two beings irreducible to each other. Furthermore, the transparency of sexual differences does not imply that wonder is inappropriate here—a thin essentialism is at work here that leaves open a vast and definitive enigma.[28] On account of this we rarely (if ever) find Irigaray employing static language to describe either man or woman, and rarely find her employing static language to describe the encounter between those who represent distinct natures/cultures.

25. Deutscher, *Politics*, 112. Deutscher is quoting Irigaray, *Ethics*, 136.
26. Perpich, "Sensible Subjects," 307–8.
27. Irigaray, *I Love to You*, 139.
28. Thus, Patricia Huntingdon will argue that, for Irigaray, woman "is not a unified category under which all particular women's identities fall and into which they could be resolved without excess. To the contrary, Woman is a formal signifier that lends itself to proliferation; it gains substance only through the manifold ways that specific women interpret their actual and dissimilar lives." See Huntingdon, *Ecstatic Subjects*, 140.

Mind the Gap

A question remains: Is it legitimate to demand wonder from one who does not spontaneously experience wonder before the face/body/being of the other? Can wonder be commanded? We are asking whether the need to cultivate wonder between two is contrary to the definition of wonder since wonder seems to be spontaneous by nature. We tentatively conclude that wonder can be cultivated by man and woman (can be required of each) in their relationship to, and encounter with, one another.

Perhaps the first step toward the cultivation of wonder would consist in a simple awareness that woman has historically been defined in relation to man; wonder would begin with an awareness that this passion has been displaced from its first locus. To become aware of this displacement, and of the logic by which woman has been defined and appropriated in relation to man, is to radically transform the relational context. That is, if man comes to the realization that woman is other than what he has known her to be, and comes to the awareness that a whole set of social structures and personal presuppositions have conspired to define her in relation to him, then his awareness that she exceeds this identification of her should (might?) have an impact on him in his relation to her. Of course, man might simply refuse woman a free space of becoming. Man might insist that the representation of woman with which he and his culture have functioned is an adequate and faithful representation, and that the notion of wonder between two is built upon a tendentious foundation. There appears to be little basis for "proving" that Western culture must take these initial steps beyond the symbolic framework with which it has functioned. As we have noted, the only proof that Irigaray seems prepared to offer in this regard is evidence of present unhappiness among men and women—an unhappiness that is also expressed, on a macro level, in environmental degradation and a culture of war. Beyond this, she might also point to the "self-evident" difference between men (boys) and women (girls) in language use, and to the "self-evident" difference in the temporal rhythms that make them men and women. On the basis of an awareness that woman is other than what has been assumed (the identity of woman is far in excess of what we thought we knew), wonder finds its appropriate locus between particular men and women.

The Caress

Irigaray's vision of the caress gives expression to, and remains indebted to, her account of wonder. In the concluding essay of *An Ethics of Sexual*

PART ONE—Irigaray and Love's Possibility

Difference, in which Irigaray engages with Levinas on the question of the caress, she writes: "Sensual pleasure can reopen and reverse this conception and construction of the world, in which the subject knows its objects and controls its relations with the world and with others. It can return to the evanescence of subject and object. To the lifting of all schemas by which the other is defined. Made graspable by this definition. *Eros* can arrive at that innocence which has never taken place with the other as other."[29] Irigaray is suggesting that the erotic encounter between man and woman can become a context in which wonder is cultivated and experienced. Irigaray will also suggest the opposite, however, when she says that wonder is "a primary passion and a perpetual crossroads between earth and sky, or hell, *where it would be possible to rework attraction between those who differ*, especially sexually."[30] Thus, the caress allows man and woman to encounter one another as for the first time (in wonder) and the cultivation of wonder leads to an ethical sensuality. Beyond the mutual implication of wonder and the caress, Irigaray's account of the caress gives expression to her ethics of the negative. Irigaray conceives of the encounter between man and woman as one in which neither is defined or appropriated or circumscribed by the other. In continuity with this, Irigaray suggests that sensual pleasure can return us to "the lifting of all schemas by which the other is defined. Made graspable by this definition."[31] Finally, before turning to a more substantive discussion of the caress, we point out that Irigaray develops her account of eros and the caress in conversation with Levinas and in terms of what she sees as Western assumptions and convictions about the nature of the erotic encounter between man and woman.

At the outset of her engagement with Levinas, Irigaray suggests that eros, of which the caress is the first gesture, should be conceived as prior to the establishment of the subject as such. She writes: "*Eros* prior to any *eros* defined or framed as such. The sensual pleasure of birth into a world where the look itself remains tactile—open to the light. Still carnal. Voluptuous without knowing it. Always at the beginning and not based on the origin of a subject that sees, grows old, and dies of losing touch with the enthusiasm and innocence of a perpetual beginning. A subject already 'fixed.' Not

---

29. Irigaray, *Ethics*, 186.

30. Ibid., 80. Italics added.

31. Ibid., 186. The relationship between the caress and wonder is in evidence here, also, since Irigaray will speak of wonder as that which does not "seize, possess, or reduce this object, but leaves it subjective, still free." See Irigaray, *Ethics*, 13.

'free as the wind.' A subject that already knows its objects and controls its relations with the world and with others."[32] To say that the caress is prior to the subject is not to suggest a temporal sequence. Rather, the caress is both "prior to *and following* any positioning of the subject . . ."[33] Thus, the caress should be seen as an interruption of subjectivity as it is lived in the everyday; or, should be seen as an interruption of a subjectivity that would reduce intersubjectivity to the subject-object encounter. Cathryn Vasseleu argues that the caress, for Irigaray, "is a never-to-be-grasped beginning, an attraction without consummation, always on the threshold of appetite, not yet anticipating or yearning for an other. The caress affirms and protects its infinite otherness in the prolongation of a birth which will never come to pass. Untouched by mastery, it is before and beyond any subject or setting. Life, made familiar in its consumption and habitation, is suspended and reopened in the gesture of the caress."[34] To caress, or be caressed, is to step back from subjectivity as it has come to expression in Western culture, in terms of subject and object, and of mastery. Eros expresses an *anticipation* of a subjectivity that may yet appear.[35] Indeed, we might go one step further and suggest that the caress (the erotic and sensual encounter between man and woman) will be a condition of the emergence of a subjectivity particular to man and woman.

The question arises as to how the caress can be construed as the condition of the emergence of a subjectivity other than that which we have known. The answer Irigaray provides is that the caress gives birth to, engenders, the subject by providing him or her with a sense of his or her boundary or outline—thus, the ego only makes its appearance when the caressing hands of the other have disclosed its outlines (physical and spiritual), without at the same time subjugating it.[36] Irigaray, then, conceives of the caress as a means of affirming the boundaries of man and woman

32. Ibid., 185.

33. Ibid., 186. Italics added.

34. Vasseleu, *Textures of Light*, 115. Elsewhere, Irigaray writes: "The caress is a reawakening to the life of my body: to its skin, senses, muscles, nerves, and organs, most of the time inhibited, subjugated, dormant or enslaved to everyday activity, to the universe of needs, to the world of labor, to the imperatives or restrictions necessary for communal living." See Irigaray, *To Be Two*, 25.

35. Diane Perpich affirms this when she says that "the subject thus preexists and precedes itself—not as potentiality precedes actuality, or capacity activity, but in a quite different manner unique to the mode of being of one who is *born*." See Perpich, "Sensible Subjects," 305.

36. Ibid., 305.

PART ONE—Irigaray and Love's Possibility

in erotic encounter, which is to say that subjectivity makes its appearance in the space of the sensual, where sexual difference is also recognized. She writes: "This gesture, which is always and still preliminary to and in all nuptials, which weds without consum(mat)ing, which perfects *while abiding by the outlines of the other*, this gesture may be called: the touch of the caress."[37] The caress is an invitation to each subject to abide by the outlines of the other and to respect his or her difference.[38]

Even more, however, the caress is a positive means by which a man or woman is provided with a sense of his or her own integrity and subjectivity—the palms of the other give me the boundaries of my own self: "Approaching and speaking to me with his hands. Bringing me back to life more intimately than any regenerative nourishment, the other's hands, these palms with which he approaches without going through me, give me back the borders of my body. . . . As he caresses me, he bids me neither to disappear nor to forget but rather to remember the place where, for me, the most intimate life is held in reserve."[39] The caress, then, has a two-fold function as it invites me to recognize the bodily/spiritual presence of the other even as her palms remind me of the space of my own becoming. If the caress has all too often become a means of grasping, holding, and appropriating the other, Irigaray would inaugurate the caress as that by which the alterity and boundaries of the other are respected, and affirmed. "[T]he caress leads each person back to the *I* and to the *you*. I give you to yourself because you are a *you* for me."[40] This *I* and this *you* are each selves of distinct nature (body) and culture (spirit), are each selves in becoming—caressing hands affirm this for each.

In order that the caress might become a genuine encounter, a "yes" must be spoken from each side of the interval. In the context of a discussion of sexuate (civil) rights, Irigaray makes the following comment: "It is important that each has been able to assent freely before the other approaches and goes beyond the sphere of subjective integrity, an integrity which should be protected by a right."[41] The question of consent, however, arises prior to and apart from the question of sexuate rights, and is ap-

37. Irigaray, *Ethics*, 186. Italics added.

38. Diane Perpich writes: "The caress neither consumes nor completes what it touches; it is a relation that follows the contours of the other, helping to define them, to show them to themselves, without either mastering or being mastered by the caressed body." See Perpich, "Sensible Subjects," 304.

39. Irigaray, *Ethics*, 187.

40. Irigaray, *To Be Two*, 27.

41. Ibid., 26.

propriately discussed with reference to intersubjectivity between man and woman. Irigaray writes:

> A *yes* from both should precede every caress.
>
> A *yes* which gives permission to go beyond the limits of communal life toward your concrete presence.
>
> A *yes* which is proof of my consent to your approach to my body, to my sensibility and to my most intimate language, all of which are foreign to the coexistence between citizens.[42]

The caress must be assented to, in part, because the encounter between man and woman entails risk. "In us, sensible nature and spirit become in-stance by remaining within their own singularity and grow through the risk of an exchange with what is irreducible to oneself."[43] A "yes" must precede the risk-filled encounter in which each hopes that he or she will be delivered separately into the world, in a rebirth and becoming that was previously inconceivable.[44]

The caress, then, is a means by which the mutual, individual becoming of man and woman, as physical and spiritual beings, is fostered. Irigaray will express it as follows in *I Love to You*: "The carnal act [the caress] ceases to be a regression to degree zero for pleasure or words; rather it is the locus for the lovers' revival and becoming."[45] In this sensual encounter, or this creation of a free space for the becoming of the other, the love between man and woman becomes also an encounter in which the two *together* are transformed: "Love, even carnal love, is therefore cultivated and made divine. The act of love becomes the transubstantiation of the self and his or her lover into a spiritual body. . . . Love is redemption of the flesh through the transfiguration of desire *for* the other (as an object?) into desire *with* the other."[46] In the caress, man and woman *together* fulfill the human, not as an abstract and neutral subjectivity but as two who are irreducible to each other yet who meet meaningfully in spirit and flesh.

It is here that Irigaray's language of fecundity comes into its own since she will argue that the caress is the source of fecundity, prior to any question of procreation. While Levinas insists that the fecundity of the

---

42. Ibid., 26–27.
43. Ibid., 29.
44. The language of this sentence is, in part, borrowed from Cathryn Vasseleu. See her *Textures of Light*, 117.
45. Irigaray, *I Love to You*, 138.
46. Ibid.

caress is expressed in the child (the son!) that results from the encounter between two, Irigaray objects: "Prior to any procreation, the lovers bestow on each other—life. Love fecundates both of them in turn, through the genesis of their immortality. They are reborn, each for the other, in the assumption and absolution of a definitive conception."[47] As each respects the other and gives the other his or her boundaries, and as they share together in physical and spiritual intimacy, man and woman fecundate one another. This fecundity owes specifically to their difference.

> From the other irradiates a truth which we can receive without its source being visible. That from which the other elaborates meaning remains a mystery for us but we can indirectly perceive something of it. Such an operation transforms the subject, enlightens the subject in a way that is both visible and invisible. The light that then reaches us illuminates the world otherwise, and discloses to us the particularity of our point of view. ... It opens new possibilities of perceiving and of elaborating space and time, delivering them from the opacity of the night while still arranging nothing—only the unfolding of another manner of looking at, of listening to, of welcoming the real, taking into account the importance of the other in their existence. It keeps alive the astonishment, the questioning, the movement of thinking and of saying.[48]

According to Irigaray, the negative at the heart of human subjectivity requires and makes possible an openness toward the mystery of the other, in relation to whom (and in the light of whom) I am set free to perceive myself differently. Thus I am transformed in myself, and we together are able to build a new world in which the mystery and intention of each is given a place. There is a "blossoming in what is proper to oneself" and a contributing toward "the blossoming of the other in what is proper to him, or her."[49] The content of this fecundity cannot be guaranteed or pinned down in advance of the encounter between two, yet as each respects the becoming of the other, and approaches the mystery and interiority of the other with attentiveness, this fecundity finds expression.

In Western culture, says Irigaray, the erotic has been bound up with the logic of sameness by which man identifies and circumscribes woman—the erotic encounter (the caress) has become a means by which man

---

47. Irigaray, *Ethics*, 190
48. Ibid., 164.
49. Ibid., 130.

possesses, grasps, or appropriates woman. Thus we find Irigaray juxtaposing her own account of the caress with this tendency toward appropriation and containment: "The gesture of the one who caresses has nothing to do with ensnarement, possession or submission of the freedom of the other who fascinates me in his body."[50] In a similar vein, Irigaray argues as follows: "Rather than grasping you—with my hand, with my gaze, with my intellect—I must stop before the inappropriable, leaving the transcendence between us to be. 'You who are not and will never be me or mine' are and remain *you*, since I cannot grasp you, understand you, possess you. You escape every ensnarement, every submission to me, if I respect you not so much because you are transcendent to your body, but because you are transcendent to me."[51] Whereas the desire to grasp the other, to take hold of the other, and to possess the other correlates with a refusal to respect the natural/cultural transcendence of the other, the caress becomes an approach in which the other's distinct nature and culture is acknowledged. Over-against the caress as an expression of woman's elision, then, Irigaray would inaugurate the caress as an expression of the negative—of the twoness of the human.

In anticipation of our discussion of air/breath/speaking, it is helpful to remember that Irigaray's account of the caress cannot be divorced from the symbolic and linguistic realms. She writes: "We need to start again from the relationship between words, gesture and meaning in an incarnate subject—a subject made of body and language—in order to revise the symbolic universe."[52] Here, "the carnal act becomes an act of speech, speech that respects woman and man, and is mindful of silence and breath."[53] In *To Be Two* Irigaray refers to the caress as a "gesture-word" and in doing so suggests that the caress can become "an offering of consciousness, a gift of intention and of word addressed to the concrete presence of the other, to his natural and historical particularities."[54] The binding together of sensible and transcendental is expressed in a gesture-word (the caress) that touches the other through words and body together—thus respecting and giving the other his or her boundaries and self, both through one's palms and one's words.

50. Irigaray, *To Be Two*, 26.
51. Ibid., 19.
52. Irigaray, "Different but United," 114.
53. Irigaray, *I Love to You*, 124.
54. Irigaray, *To Be Two*, 26.

PART ONE—Irigaray and Love's Possibility

> In this vein, Irigaray speaks of communication as a "touching upon," which respects the other, proffering him/her attentiveness, including carnal attentiveness. Here it is worth quoting Irigaray at length:
>
>> This *touching upon* asks for silence. To allow the other to emerge, silence is necessary, a silence that breaks the contiguity of a touching everything, each and every man or woman.
>>
>> This *touching upon* requires breath, the safeguard of the presence of life and of its temporalization in a becoming of self non-destructive to the other.
>>
>> This *touching upon* needs attentiveness to the sensible qualities of speech, to voice tone, to the modulation and rhythm of discourse, to the semantic and phonic choice of words . . .
>>
>> This *touching upon* cannot be appropriation, capture, seduction—to me, toward me, in him—nor envelopment. Rather it is to be the other's awakening to him/her and a call to coexist, to act together and dialogue.
>>
>> The intention of this *touching upon* would not be to tear the other away from the intimacy or interiority of his/her own self, from his/her temporality, nor to make him/her fall back into the natural immediacy of simple touching. In this *touching upon*, there is nature and spirit, breath, sensibility, body and speech.[55]

The caress is an encounter requiring *perception*—which requires not only that we be moved (passively) by sensual pleasure (as by an object) but that we remain attentive to the intention of the other—to that which is interior to the other and thus invisible to me.[56] Perception requires standing back from the other, recognizing that I cannot see the whole, and cannot possess that which is a mystery to me—I must remain open and attentive to the intention of the other, even as I recognize that I will never be able to love the other or speak to the other or perceive the other in her fullness. Thus, to perceive the other is to remain open not only to the words of the other, but also to the language of her body, to her tone of voice, and to the

---

55. Irigaray, *I Love to You*, 125.

56. A chapter of *To Be Two* is dedicated to exploring the distinction between sensation and perception. Irigaray writes: "Our spiritual senses are not trained to love. We do not yet know how to look at or listen to the other as subject. We still ignore the possibility of giving up a centered gaze, a fixed sight, a renunciation which would leave space and air around and within the other. I look at someone who, to a certain degree, remains invisible to me. I refuse the separation between the visible of this world and the invisible of the beyond. I look at you who are invisible against a background of invisibility: a background composed of our interiorities, our becomings." See Irigaray, *To Be Two*, 42.

rhythm of her speech. It means, as we shall observe, remaining attentive also to her breath.

Sharing Air—Learning Silence

Throughout the three phases of her work, pre-Socratic language of the elements pervades Irigaray's writings, and she has completed three works each dedicated to one of the elements: *Elemental Passions* (earth), *Marine Lover of Friedrich Nietzsche* (water), and *The Forgetting of Air in Martin Heidegger* (air). The fourth book, on fire, remains unwritten. While this emphasis on the elemental remains in place in Irigaray's later writings, the nature of her engagement with the elemental has changed significantly. Commenting on the place of the elemental in the earlier writings, Elizabeth Grosz suggests: "Empedocles' representation of the four elements provides a startling yet apposite *metaphor* of the meeting of different substances, a perilous meeting which, through Love, can bring productivity and unexpected creation, and through Strife can break down apparent unities and stable forms of co-existence. It is thus a rich *metaphor* for contemplating the possibilities of autonomy and interaction between the sexes."[57] To this, Whitford adds:

> The elements allow Irigaray to speak of the female body, of its morphology, and of the erotic, while *avoiding the dominant sexual metaphoricity* which is scopic and organized around the male gaze; she can speak of it instead in terms of space and thresholds and fluids, fire and water, air and earth, without objectifying, hypostatizing, or essentializing it. These terms are not so easily reduced to the body of one sex or the other. They are more pliable, accessible to the imagination of others and available for their private mental landscapes.[58]

While these interpretations of the elemental in Irigaray are not inaccurate, they are nonetheless bound up with the assumptions and preoccupations of the first and second phases of Irigaray's work.[59] In those phases the elemental was a means of surpassing the logic of Western philosophical discourses by way of an appeal to that which exceeds and undermines that logic.

57. Grosz, *Sexual Subversions*, 169. Italics added.
58. Whitford, *Luce Irigaray*, 62. Italics added.
59. Indeed, how could they do otherwise since they are published in 1989 and 1991, respectively.

PART ONE—Irigaray and Love's Possibility

From the perspective of the third phase of Irigaray's writings, however, what is striking in the passages from Grosz and Whitford is the language of "metaphor," since Irigaray's appeal to the elemental in the third phase of her work cannot be reduced to metaphor.[60] In *The Way of Love*, Irigaray writes: "Air is the environment where humans come into the world, where they grow, live and work. . . . Air is the medium of our natural and spiritual life . . ."[61] In *I Love to You* she relates the element of air to the act of respiration: "Only a mother breathes for her child. Once born, we all must, should, breathe for ourselves."[62] While the language of "metaphor" is not completely out of place in describing Irigaray's later appeal to the elemental, it remains secondary.

As we have noted, Irigaray insists that the interval between man and woman "is first of all nature as it remains left to itself: air, water, earth, and sun, as fire and light. Being par excellence—matter of the transcendental."[63] Later in *The Way of Love* she will insist on *air* as the medium and mediator of the interval/gap between sexuate beings: "This distance is never covered, always to be passed through, and ever to be started anew. And the gap has to be maintained. The transcendence between us, this one which is fecund in graces and in words, requires an interval, it engenders it also. *The space will be more or less left in its elemental form, the air* . . ."[64] While one might have thought that this gap could have been conceived of in terms of empty space or nothingness, Irigaray insists that the gap between man and woman is to be understood in terms of the materiality of air.[65] The ethical implications of this, according to Irigaray, are multiple. In the first instance, however, we note Irigaray's insistence that Western culture is implicated in a forgetting of air and in a denial of woman's access to air— that is, Western culture is caught up in attitudes toward air and toward

---

60. Diane Perpich, in her generally helpful essay on Irigaray's appeal to air/breath, nevertheless insists on the primacy of the metaphorical even in Irigaray's later writings: "In the interview in *This Sex Which is Not One*, Irigaray identifies metaphoricity with materiality in the sense of being possessed of a surplus or excess that overflows any containable or manageable meaning. *Metaphor itself is thus a figure for the possibility of creating meaning outside of and in opposition to the systems in which such metaphors appear.*" See Perpich, "Subjectivity and Sexual Difference," 400. Italics added.

61. Irigaray, *The Way of Love*, 67.

62. Irigaray, *I Love to You*, 121.

63. Irigaray, *The Way of Love*, 19.

64. Ibid., 66. Italics added.

65. On this see Oliver, "Vision, Recognition," 121–36.

woman (these two attitudes being mutually implicated) that prevent an ethical and fecund intersubjectivity.

The correlation between the forgetting of air and the denial of woman's subjectivity finds expression in Irigaray's *Elemental Passions*, in which she gives voice (in dialogic and poetic form) to the fact that man has cut woman off from air. In the first chapter of that work we find woman reflecting on her own experience and then addressing man directly:

> White, Immense spaces. White, a rush of breath. Be swift, marry this breath. Remain in it. Make haste. Let it not abandon me. Let me not turn from it. Be swept up: my song.
>
> You give me a blank white mouth. My white mouth, open, like an angel in a cathedral. You have stopped my tongue. What remains is song. I can say nothing but sing.
>
> A song, for you. But that "for you" is not a dative. Not that song, a gift. Not received from you, not produced by me, nor for you, that song: my love with you. Intermingled. Escapes from me. A cloud.[66]

Reflecting on these words in their commentary, Canters and Janzen write:

> The man, [woman] says, has made her mouth "white," like a plaster angel, and thus has stopped her speech: the "I" cannot use her tongue or her language any more. But if she is quick, if she hurries, before her metamorphosis into a statue is complete perhaps she can still sing. Perhaps her music, her song telling her love for him, will stop him from turning her into a statue, and thus will save them both. He, after all, also wants love, and a statue, even a statue of an angel, cannot give him love. Though he can control it completely, it can never fulfill his desires. Only a real live woman—a woman who is free to be herself and to speak and sing in her own voice—can do that.[67]

The cloud here (air and moisture) is a symbol or metaphor of woman's desire to attain her own subjectivity, in excess of the logic of the same. The cloud is an emblem or metaphor of woman's last gasp, her last access to air, by which she offers a song, an appeal and invitation to man. However,

---

66. Irigaray, *Elemental Passions*, 7. In *Marine Lover of Friedrich Nietzsche*, Irigaray gives voice to a similar sentiment, in that she suggests there is only a small window of opportunity for woman to reclaim her own subjectivity. She writes: "All that was left—barely—was a breath, a hint of air and blood that said: I want to live." See Irigaray, *Marine Lover*, 4. On this, see also Mortensen, *The Feminine and Nihilism*, 57.

67. Canters and Janzen, *Forever Fluid*, 61.

PART ONE—Irigaray and Love's Possibility

the devastating truth is that: "you[-man] do not hear."[68] Nevertheless, woman is not prepared to give up, and exhorts the man: "Recall yourself once more: I insist, into the air."[69] As Canters and Janzen, again, put it: "If you-man will respond to this invitation, will mingle with I-woman in harmonious song, there is hope. Until he hears her song and joins in her breath, the fruitful relationship between man and woman as two sexually different subjects remains only a promise, an invitation."[70] Already, here, air becomes more than metaphor.

For Irigaray, air is more than the merely neutral medium and stuff of human existence—as if one could consider air in an ethically neutral way. Rather, to come to an awareness of air as the medium of human becoming, and as the medium and mediator of intersubjectivity, is to see what shape the relationship between man and woman should take. As she puts it in *The Way of Love*: "Air gives what is indispensable to live, to grow, to speak—to each one, man or woman, and to a relation between two not dominated by the one or by the other. . . . Air allows for modulating sounds, speaking with different tones. . . . Air lets someone be in the present, enter into presence in the present."[71] Air is by definition shared by man and woman. Air provides the basis of life for each and makes possible the variety of communicative patterns between them. Without air, the very possibility of communication is lost. According to Irigaray, as observed, Western culture is built on a denial of the significance of air (which is tied to a denial of woman as subject), and it is only through a remembering of air that the possibility of a genuine sharing between man and woman will become possible.

In the Epilogue of *To Be Two*, Irigaray offers this poem of praise to air:

> Air,
> you the pure,
> you who make confusion vanish,
> you who render each to him or herself, the exterior to the exterior, the interior to the interior
> you who flow between one and the other but without destroying either's boundaries proper,

---

68. Irigaray, *Elemental*, 7.
69. Ibid., 8.
70. Canters and Janzen, *Forever Fluid*, 62.
71. Irigaray, *The Way of Love*, 67.

> you who respect the skin and nourish it, and who procure the medium of every contact,
> you who maintain life, protecting it beyond every morsel gaudy,
> you without whom we cannot touch each other,
> who always keep yourself between us, whose distance allows us to approach each other,
> you who distinguish each from the other and assure that each never resembles the other, except through actions with which to be alike but not in growth as such . . .[72]

As was the case with wonder, of course, one might simply refuse to accept the implications of the fact that man and woman each have a share in air, in which case man will become implicated again in the denial of full subjectivity to woman. Yet Irigaray's appeal to the element of air, and her description of the significance of air, might also become the means for envisaging an alternative approach to the other.

According to the logic of the sensible-transcendental, the natural/material and transcendent/spiritual are necessarily tied to each other—these cannot be divorced from each other. Thus we find Irigaray declaring that "Air is the medium of our natural *and* spiritual life" and that air "is the elemental of the universe, of the life starting from which it is possible to elaborate the transcendental."[73] Here, as we have already suggested, the question of respiration comes to the fore. As Perpich puts it, Irigaray's account of the relationship between air and physical respiration "represents the rejection of views for which the subject is essentially an animal body endowed in addition with consciousness or, alternatively (though it amounts to the same thing), essentially a spirit or mind subsequently encumbered with a body."[74] It is precisely in the act of breathing, in the physical act of respiration, that nature is spiritualized, that air becomes the medium of our spiritualization as two. Although Irigaray takes up this discussion in a number of her later works, it is in *Between East and West* that she offers a thorough engagement on the subject. In that text, Irigaray

---

72. Irigaray, *To Be Two*, 117.

73. Irigaray, *The Way of Love*, 67.

74. Perpich, "Subjectivity and Sexual Difference," 400–401. Immediately following this, however, in her concluding comments on air and breath in Irigaray's later writings, Perpich proceeds to undermine precisely this unity of the natural and material. She suggests that breath is conceived, by Irigaray, as "a *figure* of non-appropriative exchange between subjects and as a *model* for a reconceived subjectivity and intersubjectivity with correspondingly new possibilities for understanding individual autonomy." Ibid., 401. Italics added.

PART ONE—Irigaray and Love's Possibility

returns to the forgetting of air in the Western tradition: "We speak of elementary needs like the need to eat and to drink, but not of the need to breathe. That corresponds nevertheless to our first and most radical need. And we are not really born, not really autonomous or living as long as we do not take care, in a conscious and voluntary way, of our breathing."[75] According to Irigaray, the lack of attentiveness to physical respiration reflects the dualistic assumptions that prevail in Western culture, according to which the corporeal and spiritual are severed from each other. Unlike the Eastern tradition, which has more frequently remembered that "living is equivalent to breathing," those who live in the West "have been taught that it is necessary to despise the body in order to be spiritual; the body would be the nature that we have to surpass in order to become spirit, in order to become soul."[76]

Of primary importance in Irigaray's account of the sharing of air between man and woman is her insistence that to breathe is to become an autonomous being: "Breathing corresponds to the first autonomous gesture of the living human being. To come into the world supposes inhaling and exhaling by oneself. In the uterus, we receive oxygen through the mother's blood. We are not yet autonomous, not yet born."[77] Indeed, she will go on to say that as long as we do not become conscious of our own breath, and control our own breathing "we are not really born, not really autonomous or living."[78] This exercise of autonomy through the cultivation of breathing is the basis of an ethical intersubjectivity and she makes the connection between autonomy and ethical existence explicit: "Breathing in a conscious and free manner is equivalent to taking charge of one's life, to accepting solitude through cutting the umbilical cord, to respecting and cultivating life, for oneself and for others."[79] A failure to cultivate one's breath, a failure to "conquer one's personal life," according to Irigaray, will result in relations of appropriation, in which we encroach upon the air and space of others in order that we might live.[80]

75. Irigaray, *Between East and West*, 75.

76. Ibid., 75. Irigaray is not sufficiently attentive to those aspects of Western culture (not least in Christianity) that are resistant to this dualistic framework. Her writings, here as elsewhere, too often represent the Western tradition, and Christianity, as monolithic and inattentive to the concerns she expresses.

77. Ibid., 73.

78. Ibid., 74.

79. Ibid.

80. While the full implications of Irigaray's account of breath have not been laid out, here, Perpich is not wrong to say that Irigaray "has in mind all the ways in which

The concreteness of Irigaray's appeal to air and breath, we should add, is expressed in her appeal to her own practice: "Breathing is thus a duty toward my life, that of others, and that of the entire living world. Because the majority of people in our age do not treat with care the time of breathing, it is necessary—in any case, it is necessary for me, but I think that this necessity is general—to go for walks or to remain for a moment each day in the vegetal world in order to continue to breathe and to live outside of the surrounding social exploitation."[81] Attentiveness to air, and to one's physical respiration, is a necessary condition for the cultivation of an autonomy in which we might become confident and content in who we are and, thereby, become free to respect the breathing of the other. In referring back to the relationship between Irigaray and Hegel, we can say that recognition of the duality of the human, and respect for the breath of one who differs from me sexually, is precisely the beginning of culture. Without this mutual cultivation of breath we lapse again into an antinatural (anti air/mother/woman) mode of existence.

For Irigaray, the cultivation of breath is also conceived in terms of the *becoming divine* of man and woman. In appealing to the creation narratives of Genesis, Irigaray points out that "the God-Father creates humanity by sending his breath into matter, into earth," and goes on to suggest that the third age (of the Spirit) "corresponds to the age of cultivation, by man and woman, of the divine breath they received as human beings."[82] As observed, Irigaray conceives of the negative in terms of a transcendence that persists between man and woman, thereby resisting man's projection of transcendence onto God and the relegation of woman to natural immediacy. In developing this theme, she writes: "They divide us between natural life and divine life without our being able to ensure the passage from the one to the other at each moment. It is in sexual difference that the split between human and divine identities can be overcome thanks to a cultivation of energy, in particular a cultivation of breathing."[83] Our

---

Western late capitalist industrial societies appropriate and exploit the unpaid or underpaid labor of women in all nations and almost all strata of society, the labor of men and children in developing nations, and various natural resources in the environment." See Perpich, "Subjectivity and Sexual Difference," 399.

81. Irigaray, *Between East and West*, 50.

82. Irigaray, "The Age of Breath," 168. This requires respect, we should indicate, for the mother, who is the one who gives breath to the child—who provides air, and the freedom also to breathe. The divine does not breathe into each and every human being but entrusts this task to the woman/mother.

83. Irigaray, *Between East and West*, 90.

largely theoretical description of Irigaray's negative in the previous chapter finds realization, here, in an accession to divine existence through breath: "Centered on the divinization of humanity incarnated and not on representations of divinity—images, various figurations, abstract ideals, dead words: all kinds of idols—our epoch has to return to an awareness and to a cultivation of the breath before and beyond any representation and discourse. The accomplishment of humanity, its perfect realization, requires the cultivation of one's own breath as divine presence, in ourselves and between us." The age of the Spirit is nothing less than the spiritualization of the flesh of man and woman.[84]

In *I Love to You*, Irigaray also explores the relationship between breath and language and argues that "our language, the language we use, our dialogues and exchanges, [usually] stifle breath more than they cultivate it. Our messages, our truths are generally breathless, suffocated and suffocating.... As if the less we breathe, the nearer we come to correct thinking. Death would then be the guarantee of our nearness to truth."[85] To further explore this relation between language and breath, Irigaray juxtaposes two forms of life, one in which air is respected and breath cultivated, and one in which (as already noted) air is forgotten and breath stifled. She writes:

> It is, therefore, important to reflect upon the fact that a language, spirituality or religion that is founded on speech, yet pays no heed to the silence and breath making it possible, might well lead to a lack of respect for life; for one's own life, for the other's life, for others' lives. Using breath and the body to define or pronounce something in quite certain terms, to structure a religion or a sociological symbolic order, becomes destructive when this bearer of life is not recognized or regenerated. Cultural practices constituted in this manner soon become authoritarian as a result of immobilizing and stifling breath.[86]

The patriarchal culture of the West has missed the link between word and breath, according to Irigaray, so that language "is given over to ritual,

---

84. It would be remiss of us not to at least mention Irigaray's indebtedness to certain Eastern traditions. "Yoga taught me to return to the cultivation of sensible perception. In fact, I have always loved it. Since my childhood, nature has helped me and has taught me how to live. But yoga brought me back to this task with texts that lead me from the innocence of sensations to a spiritual elaboration that permits their development, and sometimes their communication or sharing." See Irigaray, *Between East and West*, 55.

85. Irigaray, *I Love to You*, 121.

86. Ibid., 122.

repetition, a secondary attribution of values, speculation, and to a logic unsuited to life and its breath."[87]

Here again we come up against Irigaray's insistence that man participates in, and is prone to, an anti-natural mode of existence. In "The Age of Breath" Irigaray refers to this anti-natural mode of existence as the diabolic: "The diabolic . . . delights in enclosure, it avoids the draughts, it can adapt itself to fire but not to air. Miming the living, the diabolic does not breathe, or does not breathe any longer. It takes away the air from the others, from the world. It suffocates with its sterile repetitions, its presumptuous imitations, with its wishes deprived of respect for life. It also annoys with its insistence, its pretension to dominate everything without being able to remain in itself."[88] To respect air, and to respect the mutual cultivation of breath by man and woman, is for man and woman to allow the other an existence that is sensible and transcendental. To respect air, and to respect the mutual cultivation of breath by man and woman, is to move beyond the imperatives and certainties and Truth of Western religion and culture to the possibility of a dialogue and sharing between two. Here, "the logos becomes dialogic, the relationship between living women and men, and not an ecstasy of truth in an idealized beyond. Men and women speak to one another, fecundate one another."[89] Here again, communication is no longer a matter of passing on a closed truth but of creating the space in which two irreducible worlds might meet for the first time.

In clarifying this relationship between one's approach to breath and the logic of one's religious or philosophical framework, Irigaray suggests that the Western tradition has exchanged speech for breath: "Speech, instead of bearing breath, takes its place, replaces it, which invariably stifles and preoccupies the place for silence. People who pay no heed to respiration, who breathe poorly, who are short of air, who cannot stop speaking, and are thus unable to listen. Speaking is their way of respiring, or more precisely expiring, of exhaling, in order to take a breath. And so they stifle the inspiration—in the strict sense, general or figurative—of others, even those who take bodily and spiritual care of their breath."[90] While the Christian tradition has supposedly emphasized the continuity between spirit and breath, says Irigaray, the tradition gives little evidence of the need to cultivate breath in order to become a spiritual being. Thus,

87. Ibid., 123.
88. Irigaray, "The Age of Breath," 166.
89. Irigaray, *I Love to You*, 124.
90. Ibid., 122.

the tradition exchanges speech for breath (exchanges words for life)—as happens in the case of those who cannot stop speaking and therefore cannot breathe.[91] This emphasis on speech, silence, and breath, leads Irigaray to an insistence on forms of speech other than the prepared speech or text (which tends to express laws, orders and imperatives, rather than asking questions, offering praises, or giving thanks). With the cultivation of breath in relation to speech, then, man and woman move beyond sterile and oppressive forms of dialogue into forms of dialogue that open up intersubjectivity.[92] Here language fosters the "vegetal" becoming of man and woman.[93]

Irigaray argues, in *To Be Two*, that the creation of this free space of dialogue and encounter between man and woman is also a question of cultivating silence. She suggests that silence is threefold: there is a silence particular to man, a silence particular to woman, and a third silence that persists between them.[94] If the silence of man and the silence of woman reflect their respective becoming, then the third silence is that which mediates the relationship and makes possible an ethical and fecund intersubjectivity between them. This third silence is a space between two that "must not be overcome either in words or in representations, but must be protected, cultivated, generated, also historically, so that it becomes more refined and shared."[95] Extending this, she writes: "An availability prepares a free space for a common mediation, or rather for the search for possible mediations for the two. This space is not emptiness but *a silence deliberately safeguarded* for the task that the relation with the other represents. Not starting from nothing but from what each already is, provided that neither be considered as the totality of the real. And that each be disposed

---

91. Ibid.

92. In an interview with Brena Niorelli, Irigaray suggests that the language of a culture of sexual difference "doesn't conform to traditional Western logic, with its complement: poetry. It unfolds between two modes of speaking, two languages, man's and woman's. The exchange between these two subjects creates a third language, so to speak, a language that we sill don't know, that is yet to be created." Regardless, however, it is evident that Irigaray conceives of the absence of the poetic in the relation between man and woman as evidence of a failure to cultivate breath. See Irigaray, "The Air of Those Who Love," 131.

93. This language is also from Irigaray. See Irigaray, *Ethics*, 139.

94. Irigaray, *To be Two*, 63.

95. Ibid., 62.

to dialogue with a real which is not one's own but with which one has to enter into relation as human."[96]

To achieve an ethical intersubjectivity, each must acknowledge the negative that lies at the heart of human subjectivity—that he or she is only half of the human. Indeed, in *The Way of Love* Irigaray argues that silence is "made possible by the fact that neither I nor you are everything, that each of us is limited, marked by the negative, non-hierarchical difference."[97] On the basis of this negative, non-hierarchical difference, then, and on the basis of my awareness that the other is forever a mystery to me, silence is a refusal to name or circumscribe her or him.[98] Silence is a refusal to deploy language and communication as they have been deployed according to the logic of the One, as a means of denomination and circumscription. The creation and cultivation of this free space of silence, of course, will require a high degree of self-control, particularly on the part of man, whose tendency to objectify and name the other through language is decidedly more pronounced than that of woman, according to Irigaray. If man and woman are to fulfill the human together, each must respect the becoming of the other, a respect that must be expressed in the space of silence they cultivate between them—a free space of encounter.

In concluding we do well to return to the question of fecundity. In *Between East and West*, as well as in *I Love to You*, Irigaray ties together breath and fecundity, arguing that without a cultivation of breath, man and woman are thrown back upon the death of the species (with death defined more broadly than in terms of the physical survival): "Assuring [the survival of the species] does not mean only to conceive and engender children but implies preserving human life as a life endowed with consciousness, with soul. Now this task belongs to woman as well as to man. It is not the woman's task to bring bodies into the world that man, beginning with the father, will educate. Together man and woman should engender children who are both natural and spiritual."[99] When the family begins with the third of the child, Irigaray insists, it is reduced to a natural institution implicated in all of the assumptions of patriarchy. To begin with

---

96. Irigaray, *The Way of Love*, 88. Italics added.

97. Ibid., 117.

98. Elsewhere Irigaray argues that "This silence is space-time offered to you with no a priori, no pre-established truth or ritual. To you it constitutes an overture, to the other who is not and never will be mine. It is a silence made possible by the fact that neither I nor you are everything, that each of us is limited, marked by the negative, non-hierarchically different." See Irigaray, *I Love to You*, 117,

99. Irigaray, *Between East and West*, 78.

the couple, however, is both to acknowledge nature and to spiritualize the human since the acknowledgment of sexual difference is a first step into culture. In this vein Irigaray insists that man and woman's cultivation of breath represents a new future:[100]

> It is not the reduction of the family to its natural dimension that can assure it a future, but a cultivation of the union between man and woman in respect for their differences, which implies that nature becomes consciousness. In order to be and to remain two in love, including carnal love, it is necessary, in fact, that the body become flesh awakened by consciousness. It is necessary that the man and the woman enjoy an equivalent dignity and that they discover together how to combine nature and spirituality across their differences of body and subjectivity.[101]

For Irigaray, the cultivation of breath, and respect for air as the mediator and medium of the becoming of man and woman, defines this awakening, this acknowledgment of equal dignity, and this possible discovery of sharing across difference. Only through such a cultivation of breath might the human, as man and woman together, become spiritually fecund (and in a way that does not exclude procreative fecundity).

---

100. Thus she objects to the suggestion of John Paul II that the family is the natural and fundamental element of society. See Irigaray, *Between East and West*, 118.
101. Ibid.

PART TWO

Kierkegaard and Love's Promise

3

Søren Kierkegaard

God as the Middle Term

> Similitude is the fruit of the exchange between esteem for oneself and solicitude for others. This exchange authorizes us to say that I cannot myself have self-esteem unless I esteem others *as* myself. "As myself" means that you too are capable of starting something in the world, of acting for a reason, of hierarchizing your priorities, of evaluating the ends of your actions, and, having done this, of holding yourself in esteem as I hold myself in esteem.
>
> —Paul Ricoeur, *Oneself as Another*

As we continue to set the stage for a conversation between Luce Irigaray and Søren Kierkegaard on sexual difference, it is by now evident that the gap or interval between man and woman will take centre stage—that is, that the question and reality of mediation will necessarily figure prominently in any such conversation. Within *Works of Love*, we will observe, the logic of mediation between persons centers on Christ, or God, as the middle term in every relationship. Indeed, although Kierkegaard engages in an explicit discussion of God as the middle term in only one discourse of *Works of Love*, this logic of mediation is everywhere assumed within

PART TWO—Kierkegaard and Love's Promise

Works of Love.[1] From Kierkegaard's perspective, every aspect of human intersubjectivity is defined or shaped by the relationship of each to God— the one who gives the self as gift and task. Thus, if a Kierkegaardian ethics of sexual difference can be conceived at all, this will depend on our discerning a confluence between Irigaray's account of mediation (defined in terms of the negative) and Kierkegaard's explicitly theological account. In the present chapter, then, we provide an account of this notion of God as the middle term.

MEDIATION: GOD AS THE MIDDLE TERM

In "Love is the Fulfilling of the Law," a discourse within *Works of Love*, Kierkegaard takes up the question of God as the middle term and does so while exploring a collision that necessarily occurs between Christian and worldly views of love. According to Kierkegaard, while there is significant formal overlap between Christian and worldly views of love (from each perspective love is devotion and sacrifice), this formal overlap belies a substantive difference—namely, that each provides a unique standard for judging devotion and sacrifice. Kierkegaard writes: "Love is indeed devotion and sacrifice, and therefore the world thinks that the object of love (whether it be a beloved or friend or loved ones or a social club or the contemporaries, what for the sake of brevity we shall hereafter call 'the beloved') is to determine whether devotion and sacrifice have been shown, and whether the devotion and sacrifice shown are love."[2] For Kierkegaard, those who forget God inevitably misjudge the devotion and sacrifice that true love requires and are inclined to accept the *beloved's* judgment concerning appropriate devotion and sacrifice, a judgment that is invariably mistaken. "[W]hen [God is forgotten], the beloved will regard a false kind of devotion and sacrifice as true love and will regard true love as lovelessness."[3] For Kierkegaard, the worldly point of view leaves out that which is fundamental to the Christian—that God is the creator of each person, the source of love, the proper and primary object of

---

1. We focus on the non-pseudonymous *Works of Love* in view of its emphasis on mediation, intersubjectivity, and the nature of love. We will turn to other of Kierkegaard's texts (particularly *Either/Or*) in developing a Kierkegaardian account of the self and of sexual difference. However, the content of *Works of Love* lends it to this engagement with Irigaray, as will become apparent.

2. Kierkegaard, *Works of Love*, 107.

3. Ibid., 107.

love, and the judge of love. Devotion and sacrifice, when defined outside of this theocentric framework are in collision with the Christian view of love.[4]

With this collision in mind, it is possible to consider the idea that lies at the heart of "Love is the Fulfilling of the Law"—namely, God as the middle term:

> *Worldly wisdom is of the opinion that love is a relationship between persons; Christianity teaches that love is a relationship between: a person—God—a person, that is, that God is the middle term.* However beautiful a relationship of love has been between two people or among many, however complete all their desire and all their bliss have been for themselves in mutual sacrifice and devotion, even though everyone has praised this relationship—if God and the relationship with God has been omitted, then this, in the Christian sense, has not been love but a mutually enchanting defraudation of love. *To love God is to love oneself truly; to help another person to love God is to love another person; to be helped by another person to love God is to be loved.*[5]

There is much to be unpacked in these words, but it is helpful to begin by simply diagramming the love relationship as Kierkegaard envisions it (see Figure 1).

In suggesting God as the middle term in every relationship, Kierkegaard is not saying that God stands between the two terms of the relationship such that they relate to each other only indirectly, through God.[6] Rather, Kierkegaard is suggesting that each person relates both to God and to the other person, which implies that the relationship to God sets limits on the relationship to the other person.[7] God's priority in the relationship provides a measure of the sacrifice and devotion that can be expected or required. To get clearer on this appeal to God as the middle term, a few features of the "triadic" framework must be considered.

---

4. And Kierkegaard argues that those who embrace a worldly view of love will perceive Christian love as unloving. For a discussion that contextualizes this perspective, see Kirmmse, *Kierkegaard in Golden Age*, 318–23.

5. Kierkegaard, *Works of Love*, 106–7. Italics in the original.

6. Ferreira, *Love's Grateful Striving*, 72.

7. As Ferreira puts it, "What makes Christian devotedness to the other different is that our determinations of what counts as loving in a given case are stabilized by relating first 'to God and God's requirement.'" See Ferreira, *Love's Grateful Striving*, 72.

PART TWO—Kierkegaard and Love's Promise

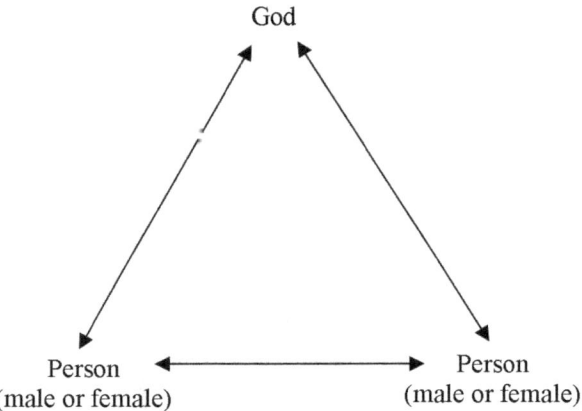

Figure 1. Kierkegaard's view of intersubjectivity

In the first instance we give attention to the vertical axis, and to Kierkegaard's insistence that each person is a bond servant of God.[8] "Every person is God's bond servant; therefore he dare not belong to anyone in love unless in the same love he belongs to God and dare not possess anyone in love unless the other and he himself belong to God in this love—a person dare not belong to another as if that other person were everything to him; a person dare not allow another to belong to him as if he were everything to that other."[9] Even in the most beautiful relationship between two people, Kierkegaard suggests, "Christianity steps forward and asks about the relationship to God, whether each individual is first related to God," which is to say that Christianity steps forward to ask whether each person's status as bond servant of God has been preserved.[10] In his own historical and cultural context, Kierkegaard observed a generalized desire

---

8. This is one of two theological assumptions that Ferreira has argued undergird Kierkegaard's account of God as the middle term. See Ferreira, *Love's Grateful Striving*, 72.

9. Kierkegaard, *Works of Love*, 107–8.

10. Ibid., 108. In the discourse "Love is a Matter of Conscience," Kierkegaard suggests that the pure heart "is first and last a *bound* heart." He also adds, there, that "God has first priority, and everything, everything a person owns is pledged as collateral to this claim." See Kierkegaard, *Works of Love*, 148–9.

72

to move beyond the "abominable era of bond service," yet he insists that "every human being, not by birth but by creation from nothing, belongs as a bond servant [to God], and in such a way as no bond servant has ever belonged to an earthly master, who at least admits that thoughts and feelings are free."[11] The relationship to God, according to Kierkegaard, binds a person in every aspect of his or her person, in every expression of life, and this necessarily sets limits on our relationships with others.[12] We are not free to belong to others in such a way that our status as bond servant of God is denied or compromised; nor are we permitted to possess the other in a way that his or her status as bond servant is compromised: "A person dare not belong to another as if that other person were everything to him, nor vice versa."[13]

The notion of bond service to God can be further clarified by reference to the parallel notion of infinite *indebtedness* to God. In "Love is the Fulfilling of the Law," Kierkegaard acknowledges that a human person might experience and live out genuine love toward God but points out that, nevertheless, God has always loved the person first, which is to say that "God is an eternity ahead—that is how far the human being is behind."[14]

> In earthly affairs we usually speak of the lamentable circumstance that one must go into debt in order to start an enterprise; in relation to God, every person begins with an infinite debt, even if we forget what the debt amounts to daily after the beginning. All too often this is forgotten in life, and why, indeed, if it is not because God also is forgotten. Then one person compares himself with another, and the one who has understood somewhat more than others congratulates himself on being something. Would that he himself might understand that before God he is nothing.[15]

The priority of God, and the eternal head-start of God in loving and providing for each human means that each person is infinitely indebted to God—it means that his or her whole life must be lived in (and out of) an

---

11. Ibid., 115.

12. Anti-Climacus suggests that the self has a deep "obligation in obedience to God with regard to its every clandestine desire and thought, with regard to its readiness to hear and understand and its willingness to follow every hint from God as to his will for this self." See Kierkegaard, *The Sickness unto Death*, 114.

13. Kierkegaard, *Works of Love*, 108.

14. Ibid., 102.

15. Ibid.

awareness of this indebtedness.[16] Thus, if one wishes to make something of oneself, and to *claim* to have made something of oneself, the only way forward is to forget about God: You must "never let it become clear to you that it is he who has created you from nothing; proceed on the presupposition that a human being does not have time to waste on keeping in mind the one to whom he infinitely and unconditionally owes everything."[17]

In speaking of our indebtedness to God, Kierkegaard also contrasts our *inability* to fulfill the law (to obey the provisions of God's law) with Jesus Christ's *ability* to fulfill the law. Before the example of Jesus Christ, who met the infinite demands of the law and who is the perfect embodiment of love, we can only humble ourselves in acknowledging that we are unable to meet the infinite demands of the law or to live a life of love.[18] Not only this, but even when we *do* offer a loving response to God (in obedience to the law of love), we are reminded—ah, but God has loved us first; God is an eternity ahead, that is how far we are behind.[19] Our accomplishments in life and love forever owe to the prior grace and love of God, which is to say that without God we are nothing, and also that in relation to God we are nothing. Any accomplishment of ours with respect to love is an accomplishment, finally, of God's.

In considering God as the middle term, we turn also to the horizontal axis and to Kierkegaard's insistence on a fundamental equality between human beings—this in virtue of the fact that each person is created by God. Kierkegaard affirms this truth, to offer just one example, when he points to those who have forgotten it: "There are people who have inhumanly forgotten that everyone should fortify himself by means of *the universal divine likeness of all people*, have forgotten that therefore, whether a person is man or woman, poorly or richly endowed, master or slave, beggar or plutocrat, the relationships among human beings ought and may never be such that the one worships and the other is the one worshipped."[20] In

---

16. As Kierkegaard also expresses it, "if you turn toward God and use ten-tenths of your strength, you will still be as nothing, at an infinite distance from having achieved something, in infinite debt!" See Kierkegaard, *Works of Love*, 102.

17. Ibid., 102–3.

18. Westphal argues that *Works of Love* is representative of Religiousness C, in which Christ is prototype to be emulated. See Westphal "Kierkegaard's Teleological Suspension," 110–29. See, also, Westphal, "Kierkegaard's Religiousness C," 535–548.

19. Kierkegaard, *Works of Love*, 101–2. In the prayer that opens *Works of Love*, Kierkegaard points to the necessity of union with God when he says, to God: "one who loves is what he is only by being in you." See *Works of Love*, 3.

20. Ibid., 125. Italics added.

drawing his insistence on the universal divine likeness of human persons into conversation with the love command of Jesus Christ ("You shall love your neighbor as yourself") Kierkegaard makes it apparent that the neighbor is precisely the one who shares in the universal divine likeness—that is, everyone is the neighbor. "The neighbor is the utterly unrecognizable dissimilarity between persons or is *the eternal equality before God—the enemy, too, has this equality*."[21] That each human being has been created in the image of God, and that each human being therefore belongs to God, and is loved by God, defines human equality. This implies that no one (not one person) can be excluded from the command of Jesus to "love your neighbor as yourself." As Ferreira points out, we must clarify that this inclusion of *everyone* in the love command is twofold: (i) every person must obey the love command—that is, everyone must be a neighbor in the way that the Good Samaritan was a neighbor—and (ii) every other person we see or encounter is the neighbor whom we are to love.[22] This insistence on the equality of every human person also implies the freedom and need of each person to live in self-love, in love toward God, and in love of neighbor, the freedom and need of each to live a life of self-denial and self-giving for the other.[23]

To return to the collision between the merely human and the Christian account of love, we recall that God's status as the middle term signifies that God is the judge of human love.

> To conform to the beloved's idea of what constitutes love is, humanly speaking, to love, and if someone does that he is loved. But, directly counter to the beloved's merely human conception of what constitutes love, to deny the wish and to that extent what the lover himself, in the human sense, might also wish, in order to hold fast to God's conception of love—that is the collision. It can never occur to the merely human view of what love is that

---

21. Ibid., 68. Italics added. In an earlier discourse of *Works of Love*, Kierkegaard writes: "The neighbor is one who is equal. The neighbor is neither the beloved, for whom you have passion's preference, nor your friend, for whom you have passion's preference. Nor is your neighbor, if you are a cultured person, the cultured individual with whom you have a similarity of culture—since with your neighbor you have the equality of a human being before God." See Kierkegaard, *Works of Love*, 60.

22. Ferreira, *Love's Grateful Striving*, 53.

23. The language of "need" is present throughout *Works of Love*, and is first mentioned in the prayer that opens *Works of Love*. There Kierkegaard speaks of the *works* of love as "a need in love itself." Kierkegaard, *Works of Love*, 4. See Ferreira's discussion of Kierkegaard's account of love's need in *Love's Grateful Striving*, 21; 26–28; 39–42.

PART TWO—Kierkegaard and Love's Promise

by being loved as dearly as it is possible to be loved by another person someone can stand in the other person's way.[24]

Kierkegaard suggests, again, that there is a tendency for lovers to submit to the demands and expectations of the beloved for devotion and sacrifice, and argues that the demands or expectations of the beloved become an obstacle to the God-relationship of the lover. The lover so devotes him or herself to the beloved that his or her relationship to God is rendered secondary or peripheral. And: "Whenever a person is so loved and admired by others that he begins to be dangerous to their God-relationship, there is a collision . . ."[25]

The logic of Kierkegaard's argument suggests that it is also possible for a person to become dangerous to his or her own God-relationship. If a person is unwilling to resist or question the demands of the beloved, then he or she has become an obstacle to his or her own God-relationship. Therefore we must, if necessary, "defend ourselves against the beloved, against the friend, against those nearest who after all are especially the object of love, insofar as they in any way want to teach us another explanation, or sidetrack us, but thank them if they want to help us to the right understanding."[26] It is the relationship to God that must be given priority if one is to live in love, and it is God's judgment concerning love that is to shape our relations of love toward others.[27]

With this general material in mind, we return to the portion of *Works of Love* that lies at the heart of Kierkegaard's argument concerning God as the middle term, where he writes: "*To love God is to love oneself truly; to help another person to love God is to love another person; to be helped by another person to love God is to be loved.*"[28] With these words Kierkegaard makes it clear that God's status as middle term requires that God become

---

24. Kierkegaard, *Works of Love*, 114.

25. Ibid.

26. Ibid., 118. Elsewhere in *Works of Love*, Kierkegaard writes as follows: "You who speak so beautifully about how much the beloved means to you or you to the beloved, remember that if a pure heart is to be given away in erotic love the first consideration must be for your soul as well as for your beloved's." In speaking of "your own soul" and "the soul of the beloved," Kierkegaard refers to the God-relationship of each. See Kierkegaard, *Works of Love*, 149.

27. Ferreira argues: "For Kierkegaard, what is at stake in [the idea of God as the middle term] is that God should remain the judge of what true love is—for example, that the relationship between husband and wife should remain under God's judgment of what is truly good for each." See Ferreira, *Love's Grateful Striving*, 71.

28. Kierkegaard, *Works of Love*, 107. Italics in the original.

the first of object of love, a requirement he sometimes expresses rather starkly: "This the world can never get into its head, that God in this way not only becomes the third party in every relationship of love but really becomes the sole object of love, so that it is not the husband who is the wife's beloved, but it is God, and it is the wife who is helped by the husband to love God, and conversely, and so on."[29] Both lover and beloved, then, are to acknowledge and preserve God as first love. "As soon as a love-relationship does not lead me to God, and as soon as I in the love-relationship do not lead the other to God, then the love, even if it were the highest bliss and delight of affection, even if it were the supreme good of the lovers' earthly life, is still not true love."[30] To express it in terms of the logic of God as the middle term, the vertical axis in the relational framework is the primary axis, and the horizontal axis can only be rightly understood and lived when the vertical is rightly lived.

What, however, does it mean to love God? One of the primary expressions of our love toward God is precisely the love of the neighbor, since God receives our love as it is extended toward the neighbor. For example, to help the neighbor love his or her neighbor is to help the neighbor love God.[31] At the same time, however, Kierkegaard will speak of our direct relationship to God, and love toward God, expressed in obedience and adoration. Making reference to Jesus' words in Matthew 22:37 (You shall love the Lord your God with all your heart, and with all your soul, and with all your mind), Kierkegaard writes: "A person should love God unconditionally in *obedience* and love him in *adoration*."[32] To love God in *obedience* is to acknowledge one's status as bond servant of God, to acknowledge God as the source of life and love, and to acknowledge that the requirement of God is expressed most fully in the example of Jesus and in the love command. Love of neighbor is evidence of love of God.[33]

Although Kierkegaard does not fill out what *adoration* toward God might consist in, the opening prayer of *Works of Love* offers at least one expression. Kierkegaard speaks directly to God in prayer: "How could one

29. Ibid., 121.
30. Ibid., 120.
31. Ferreira, *Love's Grateful Striving*, 74.
32. Kierkegaard, *Works of Love*, 20.

33. We use the word "evidence" somewhat tentatively, given Kierkegaard's contention that the outer does not transparently reflect the inner. While love has a need to express itself (true love must bear fruit), this does not imply that we have the capacity to judge whether a particular action is rooted in love or not. See Ferreira's discussion in *Love's Grateful Striving*, 21–26.

speak properly about love if you were forgotten, you God of love, source of all love in heaven and on earth; you who spared nothing but in love gave everything; you who are love, so that one who loves is what he is only by being in you. ... O Eternal Love, you who are everywhere present and never without witness where you are called upon, be not without witness in what will be said here about love or about works of love ..."[34] Evidently, Kierkegaard concurs with the long tradition of Christianity and Judaism in which adoration toward God is expressed by way of a rehearsal, before God, of the attributes and activities of God. And in this case we note again that Kierkegaard's prayer of adoration (and/or invocation) is Trinitarian in structure, confirming that the God of *Works of Love* is the God of the classical Christian tradition—Father, Son, and Holy Spirit—and confirming also that adoration toward God must be expressed by way of a Trinitarian formulation.

Before turning to consider the question of self-love, it is appropriate to extend this discussion of love of God and neighbor by briefly attending to a question that preoccupies Ferreira in *Love's Grateful Striving*. The question whether Kierkegaard has over-spiritualized love of neighbor by saying that to love the neighbor is to help the neighbor to love God, such that we become inattentive to the concrete and material needs of the neighbor. Already we have suggested that love of God finds primary expression in our service of the neighbor (keeping God in mind). Yet Ferreira contends that, for Kierkegaard, love of neighbor is indeed attentive to the physical and material needs of the neighbor. Decisive for Ferreira is Kierkegaard's discussion of the Good Samaritan, in the context of which he argues that the concrete act of helping one who is in need is a genuine and necessary expression of neighbor-love.[35] Ferreira writes, in the context of her discussion of self-love: "The Samaritan is praised for having given the man precisely what he needed, which in this case was help for his physical, material, bodily pain and suffering. Kierkegaard may not often give such concrete examples, but the Samaritan is surely an unambiguous illustration of the kind of care for another that he believes is implied by the phrase 'as yourself.'"[36] Within Kierkegaard's account of God as the middle term, then, love toward God must be the first expression of love, and yet the priority of God in no way diminishes the need to love the neighbor,

---

34. Ibid., 5.
35. Ferreira, *Love's Grateful Striving*, 79–80.
36. Ibid., 34.

both by directing the neighbor toward the love of God (in obedience and adoration) and by meeting the concrete needs of the neighbor.

The Question of Self Love

Moving beyond Kierkegaard's account of God as the middle term, we take up related questions pertinent to our stated intention to draw Kierkegaard and Irigaray into conversation on mediation and intersubjectivity. We begin with the question of self-love.

In the second discourse of *Works of Love*, in which Kierkegaard reflects on the command to "love your neighbor as yourself," Kierkegaard points out that if the love command had excluded the phrase *as yourself*, then the question of self-love, and of the selfishness in our self-love, would have been held in abeyance. He writes:

> Long and discerning addresses could be delivered on how a person ought to love his neighbor, and when the addresses had been heard, self-love would still be able to hit upon excuses and find a way of escape, because the subject had not been entirely exhausted, all circumstances had not been taken into account, because something had continually been forgotten or something had not been accurately and bindingly enough expressed and described. But this *as yourself*—indeed, no wrestler can wrap himself around the one he wrestles as this commandment wraps itself around self-love, which cannot move from the spot.[37]

As it stands, the love command includes the *as yourself* and, in virtue of this inclusion, "penetrates into the innermost hiding place where a person loves himself" and sheds light on the selfishness in our self-love.[38] That is, in commanding me to love my neighbor *as myself*, the command reveals that I invariably love myself more than my neighbor, and tells me that this is precisely what I am *not* to do. The love command, then, does not point to the illegitimacy of self-love; rather, the *as yourself* presupposes self-love while rooting out the selfishness in self-love. Kierkegaard writes: "Just as Jacob limped after having struggled with God, so will self-love be broken if it has struggled with this phrase that does not want to teach a person that he is not to love himself but rather wants to teach him proper self-love." Accordingly, Kierkegaard will rewrite the love command in the following way: "You shall love yourself in the same way as you love your neighbor

37. Kierkegaard, *Works of Love*, 18.
38. Ibid.

PART TWO—Kierkegaard and Love's Promise

when you love him as yourself."[39] That is, we are not to love ourselves more than we love our neighbor. Here Kierkegaard reveals the rigorousness of the love command, which can only be mitigated by restricting the range of the term "neighbor."[40]

In considering the love command of Matthew 22, and in defending the legitimacy of self-love, Kierkegaard argues that "the concept of the neighbor is actually a redoubling of your own self." According to the classic Kierkegaardian definition of the self, offered by Anti-Climacus in *Sickness unto Death*, the self has three dimensions: (i) it is a synthesis of opposites—of the finite and infinite, of the temporal and eternal, of necessity and possibility, (ii) it is a self-relation—a relation that relates itself to itself, and (iii) it is ultimately dependent upon God—the self is a relation that in relating itself to itself relates to another.[41] This third dimension is most important for our purposes, and Anti-Climacus clarifies this dimension by arguing that "the human self is . . . a derived relation, a relation that relates itself to itself and in relating itself to itself relates itself to [the one who established the relation]."[42] The self, whether or not the self acknowledges it, is in relation to the one who established it, is in relation to God. Thus, "to will to be oneself in the fullest sense is also to take up an affirmative stance toward one's foundation."[43] To become a self in the fullest sense, as Anti-Climacus puts it, is to rest transparently in God.

When Kierkegaard argues that the neighbor is a redoubling of your own self, he suggests that the neighbor is a self in the way that you are a self. Martin Andic expresses the point well: "[Kierkegaard] means that to see another human being as your neighbor is to address yourself to him or her as to someone who is truly, in the sight of God, exactly what you are: the spirit that each person in his or her own way can become before God in conscience, and this is the true self in each that is the other and double of the natural one, the *you* addressed eternally by God. It is this that you shall love in each human being, *and in yourself*, because you love God

---

39. Ibid., 23.

40. Ibid., 20.

41. This helpful summary description of Anti-Climacus' account of the self is offered in Glenn, "Definition of the Self," 5. It is a questionable methodological move to turn to Anti-Climacus's definition of the self, given that our preoccupation is with the argument of Kierkegaard in *Works of Love*. Nevertheless, this notion of the neighbor as a "redoubling of yourself" is not one that can be fully clarified in terms of the content of *Works of Love* itself/alone.

42. Kierkegaard, *Sickness*, 13–14.

43. Glenn, "Definition of the Self" 15.

above all, in relationship with whom each becomes what he or she truly is."[44] In the context of *Works of Love*, the legitimacy of self-love and the command to love the neighbor are together rooted in the fact that every human being is a self in relation to God, and that the becoming of this self is both a gift and task before God.[45] That is, to love *oneself* truly is to recognize the self as a gift, and is to become a self by turning toward God in faith and love; to love the *neighbor* truly is to recognize the neighbor as a self-relation related to God—as a redoubling of your own self. In terms of the logic of God as the middle term, *to love God is to love oneself truly* (or, to love God is to become a self in relation to God) and *to love another person is to help the other love God* (or, to love another person is to help her become a self in relation to God). And, "you shall love your neighbor as yourself."

Kierkegaard's adds: "[I]f anyone is unwilling to learn from Christianity to love himself *in the right way*, he cannot love the neighbor either," which is to say that an ethical intersubjectivity is only possible when one adopts an appropriate stance of self-love.[46] Kierkegaard writes of our everyday attitude toward those in whom self-love is not in evidence, thereby suggesting that self-love is the answer in each case:

> When the bustler wastes his time and powers in the service of futile, inconsequential pursuits, is this not because he has not learned to love himself rightly? When the light-minded person throws himself almost like a nonentity into the folly of the moment and makes nothing of it, is this not because he does not know how to love himself rightly? When the depressed person desires to be rid of life, indeed, of himself, is this not because he is unwilling to learn earnestly and rigorously to love himself? When someone surrenders to despair because the world or another person has faithlessly left him betrayed, what then is his fault (his innocent suffering is not referred to here) except not loving himself in the right way? When someone self-tormentingly thinks to do God a service by torturing himself, what is his sin except not willing to love himself in the right way? And if, alas, a person presumptuously lays violent hands upon himself, is not his sin precisely this, that he does not rightly love himself in the sense in which a person ought to love himself?[47]

44. Andic, "Love's Redoubling," 16. Italics added.

45. For this language, see Glenn, "Definition of the Self," 15.

46. Kierkegaard, *Works of Love*, 22. Quoted in Ferreira's *Love's Grateful Striving*, 32. Italics in the original.

47. Kierkegaard, *Works of Love*, 23.

Kierkegaard, then, would rein in a self-love that is rooted in selfishness, but would encourage a self-love that corresponds with one's status as a creature of Love. As Ferreira suggests, "many of the later deliberations in *Works of Love* will explicitly assume a certain model of our love of self; for example, Kierkegaard works with the assumption that we want to be treated with respect, not to be treated condescendingly, and that we forgive ourselves our false starts and weaknesses."[48] Throughout, then, Kierkegaard presupposes the legitimacy of self-love, and presupposes that self-affection is a necessary condition of love of neighbor.

Preferential Loves

The present work is taken up with the question of mediation and intersubjectivity between man and woman and also with particular preferential relationships. Yet in Kierkegaard's case it is not immediately obvious that he leaves room for preferential relationships. At the outset of his discussion in "You Shall Love *the Neighbor*," Kierkegaard contrasts the poetic conception of love with the Christian conception, and suggests that the praise of erotic love and friendship belongs essentially to paganism.[49] He asks:

> Is it not remarkable that in the whole New Testament there is not a single verse about friendship in the sense in which the poet celebrates it and paganism cultivated it? Or let the poet who is conscious of being a poet go through what the New Testament teaches about erotic love, and he will be brought to despair because he will not find a single word that could inspire him—and if any so-called poet nevertheless did happen to find a word that he used, it would be a mendacious use, an offense, because instead of respecting Christianity he steals a precious word and distorts it in his use of it.[50]

The primary difference between love [*Elskov*] as lauded by the poet and love [*Kjerlighed*] as understood by the Christian lies in the fact that erotic love and friendship drive toward the *one* beloved or friend while neighbor-love drives toward *every* one.[51] Kierkegaard writes: "Erotic love

---

48. Ferreira, *Love's Grateful Striving*, 34.
49. Kierkegaard, *Works of Love*, 44.
50. Ibid., 45–46.
51. Judge William describes this drive toward the one well: "[The first love] is directed upon a single specific actual object, which alone exists for it; nothing else exists

is based on a drive that, transfigured into an inclination, has its highest, its unconditional, its only poetically unconditioned expression in this—there is but *one and only one beloved* in the whole world, and this one and only one time of erotic love is love, is everything; the second time is nothing."[52] By contrast, Christian love proclaims that love cannot be reserved for one, or even a series of "ones." "Christian love teaches us to love all people, unconditionally all. Just as unconditionally and powerfully as erotic love intensifies in the direction that there is but one and only one beloved, just as unconditionally and powerfully does Christian love intensify in the opposite direction."[53] Of course for Kierkegaard it is precisely the category of "the neighbor" that points to the unconditional movement of Christian love toward all.

Beyond the scope of love (the one versus the many), preferential love may be distinguished from neighbor-love also in virtue of the fact that preferential love owes its existence to good fortune. "In the poetic sense, it is a stroke of good fortune (and certainly the poet is an excellent judge of good fortune), the best of good fortune, to fall in love, to find this one and only beloved. It is a stroke of good fortune, almost as great, to find this one and only friend."[54] Since erotic love and friendship are by definition a matter of good fortune, however, they cannot be commanded in the way that neighbor-love is commanded. Kierkegaard points out that one could travel far and wide (possibly in vain) in search of the beloved or the friend, but that, by contrast, one need not search for the neighbor. "Christianity is never responsible for having a person go even a single step in vain, because when you open the door that you shut in order to pray to God and go out the very first person you meet is the neighbor, whom you *shall* love."[55] Here again the universal divine likeness is decisive since Christian

---

at all." Kierkegaard, *Either/Or* Part II, 42.

52. Kierkegaard, *Works of Love*, 49. Italics added.

53. Ibid. This, of course, is the love that Christ modeled and commanded. Philip Quinn offers a helpful interpretation of the radical nature of Kierkegaard's claims. "But the point Kierkegaard is trying to make is not paradoxical at all, though it may seem shocking. I take it to be that the obligation to love imposed by the love command places absolutely every human, including one's beloved, one's friend, and one's very self at the same distance from one as one's worst enemy or millions of people with whom one has had no contact. And so it is an obligation that extends to all alike, excludes no one and does not even permit distinctions among persons rooted in differential preferences . . ." Quoted in Evans, *Kierkegaard's Ethic*, 204.

54. Kierkegaard, *Works of Love*, 51. Here the orientation of preferential loves toward the *one*, rather than toward *all*, is again in evidence.

55. Ibid.

love orients us toward each one who shares in this likeness (which is everyone)—the neighbor.

Kierkegaard makes a third distinction between preferential loves and neighbor-love when he argues that while preferential loves are natural (based on drives and inclinations), neighbor-love is spiritual. "In erotic love the I is defined as sensate-psychical-spiritual; the beloved is a sensate-psychical, spiritual specification. In friendship the I is defined as psychical-spiritual; the friend is a psychical-spiritual specification. It is only in love for the neighbor that the self, who loves, is defined as spirit purely spiritually and the neighbor is a purely spiritual specification."[56] In saying that "neighbor" is a purely spiritual specification, Kierkegaard is not suggesting that the neighbor is never a concrete person but is suggesting, again, that we are commanded to love each person who shares in the universal divine likeness. According to this logic, merely to love a friend or the beloved is to allow natural and individual determinants to shape one's love, rather than allowing one's love to be determined by the universal divine likeness. Thus, Kierkegaard will conclude: "Love for the neighbor is therefore the eternal equality in loving, but the eternal equality is the opposite of preference. This needs no elaborate development. Equality is simply not to make distinctions, and eternal equality is unconditionally not to make the slightest distinction, unqualifiedly not to make the slightest distinction. Preference on the other hand, is to make distinctions; passionate preference is unqualifiedly to make distinctions."[57] While preferential love requires making distinctions, distinctions rooted in the particularity of lover and beloved, neighbor-love entails a refusal to make distinctions. Neighbor-love opens radically to all. Whereas the poet knows nothing of neighbor-love and of commanded love, the life and identity of the Christian must be grounded in awareness that he or she is called/commanded to love each/every person, without distinction—this is the spirit's love.

For Kierkegaard, a final and decisive criticism of preferential love is that such loves are essentially selfish. In defending this argument, Kierkegaard points to the traditional Aristotelian definition of friendship, according to which the friend is "another self." To define the friend or beloved as "another self," according to Kierkegaard, implies that the love extended to friend or beloved redounds to the self. But this is contrary to Christian love, since Christian love is by definition oriented toward the

---

56. Kierkegaard, *Works of Love*, 56–57.
57. Ibid., 58.

good of the neighbor. Thus we find Kierkegaard suggesting that the love command would speak as follows to one who had found the beloved (in merely preferential love):

> Love your neighbor as you love the beloved. But does he not love the beloved *as himself*, as the commandment that speaks of the neighbor commands? Certainly he does, but the beloved he loves *as himself* is not the neighbor; the beloved is the *other I*. Whether we speak of the *first I* or the *other I*, we do not come a step closer to the neighbor, because the neighbor is the *first you*. The one whom self-love, in the strictest sense, loves is basically the *other I*, because the *other I* is he himself. Yet this certainly is still self-love. But in the same sense it is self-love to love the *other I*, who is the beloved or the friend.[58]

To love the beloved or the friend is to love oneself under the guise of another person, which is to say that the love we extend to the beloved or friend is self-love.[59] In neighbor-love, on the other hand, we come face to face with the *first you*—in neighbor-love we come face to face, for the first time, with one who is other than ourselves (or, we first love the other as other).[60]

In view of Kierkegaard's attack on preferential loves, one is left to wonder whether preferential loves have not only been dethroned but also been placed on the trash heap of intersubjectivity. However, Kierkegaard commences his discussion in "You Shall Love *the Neighbor*" with the following programmatic assertion: "*It is in fact Christian love that discovers and knows that the neighbor exists and, what is the same thing, that everyone is the neighbor. If it were not a duty to love, the concept 'neighbor' would not exist either; but only when one loves the neighbor, only then is the selfishness in preferential love rooted out and the equality of the eternal*

---

58. Kierkegaard, *Works of Love*, 57.
59. Ferreira, *Love's Grateful Striving*, 44.
60. In discussing preferential loves as an instance of self-love, Kierkegaard invokes the neighbor as the middle term, arguing that this self-love is revealed when someone comes between two friends or between lover and beloved: "Test it. Place as a middle term between the lover and the beloved the neighbor, whom one shall love, place as a middle term between two friends the neighbor, whom one shall love, and you will immediately see jealousy. Yet the neighbor is self-denial's middle term that steps in between self-love's *I* and *I*, but also between erotic love's and friendship's *I* and the *other I*." See Kierkegaard, *Works of Love*, 54. According to Kierkegaard, in erotic love and friendship the two become one in a selfish sense—in a way that excludes the neighbor, both the friend or beloved as neighbor and the third person as neighbor.

preserved."⁶¹ It becomes evident, here, that one of Kierkegaard's overriding concerns is to root out the selfishness in preferential loves—in addition, his intention is to undermine the priority and prominence of preferential loves. But this means, of course, that *it is not a question of rooting out preferential loves themselves.*⁶²

In "You Shall Love the Neighbor" we also find Kierkegaard arguing: "If in order to love the neighbor you would have to begin by giving up loving those for whom you have preference, the word 'neighbor' would be the greatest deception every contrived."⁶³ Kierkegaard's narrower point, here, is that the beloved or friend shares in the universal divine likeness, and thus is also a neighbor, who must be loved. But he seems also to be suggesting that preferential loves may remain in place, a suggestion that is confirmed by other explicit statements. For example: "No, love the beloved faithfully and tenderly, but let love for the neighbor be the sanctifying element in your union's covenant with God. Love your friend honestly and devotedly, but let love for the neighbor be what you learn from each other in your friendship's confidential relationship with God!"⁶⁴ Thus, although the language Kierkegaard often employs seems to suggest an either/or (either one loves in neighbor-love or one loves preferentially), the either/or that he sets up *is not a radical either/or.*⁶⁵ That is, it is not a question of one or the other. It is, rather, a question of recognizing that neighbor-love is true love (indeed, the *only* love from a Christian point of view) and that preferential loves can only ever have a secondary place in relation to neighbor-love—such loves are "thrust down". As Ferreira helpfully summarizes the matter: "In one sense there is a kind of either/or about preference—preferential love can be sharply contrasted *conceptually* with nonpreferential love. Yet [Kierkegaard] claims that the goal is to preserve love for the neighbor in erotic love and friendship—'in erotic love and friendship, preserve love for the neighbor'—and thus they can coincide materially."⁶⁶ Thus we find

---

61. Ibid., 44. Italics in the original.

62. In the same way, Judge William argues that while the aesthetic (which corresponds with erotic love) has its validity, "it is nevertheless dethroned." See Kierkegaard, *Either/Or*, Part II, 226.

63. Kierkegaard, *Works of Love*, 61.

64. Ibid., 62. Italics added.

65. Ferreira, *Love's Grateful Striving*, 45.

66. Ferreira, *Love's Grateful Striving*, 45. In this passage Ferreira quotes *Works of Love*, 62. Martin Andic makes this same point, though differently, when he writes: "Kierkegaard thus sends us out in the name of Christ to love our spouse and our friend, retaining the element of difference that has to do with his or her being our

Søren Kierkegaard

Kierkegaard arguing, in "Love Is a Matter of Conscience," that "your wife must first and foremost be to you the neighbor; that she is your wife then is a more precise specification of your particular relationship to each other. But what is the eternal foundation must also be the foundation of every expression of the particular."[67]

We might say, then, that neighbor-love transforms or disciplines preferential love, and Kierkegaard confirms this when he writes: "[J]ust as we say to the solitary person: Take care that you are not led into the snare of self-love, so it must be said to the two lovers: Take care that you are not led by erotic love into the snare of self-love. The more decisively and exclusively preferential love embraces one single person, the further it is from loving the neighbor."[68] Thus, it is the task of true love (neighbor-love) to root out the selfishness in preferential loves, a task that it accomplishes by ensuring that the neighbor is not excluded (as a third term) from the relationship and by requiring that the friend or beloved be related to not merely as an *other I* but as the *first you*. Neighbor-love allows and requires, in the context of preferential loves, that we come face to face with one (in this case, the friend or beloved) who is other than ourselves. We might say that the Spirit's love (which is love of neighbor) serves as a check against merely natural impulses and inclinations in such a way that loves based on drives and inclinations do not become an obstacle to neighbor-love. And this should be seen to imply, as we have said, both that one should not fail to love every other person, given or chosen, but also that one should not fail to love the beloved him or herself *as neighbor*.[69]

In turning toward a conclusion of this discussion, it is helpful to quote Ferreira's summary of Kierkegaard's argument:

---

spouse or our friend, remembering that he or she is to be our neighbor first." See his "Love of Neighbor," 117.

67. Kierkegaard, *Works of Love*, 141. In the same discourse, Kierkegaard writes: "Christianity, however, knows only one kind of love, the spirit's love, but this can lie at the base of and be present in every other expression of love. How wonderful!" (Ibid., 146.)

68. Ibid., 61.

69. The language of "given or chosen" is used by Kierkegaard in a variety of places in *Works of Love*, including the discourse "Our Duty to Love the People We See," where he argues that *"the task is not to find the lovable object, but the task is to find the once given or chosen object—lovable . . ."* See Kierkegaard, *Works of Love*, 159. Regarding the need to love the beloved in the spirit's love, see Ferreira's discussion in "Immediacy and Reflection," 118.

PART TWO—Kierkegaard and Love's Promise

> One is tempted to say that Kierkegaard wants to ensure that friendship and erotic love are both supplemented by nonpreferential love, but he rejects the language of supplementation or addition. He makes this clearer later on when he insists that "there is only one kind of love, the spirit's love" (p. 143). Therefore, neighbor-love should "permeate" every expression of love (p. 112); it can and should "lie at the base of and be present in every other expression of love"; "it is in all of them, that is, it can be, but Christian love itself you cannot point to." (p. 146). It is a "misunderstanding" to think that "in Christianity the beloved and the friend are loved faithfully and tenderly in quite a different way than in paganism (p. 53); neighbor-love allows "drives," "inclinations," "feelings," "natural relations," and "prescriptive rights . . . to remain in force"; it is not indifferent to family relations" or "friendship" or "fatherland" (p. 144).[70]

Thus, we find Kierkegaard arguing, again: "No, love the beloved faithfully and tenderly, but *let love for the neighbor be the sanctifying element in your union's covenant with God.* Love your friend honestly and devotedly, but let love for the neighbor be what you learn from each other in your friendship's confidential relationship with God!"[71]

As Stephen Evans points out, Kierkegaard is not entirely clear on how the transformation of preferential loves by neighbor-love might take place in everyday life—he provides no account of what this transformation might look like. However, as Evans rightly adds, "this lack of precision on his part may be intentional since part of his view is that individuals must attempt to work out what the obligation means for them in the absence of algorithmic procedures."[72] Kierkegaard's account of neighbor-love, then, is such that love may come to fruition or expression in a great variety of ways and circumstances. We cannot fully anticipate the requirement of love in a given situation, and cannot foreclose on possibilities ahead of time. This

70. Ferreira, *Love's Grateful Striving*, 45–46.

71. Kierkegaard, *Works of Love*, 62. Italics added. We can only disagree with Vanessa Rumble's suggestion that, in *Works of Love*, "the one who truly loves will not attend to this distinction [between preferential and agapic love]," by which she means to say that the one who truly loves will ignore those aspects of a preferential relationship that make it preferential. As observed, Kierkegaard does not argue that the one who loves truly will not attend to preferential loves as preferential. Neither can we accept Rumble's suggestion that the first part of *Works of Love* entails a "Kantian denigration of earthly love" since we have observed that Kierkegaard's goal is not to denigrate earthly loves but to rightly situate them in relation to the love of neighbor. On each of these points, see Rumble "Love and Difference," 163–65.

72. Evans, *Kierkegaard's Ethic*, 207.

Søren Kierkegaard

will become particularly important as we draw Irigaray and Kierkegaard into conversation on the nature of human subjectivity and on an ethical intersubjectivity between persons (between man and woman).

LOVE DOES NOT SEEK ITS OWN

As we continue to explore the notion of God as the middle term, we take up a question that will also be important for the conversation between Irigaray and Kierkegaard—namely, the question of distinctiveness.[73] Kierkegaard develops the notion of distinctiveness in the context of a consideration of the requirement that we love the other's own.[74] He argues that the refusal to seek one's own, the refusal to look out for one's own interest, implies also that we seek, positively, the "distinctiveness" of the other. In referring to the distinctiveness of the other, Kierkegaard refers to God's creation of each person, *ex nihilo*, in his or her particularly. Kierkegaard invites the reader to consider the natural world:

> With what infinite love nature or God in nature encompasses all the diverse things that have life and existence! Just recollect what you yourself have so often delighted in looking at, recollect the beauty of the meadows! There is no difference in love, no, none—yet what a difference in the flowers! Even the least, the most insignificant, the most unimpressive, the poor little flower disregarded by even its immediate surroundings, the flower you can hardly find without looking carefully—it is as if this, too, had said to love: Let me become something in myself, something distinctive. And then love has helped it to become its own distinctiveness, but far more beautiful than the poor little flower had ever dared to hope for. What love! First it makes no distinction, none at all; next, which is just like the first, it infinitely distinguishes itself in loving the diverse. Wondrous Love! For what is as difficult as to make no distinction at all in loving, and if one makes no distinction at all, what is as difficult as making distinctions! Just suppose nature were like us human beings—rigid, domineering, cold, partisan, small-minded, capricious—and imagine, yes, just imagine what would happen to the beauty of the meadow![75]

---

73. With the title of this discourse, Kierkegaard makes reference to 1 Corinthians 13:5.

74. Kierkegaard, *Works of Love*, 264.

75. Ibid., 270.

Just as the beauty of the meadow consists in the diversity of its flowers and grasses and birds and shrubs, so the beauty of the human consists in its diversity. The God who creates the human person does so *ex nihilo* "yet creates distinctiveness, so that the creature in relation to God does not become nothing even though it is taken from nothing and is nothing but becomes a distinct individuality."[76] According to Kierkegaard, belief in one's own distinctiveness correlates with belief in the distinctiveness of every other person.[77]

In uniting this account of distinctiveness with the rigorousness of the love-command, Kierkegaard writes: "*Love does not seek its own. The truly loving one does not love his own distinctiveness but, in contrast, loves every human being according to his distinctiveness; but 'his distinctiveness' is what for him is **his own**; that is, the loving one does not seek his own; quite the opposite, he loves what is the other's own.*"[78] Kierkegaard expresses the rigorousness of the love command most clearly when he suggests that "loving the other's distinctiveness will entail the sacrifice and self-denial of not seeking one's own."[79] True love seeks not its own distinctiveness but that of the other.[80] As Andic puts it, "we should love each human being as he or she actually is, and may authentically become as an ethical subject before God, boundlessly different and irreplaceable and valuable."[81]

To clarify what he means by this, Kierkegaard gives two examples of those who fail to love and respect the other in his or her distinctiveness. On the one hand, the rigid and domineering person "lacks flexibility, lacks the pliability to comprehend others; he demands his own from everyone, wants everyone to be transformed in his image, to be trimmed according to his pattern for human beings." This is the person who, by refusing to acknowledge the neighbor's distinctiveness, diminishes or even destroys the

---

76. Ibid., 271–72.

77. Kierkegaard writes: "To have distinctiveness is to believe in the distinctiveness of everyone else, because distinctiveness is not mine but is God's gift by which he gives being to me, and he indeed gives to all, gives being to all." (Ibid., 271.)

78. Ibid., 269. Italics and bold in the original.

79. Ferreira, *Love's Grateful Striving*, 153. According to the "like for like" of *Works of Love*, when I love the other's distinctiveness, I am affirmed and established by God in my own distinctiveness. Priority is not given to self-love, but self-love is nevertheless affirmed. There is no opposition between what we've said here and what we've said, above, regarding the necessity of self-love.

80. Kierkegaard, *Works of Love*, 274. As Arne Grøn points out, this does not mean that one's own distinctiveness is denied or diminished. See his "The Dialectic of Recognition," 147–57.

81. Andic, "Love of Neighbor," 119.

other's particularity. Kierkegaard continues, "if the rigid and domineering cannot ever create, he wants at least to transform—that is, he seeks his own so that wherever he points he can say: See, it is my image, it is my idea, it is my will."[82] And lest we think that only military commanders or royal personages are prone to such a rigid and domineering approach to others, Kierkegaard points out that the rigid and domineering can be a tyrant in an empire or a domestic tyrant in a little attic room. "The nature is the same: domineeringly refusing to go out of oneself, domineeringly wanting to crush the other person's distinctiveness or torment it to death. The nature is the same—the worst tyrant who ever lived and had a world to tyrannize became bored with it and ended up tyrannizing flies, but he really remained the same."[83] True love makes no distinction at all, extends love to every person, yet remains profoundly aware of the other's distinctiveness.

Beyond the domineering person, Kierkegaard also gives the example of the small-minded person who has never had the courage to become a distinct self before God—this person does not believe in his own distinctiveness and so cannot believe in the distinctiveness of the neighbor. Kierkegaard writes: "The small-minded person has clung to a very specific shape and form that he calls his own; he seeks only that, can love only that. If the small-minded person finds this, then he loves."[84] The small-minded person receives the distinctiveness of the other as a refutation of himself: "therefore [the small-minded person] feels a clammy, uncomfortable anxiety upon seeing an unfamiliar distinctiveness, and nothing is more important for him than to get rid of it. Small-mindedness demands of God, as it were, that every such distinctiveness be destroyed so that small-mindedness will be shown to be in the right and God to be a jealous God—jealous for small-mindedness."[85] There is, in small-mindedness, insecurity about one's identity and a desire for self-preservation that drives the small-minded person to "get rid of everything else but its own. . . . In its asthmatic tightness that gasps for relief, we hear how it would perish if it did not get rid of this discomfort, this anxiety. One sees in its glance how basically unsure it is of itself deep down, and therefore how sneakily and how rapaciously it lies in wait for its prey—in order that it may become

---

82. Kierkegaard, *Works of Love*, 270.

83. Ibid., 271. The reference, according to the editors of *Works of Love*, is to the Roman Emperor Domitian.

84. Ibid., 272.

85. Ibid., 273.

PART TWO—Kierkegaard and Love's Promise

apparent that small-mindedness nevertheless is right and has the victory."[86] Thus, small-mindedness, in its insecurity about its own distinctiveness, becomes petty and self-protective. For both the domineering person and the small-minded person, the result is the same—the distinctiveness or particularity of the neighbor is diminished or denied. As Kierkegaard summarizes it in an earlier discourse: "The one who seeks *his own* must of course push everything else to the side, must tear down in order to make room for his own, which he wants to build up."[87]

To consider a question that will become important for us below, we ask what place a person's sensate-psychical nature has within Kierkegaard's account of distinctiveness. On the one hand, we could construe Kierkegaard as suggesting that distinctiveness refers only to the self as a spiritual being—it refers to the individual's dynamic and private relation to God—in which case the sensate-psychical nature of the person is not an aspect of his or her distinctiveness. In fact, in the context of his discussion of distinctiveness Kierkegaard does not raise the question of a person's particular sensate-psychical nature. However, we should not conclude that these are not an aspect of a person's distinctiveness before God.

That a person's sensate-psychical being *is* part of a person's distinctiveness can be affirmed on the basis of Kierkegaard's insistence that preferential loves are appropriate to Christian life and love. For Kierkegaard, each person is drawn to others (in love and friendship) on the basis of desires and inclinations that are particular to him or her—and *Works of Love* affirms that Christianity does not wish to remove or ignore such desires and inclinations.[88] If such desires and inclinations (the sensate and psychical aspects of the person) are a good and legitimate feature of human being, then a person's sensate and psychical nature can be construed as an aspect of his or her distinctiveness. That I have *this* particular set of skills, that I am attracted sexually to *this* person, that I find *this* set of characteristics desirable in a friend, and that I have *this* physiological makeup, makes me the being I am. To some degree, at least, I cannot be

---

86. Ibid. In what we can read as an echo of Irigaray's thought, the small-minded person does not know how to breathe, and therefore is unable to grant the other person space to breathe. Only as the asthmatic finds relief (by acknowledging one's own distinctiveness, as well as that of the other) will he or she become free to allow the other space to breathe and to become.

87. Ibid., 220. Italics added.

88. "Christianity does not want to make changes in externals; neither does it want to abolish drives or inclinations—it wants only to make infinity's change in the inner being." See Kierkegaard, *Works of Love*, 139.

other than I am—thus it is appropriate to use the language of "givenness" with respect to our sensate-psychical nature. According to Kierkegaard's argument concerning "distinctiveness," then, to love another is not only to acknowledge him or her as an individual secretly related to God, but is to acknowledge and affirm the particular sensate-psychical, spiritual being he or she is. Thus also, we must recognize that the human tendency to diminish or deny the distinctiveness of the other (whether through a domineering or small-minded spirit), takes place at every level of our human identity—at the level of the sensate-psychical and also at the level of the other's becoming in relation to God.

In anticipation of a possible confluence between Irigaray and Kierkegaard, it is helpful to consider Kierkegaard's insistence, in this same discourse, on each person's need "to become himself, free, independent, his own master," to stand alone.[89] With respect to this need Kierkegaard argues that the greatest gift we can offer another is to help the other stand alone, to help the other become free and independent. Of course, Kierkegaard recognizes that this ethical imperative is paradoxical in nature, and acknowledges that if I have helped another to stand by himself, "then he has indeed not become his own master [since] it is to my help that he owes all this—and he is aware of it."[90] According to Kierkegaard, to help another in this way (such that the other becomes aware of my helping him stand alone) is actually to betray the other—it is to help the other in the wrong way.

In order to alleviate the problem of the neighbor's *dependent* independence Kierkegaard argues that "the greatest benefaction . . . cannot be done in such a way that the recipient comes to know that it is to me that he owes it, because if he comes to know that, then it simply is not the greatest beneficence."[91] The best thing that a person can do, then, is to hide his or her help so that it can be said that the other person "is standing by himself—through my help." Kierkegaard makes much of the dash. When you hide behind the dash, Kierkegaard says: "You see no help or support, no awkward bungler's hand holding on to him, any more than it occurs to the person himself that someone has helped him. No, he is standing by himself—through another's help. But this person's help is hidden from him—the one who was helped. No, from the eyes of the independent one (for if he knows that he has been helped, then in the deepest sense he of

---

89. Kierkegaard, *Works of Love*, 274.
90. Ibid.
91. Ibid., 275.

course is not the independent one who helps and has helped himself); [the help] is hidden behind the dash."[92] According to Kierkegaard, it is the responsibility of the helper to make him or herself anonymous, to magnanimously will to annihilate him or herself in helping the other to stand.[93] Those who truly love do not seek their own, and they give to another in such a way that it looks as if the gift were the recipient's property.

Why this insistence on the anonymity and even the annihilation of the giver? For Kierkegaard, the answer is theological. When a person can declare that this individual is standing by himself—with my help, "there is no self-satisfaction in the last phrase, because the loving one has understood that essentially every human being indeed stands by himself—through God's help—and that the loving one's self-annihilation is really only in order not to hinder the other person's God-relationship, so that all the loving one's help infinitely vanishes in the God-relationship."[94] Every human person, in virtue of his or her status as a creature of God, as a synthesis and self-relation related to God, is helped to stand by God—and to be a self before God is to stand as the distinctive person that one is. Thus, to love the neighbor is to become a co-worker with God in the work that God has done and is doing. In love toward the neighbor there is to be a constant awareness that it is God who gives the other distinctiveness and that it is God who relates decisively to the other in her becoming a self, which is to say that neither my love toward her nor my ideas about her are decisive for her becoming a self before God. To build up the other in love, and to contribute to the becoming of the neighbor, then, is not "to transform the other person" or to produce love in her "through the exercise of control."[95] Rather, love of the neighbor is, by definition, a matter of self-control on my part. To control oneself, here, is to self-sacrificially offer love, encouragement, and support to the other, and to withdraw from view in such a way that it is God, the source of love, who is acknowledged as Love and who receives love.

Love Builds Up

Kierkegaard begins the discourse "Love Builds Up" with a discussion of the relation between the sensate-psychical and spiritual aspects of the

92. Ibid.
93. Ibid., 276.
94. Ibid., 278.
95. Ibid., 217.

human person and argues that while each person is born as both a natural and a spiritual being, each person in fact lives a merely sensate-psychical existence before arriving at a moment of spiritual awakening. At this moment of awakening, he suggests, a person does not cast off the sensible and psychical nature (as in the disposal of a dirty shirt); rather, this sensible and psychical nature is "taken over" by spirit, and is embraced within the new context of the spiritual.[96] Kierkegaard uses this discussion of the relationship between the sensate-psychical and the spiritual in order to introduce a discussion of language, arguing that language itself may be conceived of in terms of this distinction between the sensate-psychical and the spiritual. He suggests that while language has a plain meaning that is available to every person (which correlates with the sensate-psychical), language also has a metaphorical function, according to which meaning is hidden or secret (which correlates with the spiritual): "Therefore, in one sense the spiritual person and the sensate-psychical person say the same thing; yet there is an infinite difference, since the latter has no intimation of the secret of the metaphorical words although he is using the same words, but not in their metaphorical sense. There is a world of difference between the two; the one has made the transition or let himself be carried over to the other side, while the other remains on this side; yet they have the connection that both are using the same words."[97]

According to Kierkegaard, while a person who has experienced spiritual awakening continues to use words and concepts that would be recognized by the merely sensate-psychical person, the spiritually alive person will nevertheless use these words and concepts in a way that transcends the meanings ascribed to them by the person living a merely sensate-psychical existence. Kierkegaard speaks of the person who has experienced spiritual awakening in the following way: "Although conscious of himself as spirit, he continues to remain in the visible world and to be visible to the senses—in the same way he also remains in the language—except that his language is the metaphorical language."[98] The difference between the person who lives a merely sensate-psychical existence and the spiritually

---

96. Ibid., 209. This corresponds with our earlier assertion that the distinctiveness of the person includes not only the spiritual aspect of his or her being but also the sensate-psychical aspect. That Kierkegaard argues for an embrace of the sensate-psychical within the spiritual will become important for us when we turn to consider the continuity between *Works of Love* and the account of human becoming that is developed in the pseudonymous works.

97. Kierkegaard, *Works of Love*, 209.

98. Ibid.

alive person, according to Kierkegaard, is by no means an obvious or visible difference. As he says, the spirit's way is to offer a quiet, whispering secret, *"for the person who has ears to hear."*[99]

With this distinction between the literal and the metaphorical in mind, Kierkegaard turns to the phrase/concept that concerns him in the present discourse—namely, "to build up." While Kierkegaard uses the phrase/concept "to build up" in order to illustrate the difference between the literal and the metaphorical, it becomes clear that he is preoccupied with another more substantive question: with a *living out* or *embrace* of the metaphorical and spiritual meaning of "to build up." Remaining for a moment with the linguistic question however, Kierkegaard points out that the literal or plain meaning of "to build up" has to do with erecting a building, from the ground up. And he is particularly keen to emphasize that the plain or literal meaning of "to build up" includes consideration of the *foundation* of the building that is constructed: "Therefore if a man builds upward and from the ground but the depth does not correspond properly to the height, we say that he built up but also that he built it up poorly . . ."[100] It is said that this person has built it up poorly, of course, because he has not accounted for the fact that the foundation is implicated in "building up." Thus, Kierkegaard argues that if a man is going to build a tower "then by all means have him be careful to dig deep, because even if the tower reached the sky, if this were possible, if it lacked a foundation it would not actually be built up."[101] Plainly speaking, "to build up" means to build in an upward direction while also establishing a foundation that corresponds to the weight and height of the building.

Beyond the literal meaning of "to build up" there is also a metaphorical meaning, and this metaphorical meaning is appealed to in the Christian Scriptures—for example in the Apostle Paul's argument that "love builds up."[102] According to Kierkegaard, the words of the Apostle imply that there is a necessary connection between the loving and the upbuilding—the spiritual meaning of the upbuilding is bound up with the invitation and command to *love*. Indeed, Kierkegaard suggests that the relationship between loving and upbuilding (in Scripture) is so close that the command rendered by the Apostle Paul as "Do everything for upbuilding"[103] could

---

99. Ibid., 210.
100. Ibid., 211.
101. Ibid., 211–12.
102. This particular discourse, of course, takes its name from 1 Corinthians 8:1.
103. This is a reference not to 1 Corinthians 8:1 but to 1 Corinthians 14:26.

equally have been rendered: "Do everything in love."[104] Thus, the upbuilding is the loving and the loving is the upbuilding—the upbuilding can only be done in love, and the evidence of upbuilding is the love it produces in another. This is the metaphorical and spiritual meaning of "to build up."

It is evident here, however, that Kierkegaard is already moving beyond merely linguistic considerations—he is suggesting that a *living out* or *embrace* of the metaphorical and spiritual meaning of "to build up" requires a spiritual transformation of the person. That is, to accept that the upbuilding is the loving and that the loving is the upbuilding requires a spiritual transformation in the person. Thus, although the merely sensate-psychical person could understand the difference between the literal and metaphorical meaning of "to build up," the merely sensate-psychical person could not *embrace* the metaphorical meaning (which is love) in life and action.

That Kierkegaard is not simply concerned with the literal or the metaphorical use of the phrase "to build up" becomes evident when he offers the example of an infant sleeping comfortably with its mother. Kierkegaard writes:

> We would not think that the sight of a person sleeping could be upbuilding. Yet if you see a baby sleeping on its mother's breast—and you see the mother's love, see that she has, so to speak, waited for and now makes use of the moment while the baby is sleeping really to rejoice in it because she hardly dares let the baby notice how inexpressibly she loves it—then this is an upbuilding sight. If the mother's love is not visible, if in vain you search her face and countenance for the slightest expression of maternal joy or solicitude for the baby, if you see only apathy and indifference that is happy to be free of the child so long—then the sight is not upbuilding. Just to see the baby sleeping is a friendly, benevolent, soothing sight, but it is not upbuilding. If you still want to call it upbuilding, it is because you see love present, it is because you see God's love encompass the baby.[105]

On the one hand, Kierkegaard uses this example to show that we deploy the metaphorical meaning of "upbuilding" in everyday speech only where love is present. Thus, in our everyday speech we affirm what the Apostle Paul has implied—namely, that the loving is the upbuilding, and the

---

104. Kierkegaard, *Works of Love*, 213.
105. Ibid., 214.

PART TWO—Kierkegaard and Love's Promise

upbuilding is the loving. However, there is more at stake in this example than a mere filling out of the meaning of the phrase "to build up."

With this example Kierkegaard points beyond the immediate and obvious to that which can only be seen by spiritual eyes—namely, that the love of God embraces the child. While the average person will likely describe the first scene of mother with child (where the mother obviously loves and delights in her child) as upbuilding, because love is in evidence, only a person who has experienced a spiritual transformation (a transformation of vision) will see the second scene as upbuilding. The latter scene can only be described as upbuilding by the person who "looks a littler harder" and is able to see with the eyes of faith—thus seeing the scene in terms of the presence of God's love. When love is perceived, the scene becomes an upbuilding one. So Kierkegaard's preoccupation is not simply with language (and the difference between the literal and the metaphorical)—rather, this discussion of language becomes a way into a consideration of how one might live and love (fully, spiritually) in the world.

In returning to Kierkegaard's discussion of the literal and metaphorical meaning of "to build up," and to his discussion of the relation between the upbuilding and the loving, the question of intersubjectivity comes to the fore. Kierkegaard writes: "In ordinary talk about a house, a building, everyone knows what is meant by the ground and the foundation. But what, in the spiritual sense, is the ground and foundation of the spiritual life that is to bear the building? It is love. Love is the source of everything and, in the spiritual sense, love is the deepest ground of the spiritual life. In every human being in whom there is love, the foundation, in the spiritual sense, is laid."[106] If love is the foundation of the building, then love is that which builds it up, and is that which is built up, also. As Kierkegaard puts it: "Love is the ground, love is the building, love builds up."[107] While there may be other ways that we speak of the upbuilding, according to Kierkegaard (for example, through knowledge, in insight, in expertness, in integrity), "insofar as it does not build up love, [it] is still not upbuilding in the deepest sense."[108] According to Kierkegaard, the close relationship between the upbuilding and the loving requires that we conceive of the *work* of love in either of two ways—as the implanting of love in another or as the presupposing of love in another. As should already be obvious, Kierkegaard will argue that it can never be a human work of love to implant or create love in another. "It is God, the Creator, who must implant

106. Kierkegaard, *Works of Love* 215.
107. Ibid., 16.
108. Ibid.

love in each human being, he who himself is Love. Thus it is specifically unloving and not at all upbuilding if someone arrogantly deludes himself into believing that he wants and is able to create love in another person; all busy and pompous zeal in this regard neither builds up love nor is in itself upbuilding."[109] Thus, a human person is neither able to create love in another nor to implant love in another; rather, the human person can only presuppose that which is already present—namely, love.[110]

From Kierkegaard's perspective, it is by presupposing love in another that one builds the other up in love.[111] "The one who loves presupposes that love is in the other person's heart and by this very presupposition builds up love in him—from the ground up, provided of course, that in love he presupposes its presence in the ground."[112] According to the logic of God as the middle term, to love another is to presuppose his or her relation to Love (God is Love), is to presuppose that God has created the other in Love, and is to presuppose that love lies at heart and ground of the other's being.[113] Thus, a discourse about the work of Love in building up the other (in love) "cannot be about what the loving person, who wants to build up, is to do now in order to transform the other person or in order through the exercise of control to produce love in him, but it is about how the loving one upbuildingly controls himself. As you see, it is already upbuilding to bear in mind that the one who loves builds up by controlling himself!"[114] To love another person, and to encourage him or her in love of God and love of neighbor, is to exercise a degree of self-control that

---

109. Ibid.

110. In *Philosophical Fragments*, Johannes Climacus offers a Socratic approach to knowledge and truth that resonates with the argument of Kierkegaard here. Climacus argues that "between one human being and another maieuesthai [to deliver] is the highest; giving birth indeed belongs to the god." See Kierkegaard, *Philosophical Fragments*, 11.

111. In relating the need to presuppose love in the other to the question of self-love, Pia Søltoft writes: "But this foundation is of course also present in the one who builds up and presupposing it in the other is only possible by being aware of its presence in oneself. And acting upon this awareness is to do something to oneself." See Søltoft, "To Let Oneself Be Upbuilt," 25.

112. Kierkegaard, *Works of Love*, 216–17.

113. Earlier in *Works of Love*, Kierkegaard writes: "Just as the quiet lake originates deep down in hidden springs no eye has seen, so also does a person's love originate even more deeply in God's love. If there were no gushing spring at the bottom, if God were not love, then there would be neither the little lake nor a human being's love." (Ibid., 9–10.)

114. Ibid., 217.

PART TWO—Kierkegaard and Love's Promise

correlates with the fact that I am not able to produce love in the other.[115] "A person can be tempted to be a builder, a teacher, a disciplinarian because this seems to be ruling over others; but to build up the way love does cannot tempt, because this means to be the one who serves; therefore, because it is willing to serve, only love has the desire to build up."[116] Accordingly, the person who loves the other is someone who works quietly, and yet the forces of eternity are in motion in this person: "Love humbly makes itself inconspicuous just when it is working the hardest—indeed, its work seems as if it did nothing at all."[117]

As Kierkegaard's example of the sleeping child makes clear, it is frequently far from obvious that love is present in the other person—often it seems to us that love is absent from the other's life. However, in a discussion of the Apostle Paul's insistence that love, among other things, (i) believes all things, (ii) is patient, and (iii) hopes all things, Kierkegaard explains how it is that one might presuppose love in the other. With respect to "love believes all things," Kierkegaard suggests that while mistrust takes away the foundation by denying the presence of love, belief assumes the presence of love even in the misguided, the corrupted, and the hateful.[118] In terms of "love is patient," Kierkegaard argues that love bears with the misunderstandings of the other—bears even with his or her ingratitude or anger—by patiently assuming that love lies beneath these.[119] Finally, with respect to "love hopes all things," Kierkegaard points to the example of the waiting father who did not know that he had a prodigal son because he presupposed the love that was in his son—he loved forth the love of his son.[120] For Kierkegaard, to presuppose love in another is to love forth love and is to enable the other to love. He asks:

> If anyone has ever spoken to you in such a way or treated you in such a way that you really felt built up, this was because you very vividly perceived how he presupposed love to be in you. Or what kind of person do you think one would be who could truly build you up? Is it not true that you would desire him to have insight and knowledge and talent and experience? But you

---

115. Kierkegaard will, in fact, speak of the building up of another in terms of a "conquering of oneself." (Ibid., 219.)

116. Ibid., 217.

117. Ibid., 218.

118. Ibid., 221.

119. Ibid., 220

120. Ibid., 221.

> still would not consider that it depended crucially on this, but rather on his being a trustworthy, loving person—that is, truly a loving person. Therefore you consider that to build up depends crucially and essentially upon being loving or having love to such a degree that one can rely upon it.[121]

To presuppose love in another is to see him or her as a creature of God, created in Love, whose very being is grounded in the Love of God. And Kierkegaard supposes that our everyday experience of being loved confirms for us that to be loved is to be built up—as I am loved by another (as I am trusted and acknowledged as loving) I indeed love the neighbor as I love myself.

According to Kierkegaard's account of the upbuilding, then, love is a refusal to see the other as the object of a stratagem by which I might plant love in her, and is a refusal to take responsibility for the life to which the other is called. Indeed, my first task in love is to assume the presence of love in the other—my first task is to assume that the other finds his or her foundation and being in Love. On the basis of this presupposition, I also assume the other's capacity for love of self, love of God, and love of neighbor, regardless of whether or not this capacity is in evidence for me.[122] To presuppose that love is present in this way is to refuse the temptation to tear down and to push aside everything that is contrary to my liking, or contrary to my vision of what the other person is or should be. "The one who seeks his own must of course push everything else to the side, must tear down in order to make room for his own, which he wants to build up. But love presupposes that love is present in the ground and therefore builds it up."

Thus, to presuppose love in the other is not only to acknowledge that the other owes her being to Love (in an abstract kind of way), but is to acknowledge that her substantive becoming owes to the mercy and love of God—and not to me. Her becoming and upbuilding in love are rooted in the purposes of God and cannot be reduced to my intention for her. In saying that love is present as ground in the other, Kierkegaard

---

121. Ibid., 222.

122. In a parallel argument (and one that gives a more substantive bearing to the present discussion) Kierkegaard argues, in "Love Hides a Multitude of Sins," that "Every event, every word, every act, in short, everything can be explained in many ways." It is, then, the responsibility of one who loves to seek a mitigating explanation for a word or action that, in the first instance, appears unloving—perhaps, Kierkegaard suggests, there is another explanation than that upon which our mind first settles. (Ibid., 291–94.)

is suggesting that the other can never become merely a project for me, and that the upbuilding of the other in love can never be a matter of my foisting a blueprint of becoming on her. As was the case in the discourse "Love Does Not Seek Its Own," so it is the case in this discourse that love is in the first instance a matter of self-control—it is a matter of assuming that I cannot, and ought not, perceive the other's becoming as owing anything to my own wisdom or capacities. Love, therefore, "is not irritable and impetuous, impatient, almost hopelessly busy with what it must tear down in order to build up again; no, it continually presupposes that love is present in the ground."[123]

Preferential Loves, Again

In our engagement with Irigaray and Kierkegaard we are preoccupied with the relationship between man and woman generally, yet also with particular relationships. It will be helpful, then, to conclude the present chapter by providing a sketch of how a preferential love relationship between man and woman (marriage, in his terms) might take shape under the terms of Kierkegaard's account of neighbor-love, and with God as the middle term. As noted, Kierkegaard argues that Christianity casts erotic love and friendship from the throne of our lives and imaginations and sets up the spirit's love in their place.[124] However, he does not thereby place preferential loves on the scrap heap of intersubjectivity—rather, he suggests that the priority and primacy of neighbor-love entails a transformation of preferential loves. Thus, neighbor-love entails a (radical?) reconsideration of what it is to participate in and live such relationships. In providing some sense of what this reconsideration entails, we focus on self-love, distinctiveness, and the upbuilding.

For Kierkegaard, the marital relationship is, in the first instance, a relationship of sensual immediacy—temporally speaking marriage is first

---

123. Ibid., 222.

124. In his *Journals*, Kierkegaard writes: "I must once again deal with erotic love [*Elksov*] and friendship. It is obvious that in Christendom we have completely forgotten what love [*Kjerlighed*] is. We pander to erotic love and friendship, laud and praise them as love, that is, as a virtue. Nonsense! Erotic love and friendship are earthly happiness, a temporal good just like money, abilities, talents, etc., only better. They are to be complemented, but should not be made delusively important ..." See *Journals and Papers* III, 2410. Again, we find here both an affirmation of erotic love, but also a sense that erotic love and marriage should not be set up on the throne of our lives and imaginations.

a romantic encounter and relationship between a man and a woman.[125] As a preferential and erotic/sensual relationship, it is also possible to say that marriage finds its origin in the good fortune of a man and woman who "discover" each other—a discovery in which mutual attraction and affection are realized. A man and woman who, through good fortune, find themselves bound together in romantic and sensual attraction, may be inclined to move beyond this merely sensual moment of attraction and intersubjectivity into the institution of marriage; they may be inclined to accept the rights and responsibilities that correspond with the estate of marriage. In terms of Kierkegaard's *Works of Love*, we should note that it is at times difficult to distinguish his description of neighbor-love and his description of marital love since his account of marital love is frequently an account of marital love as it is disciplined by neighbor-love. Notwithstanding this overlap in his descriptions of marital love and neighbor-love, however, there remain certain features of marriage that clearly distinguish it from neighbor-love and from other preferential relationships; namely, the orientation of this relationship toward procreation, the rule of the husband over the wife,[126] and the duty of each to remain in the relationship.

For Kierkegaard, then, marriage is (i) a particular form of preferential intersubjectivity, (ii) an erotic/sensual relationship, (iii) rooted in the good fortune of a man and woman in discovering each other, (iv) entered into by an act of resolution and will, (v) a relationship of conscience before God (in virtue of its solemnization in the presence of God), (vi) oriented toward procreation, (vii) a relationship in which the husband in some sense rules over the wife, and (viii) a relationship marked by the duty of each to continue in this love relationship. Although a central feature of the marital relationship, according to the liturgy of wedding ceremony, is precisely God's status as middle term (inasmuch as the wedding liturgy invites each to consult with conscience), Kierkegaard points out that men and women invariably live the marital relationship as if God's status as the middle term was of little import. Kierkegaard seems convinced that those who live in marital relationships invariably deny the neighbor (whether the third party neighbor or the spouse as neighbor), compromise the God-relationship of the spouse, and fail to submit to God's judgment concerning the nature of true love. This failure to acknowledge God, Kierkegaard

---

125. This is not to say that neighbor-love cannot be present in erotic love (transforming it from the outset). It is to say, however, that, according to Kierkegaard's account of marriage, the erotic invariably represents the temporal beginning of such a relationship.

126. Kierkegaard, *Works of Love*, 138.

PART TWO—Kierkegaard and Love's Promise

would likely argue, owes precisely to the fact that Christians think that preferential loves are the primary expression of love and that Christianity has simply come into the world to remind husband and wife to "think a little bit about the neighbor too."[127] According to the logic of Kierkegaard's argument, then, we turn now to consider what it means that the spirit's love (neighbor-love) is love and must lie at the heart of the marital relationship.

According to Kierkegaard, every person shares in the divine likeness and, in virtue of his or her creation by God, belongs to God as a bond servant. "[T]herefore, he dare not belong to anyone in love unless in the same love he belongs to God and dare not possess anyone in love unless the other and he himself belong to God in this love . . ."[128] This also applies to the marital relationship, within which God as the middle term requires that husband and wife acknowledge that the other is first and foremost in a relationship to God—which in turn implies that neither spouse is free to posses the other in a way that his or her bond service to God (his or her obedience and adoration toward God, his or her indebtedness before God) is compromised. While this status of each spouse as bond servant of God is expressed in rather formal terms (and provides little in terms of substantive content for an ethical intersubjectivity between husband and wife), the minimal content that the concept provides is by no means insignificant.

For example, it is not difficult to conceive of a marital relationship within which one partner construes the other as an object to be possessed, or to conceive of a marital relationship in which one partner takes the other as the primary object of his or her love (without reference to the requirements of God). In either case, God's status as middle term, and the bond-service of each spouse before God, is compromised—the ability and freedom of one spouse or the other to worship and serve God is compromised. In such circumstances, Kierkegaard suggests, "Christianity steps forward and asks about the relationship to God," asks whether husband and wife are first related to God, first bound (as individuals) to the God who is the author of their respective lives and love.[129] Again, it is neces-

127. Here Kierkegaard takes aim at what Evans identifies as the "deluded pagan": "The deluded pagan is the individual who believes that neighbor-love can be identified with such natural, merely human loves celebrated by the poet as friendship or romantic love, or at best sees neighbor-love as something that one has alongside or in addition to these natural forms of love." See Evans, *Kierkegaard's Ethic*, 116.

128. Kierkegaard, *Works of Love*, 107–8.

129. Ibid., 108.

sary to acknowledge that this theocentric account of mediation offers only limited corrections in the face of historical failures of intersubjectivity between man and woman, and it is for precisely this reason that it will be necessary to explore the question of sexual difference and to develop a tentative, Irigaray-informed Kierkegaardian theory of sexual difference.

As beings created in Love, by the God who is Love, both husband and wife are free to love themselves in a self-love that has rooted out selfishness. Self-love, in fact, may be construed in terms of freedom to become oneself before God, to become a self before God, in the same way that the neighbor is free to become him or herself before God. Whether the neighbor is a spouse, a friend, or a new acquaintance from the workplace, the relationship between two is mediated by God, which implies that each partner to the relationship must acknowledge the self-love or self-affection of the other—must grant the other a free space of becoming in relation to God. Here Kierkegaard's ethical vision extends beyond the rather limited implications of bond-service to God. According to Kierkegaard's account of self-love, I am not only obliged to respect the other as belonging first to God, I am also obliged to respect and make space for the other's self-affection before God.

Once again, we could easily conceive of a preferential relationship in which one partner or the other becomes overbearing so that the other's freedom to become a self in relation to God, the other's freedom to experience and pursue love of self, is compromised. And yet it is precisely this possibility that Kierkegaard's thought resists, since the legitimacy of self-love implies that an ethical intersubjectivity is one in which each party to the relationship provides the other with space and time and resources to become (and love) him or herself before God.

Kierkegaard's discussion in "Love Does Not Seek Its Own" also has implications for preferential relationships, which could be expressed as follows: Whether the neighbor is a friend, a spouse, or a stranger, love of neighbor requires that we distance ourselves from the other in the sense that we acknowledge the distinctiveness and autonomy of the other. Whether our neighbor is the spouse with whom we share a home and a bedroom (someone to whom we are bound by promises of fidelity, in whose presence we take comfort, and with whom we may be raising children), or is the stranger across the aisle of a train, the same attitude of love is required, according to which we recognize the other as a distinctive being created by God. This neighbor (the beloved!) has his or her distinctiveness in virtue of the gracious and creative ways of God, which is to say that I am to acknowledge and love him or her as *this* being rather than foisting upon the beloved my sense of who he or she is or ought to be (either through a domineering or small-minded spirit). Kierkegaard argues: "[W]hen it is a duty to love the people we see, *one must first and foremost give up all imaginary and exaggerated ideas about a dreamworld where the object of love should be sought and found—that is, one must become sober, gain actuality and truth* . . ."[130] To love the neighbor (the spouse), for Kierkegaard, is to love him or her in actuality, and to love him or her in the distinctiveness that God has given. Rather than requiring the beloved to conform to my vision, and rather than living in an imaginary world where the beloved becomes other than he or she is, neighbor-love requires that we love the beloved in the distinctiveness that he or she receives from God.

It is perhaps not difficult to imagine a marital relationship in which one partner or the other refuses to acknowledge or love the other in his or her distinctiveness; it is perhaps not difficult to image a marital relationship in which one partner or the other lives with only an imaginative vision of who the other might be. Kierkegaard's account of neighbor-love, and of God as the middle term, is such that these failures of intersubjectivity are acknowledged as such.

Finally, to love one's spouse or friend as neighbor requires that we presuppose love in the ground of the other, and that we love forth the love God has placed in the ground. As Kierkegaard has said, "A person can be tempted to be a builder, a teacher, a disciplinarian because this seems to be ruling over others; but to build up the way love does cannot tempt, because this means to be the one who serves, therefore, because it is willing to serve, only love has the desire to build up."[131] Love does not wish to tear down and make room for one's own, but wishes only to build up, which is to love forth the love that God has planted in the ground. To presuppose love in another is not only to acknowledge that the other owes her being to Love, but is to acknowledge that her substantive becoming owes to the mercy and love of God, and not to me. The other is not an object of my machinations but is his or her own person, according to the creative and loving purposes of God. Again, it is not difficult to conceive of a relationship in which one spouse takes the other as the object of his or her creative and constructive abilities (that are negligible), rather than assuming that God has given and will give everything for the other's upbuilding in love. The other's becoming owes nothing to me, and owes everything to God.

130. Ibid., 161.
131. Ibid., 217.

Neighbor-love (and love of friend or beloved as chastened and transformed by neighbor-love) is, in the first instance, a matter of self-control since our sinful nature, according to Kierkegaard, militates against the vision and form of life that is required by the love command. To love another, whether spouse or friend or stranger, is to exercise self-control by refusing to take on the posture of one who might control, or create, or possess, or circumscribe the other according to the logic of my own subjectivity or according to my own (transient) values. To love another (any other) is to understand that he or she belongs first to the God who is Love, that he or she is a distinctive being created in the image of God, that he or she must be construed as free to become a self (and to love self) in relation to God, and that his or her being is finally and decisively rooted in the Love of God. That this orientation of love must persist whether the object of love is friend, spouse, acquaintance, or stranger, does not mean that each of these relationships is reducible to the other.[132] It is to say, however, that each of these persons is the neighbor whom we are to love.

---

132. Ibid., 141.

4

Judge William

Human Becoming and Sexual Difference

> This is why I hate all that detestable rhetoric about the emancipation of women. God forbid that it may ever happen.
>
> —Judge William, *Either/Or*, Part II

As we work toward a Kierkegaardian theory and ethics of sexual difference, it has to be asked again whether Irigaray and Kierkegaard have anything to say to one another on the nature of sexual difference. The question becomes particularly pressing when we observe that Kierkegaard and his pseudonyms offer a traditional and patriarchal account of sexual difference, where woman is not a subject in her own right but is defined in terms of man—as his helper, opposite, or complement. Within the writings of Judge William, for example, woman is assimilated to the natural/finite/immediate while man is correlated with the spiritual/infinite/reflective. Indeed, while Judge William defends woman against an aesthetic framework that would reduce her to an object that serves the tastes and whims of man, his theory of sexual difference nevertheless elides woman as subject and defines her according to the identity and needs of man. The logic of Judge William's resistance to the "emancipation of woman," in particular, points to the patriarchal and dualist assumptions that underlie his essentialist theory of sexual difference.

In spite of his denial of woman's subjectivity, however, we will insist that Judge William's account of human becoming is, in important ways, consistent with Irigaray's theory of sexual difference. That is, his account of human being and becoming opens up toward the possibility of full subjectivity for both man and woman. Judge William's perspective on human becoming and sexual difference, we will observe, centres on the imaginative process by which a person receives himself (in his natural and social givennness) and re-imagines himself, taking responsibility for the self that he is and is becoming. In exploring this account of human being and becoming it will be important to demonstrate the extent to which the Judge's thought is also consistent with the mature thought of Kierkegaard as this comes to expression in Anti-Climacus' *The Sickness unto Death* and in Kierkegaard's own *Works of Love*. In exploring the writings of Judge William, then, we assume that his thought (with some important caveats noted along the way) is repeated and embraced in the later and mature thought of Kierkegaard. Thus, we are on the way to proffering an account or theory of the human and of sexual difference that can accurately be described as "Kierkegaardian."

The present chapter will unfold in four sections. In the first we describe Judge William's explicitly held theory of sexual difference, and demonstrate his elision of woman's subjectivity. In the second section we explore Judge William's account of self-choice and human becoming. In the third we consider the ways that Judge William's ethical and religious vision is subject to critique from the perspective of later pseudonymous and non-pseudonymous writings of Kierkegaard. In the fourth and final section we highlight an important and decisive continuity between Judge William and Kierkegaard himself. This is all with a view to the subsequent chapters, in which we will present a Kierkegaardian theory of sexual difference, in conversation with Irigaray.

Sexual Difference, according to Judge William

In describing Judge William's account of sexual difference, we take as a point of departure his comments surrounding women's emancipation. In his second letter to the Aesthete, Judge William asks: "Could there really be one woman simple and vain and pitiable enough to believe that within the definition of man she would become more perfect than man, not to

PART TWO—Kierkegaard and Love's Promise

perceive that her loss would be irreparable? No black-hearted seducer could think up a more dangerous theory for woman than this, for once he has deluded her into thinking this, she is completely in his power, abandoned to his conditions; she can be nothing for the man except a prey to his whims, whereas as woman she can be everything to him."[1] These words represent an interesting parallel to Irigaray's thought inasmuch as the Judge insists that woman must preserve a distinct identity and that she can only suffer loss if subsumed under the masculine. According to Judge William, woman's emancipation will result in a diminishment of both man and woman since each will end up less than they are.[2] With a forcefulness not uncharacteristic of Irigaray, Judge Williams insists that the difference between man and woman must be preserved if the human is to reach fulfillment. Furthermore, in another seeming parallel, the Judge will insist that there is a fundamental equality between man and woman: "My brief and simple opinion is that woman is certainly just as good as man—period. Any more discursive elaboration of the difference between the sexes or deliberation on which sex is superior is an idle intellectual occupation for loafers and bachelors."[3]

Nevertheless, Judge William's account of sexual difference is as far removed from Irigaray's thought as could be imagined—indeed, his account of the essential nature of man and woman closely mirrors that of Hegel (as described by Irigaray), and is thus susceptible to Irigaray's decisive critique. Judge William's account of woman and of man emphasizes complementarity between the sexes in such a way that woman is defined in terms of the needs of man (thus, according to the logic of the same). Here woman is, for example, a helpmeet to man; she is a complement who fills particular gaps in the masculine identity.[4] It is precisely in the context

1. Kierkegaard, *Either/Or*, Part II, 312.
2. Ibid. Explaining his vision of sexual difference and his resistance to emancipation, the judge refers to a "not unwitty jibe at the emancipation of women" that he had recently heard, according to which both man and woman are to be attired in the same clothing. There is an interesting parallel to the Judge's comments in an article written by Jean-Joseph Goux in which he discusses Irigaray's thought over against the projection of an androgynous future. See Goux, "Luce Irigaray Versus," 175–90.
3. Kierkegaard, *Stages*, 124. We recall Stone's argument, mentioned in chapter 1, that Irigaray's thought is open to an equality of man and woman, articulated in terms of their equal freedom to become.
4. Céline Léon quotes Leslie Howe in suggesting that woman is "first and foremost a 'helpmeet' to man's existence—she enhances his life in one way or another, but thus she is always seen as an instrument, an addendum, whether aesthetically, or as the occasion for an ethical decision on *his* part." See Léon, "(A) Woman's Place," 108.

of Judge William's resistance to the logic of emancipation that his definition of woman as complement to man becomes obvious, inasmuch as his primary concern is that woman's emancipation will leave man unable to fulfill his identity as man.[5] Thus, he suggests that woman is man's "deepest life" and "absolute refuge," and argues that "without [woman], [man] is an unstable spirit, an unhappy creature who cannot find rest, has no abode."[6]

We are not surprised, perhaps, when Judge William pulls out all of the rhetorical stops to defend his view of emancipation:

> Indeed, if the serpent could manage to delude her [about the need for emancipation], could tempt her with this seemingly delightful fruit, if this infection were to spread, if it pushed its way through even to her whom I love, my wife, my joy, my refuge, the root of my life, yes, then my courage would be crushed, then freedom's passion in my soul would be exhausted. Then I know very well what I would do—I would sit in the market place and weep, weep like that artist whose work had been destroyed and even he could not remember what it represented.[7]

As Céline Léon puts it, in stark terms: "What in effect annoys him is the thought that a woman could become deficient in qualities he holds to be supremely desirable in a subordinate: What of the poor man—think!—left to fend for himself. ... By being protected from men, she is in fact protected for him. Because a man's pleasure manifestly lies in receiving, hers, it is 'naturally' assumed, lies in the bestowing."[8] For Judge William, the abandonment of sexual difference, rooted as it is in the logic of symmetry and complementarity, implies loss for both man and woman; yet his preoccupation is with the loss that emancipation implies for his own sex.[9]

---

5. In response to Judge William, Amy Laura Hall points out: "In a world constructed to please men, women are rewarded to the extent that we make our lovers' interest and then our husbands' comfort the measure of our existence." See Hall, *Kierkegaard and Treachery*, 134.

6. Kierkegaard, *Either/Or*, Part II, 308; 311; 313.

7. Ibid., 311–12.

8. Léon, "(A) Woman's Place," 123.

9. Of course, Judge William also believes that emancipation will be bad for women. As Malantschuk argues, "Judge William's belief that the emancipation of women is a dangerous movement for woman is prompted by the consideration that if woman makes herself equal with man—for example, in the domain of the erotic—he will have no special obligation to her; she will be completely at his disposal, and, as the weaker one in the erotic and sexual sense, she will be the one who loses most." See Malantschuk, *Controversial Kierkegaard*, 43.

PART TWO—Kierkegaard and Love's Promise

In attending to words of Judge William already quoted it is possible to identify the specific qualities of woman that substantiate his claim that man is lost without her. According to the Judge, without woman "[man] is an unstable spirit, an unhappy creature who cannot find rest, has no abode."[10] What is expressed here *in nuce* is expressed fully elsewhere:

> On the whole, woman has a native talent, an original gift, an absolute virtuosity for explaining the finite. When man was created, he stood there as nature's lord and prince, nature's magnificence and splendour; all the riches of finitude awaited only his nod, but he did not comprehend what he should do with it all. He looked at it, but everything seemed to vanish under his intellectual gaze; it seemed to him that if he moved he would be past it all in one single step. Thus he stood, an imposing figure, lost in thought and yet comic, because one had to smile at this rich man who did not know how to use his riches, but also tragic, because he could not use them. Then woman was created. She was in no quandary, knew at once how one should take hold of the situation; without any fuss, without any preparation, she was ready to start at once.[11]

As Judge William goes on to say, this was the first solace that was given to man—that woman was able immediately and instinctively to understand nature (she had a native talent for explaining the finite) whereas he was immediately lost in reflection before the created world. "She is nature's mistress; her it understands, and she it; it is at her beck and call."[12]

Consistent with the logic of patriarchy, then, woman is assimilated to the natural and finite while man accedes to the spiritual and the infinite, a point that Judge William makes with dramatic clarity: "Woman explains the finite; man pursues the infinite. This is the way it must be, and everyone has his pain, for woman bears children in pain, but man conceives ideas in pain . . ."[13] Sylviane Agacinski summarizes this framework well, though in the context of a discussion of *Repetition*, and not of *Either/Or*: "To woman, the Jew, the animal, belong: sex, sensuality, enjoyment, children, number, life, immediacy, the finite temporal world. To man, the Christian, belong: virile castration, spirit, dialectical reduplication, the ideal, infinite sacrifice, suffering, solitude, eternity."[14] The threat of emancipation is that

---

10. Kierkegaard, *Either/Or*, Part II, 313.
11. Ibid., 310.
12. Ibid., 313.
13. Ibid., 311.
14. Agacinski, "An Aparté," 141. We find Judge William declaring, unwaveringly,

man will lose that which has bound him to, and explained for him, the natural—if emancipation comes to pass, the Judge fears, man's edification (his life of reflection and spirit) will become impossible.

That woman is assimilated to the natural and the finite is expressed also in the Judge's insistence that woman is able to explain time and does so by fulfilling her task in the domestic sphere: "Yes, my wise fellow, it is unbelievable what a natural virtuoso a woman is; she explains in the most entertaining and beautiful manner the question that has cost many a philosopher his reason: time. . . . She explains this question, as she explains so many others, in a manner that arouses the most profound amazement."[15] Woman's ability to explain time, for Judge William, is expressed in her ability to "make time go by." "My wise fellow, go to the ant and become wise; learn from a girl how to make time go by, for in that she is a natural virtuoso. She may not have the conception of rigorous and sustained work that a man has, but she is never idle, is always busy; time never drags for her. I am able to speak about this from experience."[16] Thus, woman's ability to explain the finite, the temporal, the natural, is bound up with her role as wife and mother—with her role in the domestic sphere.[17] At the same time, as the Judge stands back and observes his wife in action, he finds himself unable to fully understand or explain her immediate relation to time and the finite: "I come back to my wife—I never grow weary of watching her. What she does I cannot explain, but she does it all with a charm and graciousness, with an indescribable lightness, does it without preliminaries and ceremony, like a bird singing its aria. Indeed, I do believe that her occupation can best be compared to a bird's work, and yet her arts seem to me to be genuine magic. In this respect, she is my absolute refuge."[18]

Judge William's account of sexual difference, then, is one in which man has need of woman, and yet in which she never accedes to an existence that is valuable and substantial in its own right. "This association of woman's natural telos with 'the little matters' apparently correlates with the Judge's unconsciously comic picture of the creation of man as involving the bringing into existence of 'nature's lord and prince' who bungles

---

that woman "ought to remain in the pure and innocent peace of immediacy." See Kierkegaard, *Either/Or*, Part II, 207.

15. *Either/Or*, Part II, 308.

16. Ibid., 307.

17. In addition to her being essentially bound to the marital and domestic spheres, we could add, woman is characterized "by a need to fulfill herself, to become her true self, through devotedness." See Howe, "Kierkegaard and the Feminine," 221.

18. Kierkegaard, *Either/Or*, Part II, 308.

existence because 'he did not know what to do with it.' By contrast, the woman is 'essentially' exquisite, lovely and happy, because 'the finite can presumably make a person happy, the infinite per se never.'"[19] Thus, woman is relegated to the domestic and natural sphere, to matters that preclude reflective and spiritual existence—her primary task is simply to wed man to the natural, such that he not lose himself utterly in the abstract existence that is "naturally" his.[20]

Notwithstanding his reduction of woman to the natural/immediate/finite, we should not overlook the Judge's desire to instantiate a more ethical intersubjectivity between man and woman in marriage. Even though this is offered in an inconsistent way, and is undermined by his wider account of sexual difference, the Judge nevertheless points to a more healthy relationship between man and woman. To offer just one example, he insists that "honesty, frankness, openness, and understanding [are] the life principle in marriage."[21] The Judge makes this argument for openness and understanding between husband and wife in the context of an attack on what he refers to as the "secrecy system." In its most seductive form, the secrecy system insists that woman is weak, and that "she cannot bear troubles and cares—the frail and weak must be dealt with in love." That is, there are things that must not be shared with her—must be kept from her. In reply to this the Judge insists: "Falsehood! Falsehood! Woman is as strong as man, perhaps stronger. And do you really deal with her in love when you humiliate her in this way?"[22] He insists, then, on transparency in the relationship between husband and wife, and insists that woman is able to bear the difficulties of life as much as man is able to—in this there is a seeming affirmation of the equality and mutuality of husband and wife in marriage.

On the other hand, the Judge's demand for openness and understanding is offered within the framework of his theory of sexual difference.

---

19. Berry, "Judge William Judging," 38.

20. Judge William writes, to the aesthete: "Watch her when she bows her head toward earth, when her luxuriant braids almost touch the earth, and they look as they were the flower's tendrils by which she has grown fixed to the earth; does she not stand there a more imperfect creature than man, who gazes up toward heaven and only touches earth? And yet this hair is her beauty, yes, what is more, her strength, for it is with this that she captivates man and binds him to the earth." Kierkegaard, *Either/Or*, Part II, 313.

21. Kierkegaard, *Either/Or*, Part II, 116.

22. Ibid. In fact, the Judge suggests that the wife may be stronger than the man, for she was able to bear that which he could not.

Woman's very capacity to bear the difficulties and grief of life seems to lie in her immediate religious nature—in her non-reflective approach to faith and in her nature as self-giving. Thus, even as the Judge endeavours to articulate a more positive vision of an ethical intersubjectivity between man and woman, his vision is undermined by his account of sexual difference.

Choosing Yourself, Becoming a Self

Having provided a sketch of Judge William's theory of sexual difference, we turn to his account of human becoming in order to set the stage for a Kierkegaardian theory and ethics of sexual difference. In view of Judge William's vision of sexual difference, it is perhaps surprising to suggest that his writings might yield an account of the human that correlates with the thought of Irigaray. Yet this is the argument we will make.

The letters of Judge William in *Either/Or*, Part II are written to an unnamed young man implicated in an aesthetic form of life, and are offered as an appeal that he move beyond the aesthetic into the ethical. The Judge's first letter argues that the aesthetic dimension of love (the erotic, or that which is embodied in the "first love") can be preserved within marriage and, furthermore, that it is only within the ethical sphere that the aesthetic reaches fulfillment and comes into its own.[23] The Judge's second letter, on the other hand, paints a picture of an ethical self—of a person who reaches the full stature of human selfhood and who achieves what may genuinely be described as "personality." While the first letter of the Judge is not unimportant for the Judge's theory of human being and coming, we focus on the second letter.

In his second letter to the Aesthete, Judge William suggests that the limitations of the aesthetic form of life can only be overcome by way of an absolute choice (*the* Either/Or). The Aesthete, according to the Judge, is a non-entity, a mysterious and insubstantial person, precisely in virtue of his refusal to choose, his refusal to embrace the Either/Or: "Life is a masquerade, you explain, and for you this is inexhaustible material for amusement, and as yet no one has succeeded in knowing you, for every disclosure is always a deception. . . . Your occupation consists in preserving your hiding place, and you are successful, for your mask is the most enigmatical of all. . . . You yourself are a non-entity, an enigmatical figure on whose brow stands Either/Or."[24] That the Aesthete is a non-entity, and

---

23. See Walsh's discussion of the first letter in *Living Poetically*, 99–125.
24. Kierkegaard, *Either/Or*, Part II, 159.

that Either/Or stands on the Aesthete's brow means, for the Judge, that the Aesthete is incapable of choice—the Aesthete is incapable of committing himself to relationships, to a vocation, or to the social structures that give meaning and substance to the human person. A key question this raises is why the Aesthete refuses to choose—the simple answer being that choice implies constraints on his freedom to actualize the multiple possibilities inherent within him and set before him.[25] To choose one course of action as opposed to another, one vocation as opposed to another, one woman as opposed to another, is to foreclose possibilities that entice the Aesthete or are available to him.

Beyond this desire to preserve his "freedom," however, there is the Aesthete's profound doubt that a meaningful and stable existence can be achieved by way of particular decisions or commitments. As Ronald Hall puts it, the aesthete "knows how dangerous the historical actuality is; he seems to know just how deep the anxiety of worldly existence invariably is, just how much worldly existence is always threatened with loss, pain, suffering, just how vulnerable, how dangerous, actually existing as a concrete individual in the world before others is . . ."[26] Whatever one chooses, the end result will be the same. Or, "you're damned if you do and damned if you don't." Thus, the Aesthete simply refuses to choose, refuses to decisively embrace any particular vocation or relationship. As the Judge puts it: "You continually hover above yourself, but the higher atmosphere, the more refined sublimate, into which you are vaporized, is the nothing of despair, and you see down below you a multiplicity of subjects, insights, studies, and observations that nevertheless have no reality for you but which you very whimsically utilize and combine to decorate as tastefully as you can the sumptuous intellectual palace in which you occasionally reside . . ."[27] Thus, the Aesthete dissolves into a multiplicity not unlike the demoniac of the Gospels—the Aesthete loses personality in the shifting sands of mood and desire and in perpetual reflection (sustained by profound intellectual gifts).[28]

25. As Anthony Rudd rightly points out, "The aesthete cannot wholly avoid occupying social roles, but he will refuse to admit that they do anything to define him as a person." See his *Kierkegaard and the Limits*, 73.

26. Hall, *The Human Embrace*, 43.

27. Kierkegaard, *Either/Or*, Part I, 198.

28. Judge William asks the Aesthete: "Or can you think of anything more appalling than having it all end with the disintegration of your essence into a multiplicity, so that you actually become several, just as that unhappy demoniac became a legion, and thus you would have lost what is the most inward and holy in a human being, the binding power of personality." Ibid., 160.

Judge William

In response to the Aesthete, then, Judge William argues: "The choice itself is crucial for the content of personality: through the choice the personality submerges itself into that which is chosen, and when it does not choose, it withers away in atrophy[;] . . . you cannot keep yourself continually on the spear tip of the moment of choice."[29] Here the Judge suggests that the Aesthete has cut himself off from the possibility of personality since it is only in taking the plunge of choice that the self gains its substance. Of course, the Judge's notion of the Either/Or is complex and multi-faceted; yet it will be helpful to highlight those aspects of choice most pertinent to his broader theory of human being and becoming (and thus most pertinent to the constructive project we undertake, here).

In the first place Judge William argues that the Either/Or is a matter of choosing despair, by which he means to say that the Either/Or requires acknowledgment of the fragility and instability that characterize life in the world.[30] According to the Judge, to choose despair is not simply to despair over something specific in the world (i.e., over some aspect of the multiplicity outside oneself), nor is it to be confused with doubt, since doubt is an expression only of thought and not of the total personality.[31] Peter Mehl writes: "But to 'despair completely,' to see that life in the finite empirical world is despair and to choose this, is to see that any and all possible finite empirical realities can never provide the grounding for myself, the absolute point of departure, the firm foundation for praxis, that I seek. If I am to choose absolutely, I cannot choose the relative. What is left for me? Myself as spirit, as self-transcendence."[32] The Judge himself argues: "When a person has truly chosen despair, he has truly chosen what despair chooses: himself in his eternal validity. The personality is first set at ease in despair, not by way of necessity, for I never despair necessarily, but in freedom, and only therein is the absolute attained . . ."[33] In freedom I acknowledge that my merely finite existence can never be the source of a meaningful and

---

29. Ibid., 163. For the Judge's sketch of the Aesthete's process of perpetual deliberation, see *Either/Or*, Part II, 195–202.

30. This is not to say that the Aesthete is not already in despair, from the Judge's perspective. As Walsh suggests: "The romantic-aesthetic life-view—or, more accurately, what resembles a life-view—is one of despair in that its egoistic, hedonistic philosophy of enjoyment does not penetrate beyond the immediate level of personality to an awareness of any higher form of existence." See Walsh, *Living Poetically*, 114.

31. For the Judge's comparison of doubt and despair, see Kierkegaard, *Either/Or*, Part II, 211–13.

32. Mehl, *Thinking through Kierkegaard*, 22.

33. Kierkegaard, *Either/Or*, Part II, 213.

PART TWO—Kierkegaard and Love's Promise

stable life or self, and in freedom I acknowledge and choose that which in some profound sense transcends the temporal—I choose myself in my eternal validity.[34] As I choose despair, and as I choose myself in my eternal validity, I become a self—or, I am in a process of becoming that defines the self. As Rudd points out, this ethical framework implies that "the self is not a—Cartesian or other—substance that is simply given; it is something that must be achieved."[35] This self is achieved, from the perspective of Judge William, precisely when one despairs over the temporal and chooses oneself as that which decisively transcends the finite.

Judge William cautions, however, that in choosing oneself in one's eternal validity, one must not lose oneself in the "despair of infinitude" (to use the language of Anti-Climacus from *The Sickness unto Death*). He describes a possible scenario of self-choice:

> When the individual has grasped himself in his eternal validity, this overwhelms him in his fullness. Temporality vanishes for him. At the first moment, this fills him with an indescribable bliss and gives him an absolute security. If he now begins to stare at it one-sidedly, the temporal asserts its claims. These are rejected. What temporality is able to give, the more or less that appears here, is so very insignificant to him compared with what he possesses eternally. Everything comes to a standstill for him; he has, so to speak, arrived in eternity ahead of time. He sinks into contemplation, stares fixedly at himself, but this staring cannot fill up time. Then it appears to him that time, temporality is his ruination; he demands a perfect form of existence, and here in turn there appears a weariness, an apathy, that resembles the lethargy that accompanies enjoyment. This apathy can so engulf a person that suicide seems the only escape for him.[36]

In the moment of self-choice there is a risk that the self will lose itself in infinitude, which is a sign that the person has not chosen in the right way,

---

34. The Judge writes: "The person who lives ethically always has a way out when everything goes against him; when the darkness of the storm clouds so envelops him that his neighbor cannot see him, he still has not perished, there is always a point to which he holds fast, and that point is—himself." See Kierkegaard, *Either/Or*, Part II, 253.

35. Rudd, *Kierkegaard and the Limits*, 75. As David Gouwens expresses it: "To be a self is to be engaged in a dynamic process, one involving a journey or progress of self-purification of one's moods and emotions on the way to self-clarification, what Kierkegaard calls 'becoming a self before God.'" See his *Kierkegaard as Religious Thinker*, 91–92.

36. Kierkegaard, *Either/Or*, Part II, 231.

since to choose oneself is to choose oneself precisely as a particular, finite, and temporal being. There is a clear parallel, here, between the Judge's account of the "flight into infinitude," and Anti-Climacus's account of the "despair of infinitude" as described in *The Sickness unto Death*.[37] Anti-Climacus argues that the self's becoming is "an infinite moving away from itself in the infinitizing of self, and an infinite coming back to itself in the finitizing process . . ."[38] According to this account of the self, despair can be either the despair of infinitude (which lacks finitude) or the despair of finitude (which lacks infinitude). It is the despair of infinitude that Judge William perceives in the person who loses himself in the eternal, a despair in which a person is led fantastically "out into the infinite in such a way that it only leads him away from himself and thereby prevents him from coming back to himself."[39] The Judge's point, then, is that the finite is an essential aspect of the person.

The self that a person chooses, then, is the finite self, since "to choose only the abstract infinite self is to lose myself as a whole human being . . ."[40] The self that one chooses is the concrete self that in a fundamental sense precedes the choice of self: "He chooses himself—not in the finite sense, for then this 'self' would indeed be something finite that would fall among all the other finite things—but in the absolute sense, and yet he does choose himself and not someone else. This self that he chooses in this way is infinitely concrete, for it is he himself . . ."[41] In choosing himself a person is no longer himself in finite immediacy but becomes a reflective and transcendent self who takes responsibility for his own life.

> The choice here makes two dialectical movements simultaneously—that which is chosen does not exist and comes into existence through the choice—and that which is chosen exists; otherwise it is not a choice. In other words, if what I chose did not exist but came into existence absolutely through the choice, then I did not choose—then I created. But I do not create myself, I choose myself. Therefore, whereas nature is created from nothing, whereas I myself as immediate personality am created from nothing, I as free spirit am born out of the principle of contradiction or am born through my choosing myself.[42]

37. Mehl, *Thinking through Kierkegaard*, 87.
38. Kierkegaard, *Sickness unto Death*, 30.
39. Ibid., 31.
40. Mehl, *Thinking through Kierkegaard*, 24.
41. Kierkegaard, *Either/Or*, Part II, 215.
42. Ibid., 215–16.

From this dense passage, we take away Judge William's conviction that the self chosen is the concrete and finite self that is prior to the moment of choice.[43] "The person who has ethically chosen and found himself possesses himself defined in his entire concretion. He then possesses himself as an individual who has these capacities, these passions, these inclinations, these habits, who is subject to these external influences, who is influenced in one direction thus and in another thus . . ."[44] In the moment of self-choice it is precisely this finite self that I choose absolutely—it is this self (also the choosing self) that is endowed with freedom and autonomy in the choosing. To deny the particularities (whether physical or social) that define me as a person is to become implicated in the despair of infinitude, which is a forgetfulness or denial of the finite. The aesthetic, then—that which I am in my immediacy, prior to any reflection—is acknowledged and embraced in the ethical sphere since it is precisely myself in my immediate being that I choose.[45] Yet at the moment when the self chooses itself, the aesthetic is relativized and, in language that brings to mind Kierkegaard's *Works of Love*, the aesthetic is cast down from the throne.[46]

It is important to note that, in this framework, self-choice is more than a backward looking moment in which a person chooses or receives the self: in fact, this rearward orientation is only one aspect of the dialectical process of becoming. This is apparent when we consider the Judge's idea that a person is *responsible* for himself.[47] As already observed, Judge

---

43. Judge William employs both the language of self-choice and the language of self-reception—the latter emphasizing that the self finds its source outside of itself. For a helpful discussion see Mooney, "Kierkegaard on Self-Choice," 5–32.

44. Kierkegaard, *Either/Or*, Part II, 262.

45. As the Judge says, "In the ethical, the personality is brought into a focus in itself; consequently, the aesthetic is absolutely excluded or is excluded as the absolute, but relatively it is continually present. In choosing itself, the personality chooses itself ethically and absolutely excludes the aesthetic; but since he nevertheless chooses himself and does not become another being by choosing himself, all the aesthetic returns in its validity." See Kierkegaard, *Either/Or*, Part II, 178.

46. The logic of self-choice shapes Judge William's theological convictions, also, since he reinterprets classical doctrines through this lens. Repentance, for example, is simply another way of describing the intentional act of self-choice. It is not a matter of seeking God's forgiveness, or of confessing wrongdoing before a gracious God, but is the autonomous act of a person by which he or she is launched into genuine selfhood. As Hall reminds us, the Judge concomitantly believes that "Sin may at times be limiting, but it is also limited; and one should not become overly concerned with transgression." See Hall, *Treachery of Love*, 124.

47. We have tended to employ masculine pronouns throughout this section of the chapter for the simple reason that Judge William speaks of human becoming largely

William argues that to choose oneself is to accept responsibility for what one is or has been.[48] It is to acknowledge: "*This* is who I am." The logic of "responsibility," however, includes an orientation also toward what one might become. That the self gives birth to the self in self-choice implies not only that the self receives and acknowledges what has existed prior to the choice, but also that the self accepts responsibility for what the self is to become. It is here that the self becomes a task—or, it is here that becoming a self becomes the task of the self. As Rudd puts it, "Each individual human being has a potentiality for selfhood, but to realize this potential, to become a self, is, Kierkegaard argues, a strenuous task."[49] To a consideration of this task we now turn.

In exploring the continuity between the self that is chosen and the self that is constituted in self-choice, Judge William writes:

> An individual thus chooses himself as a complex specific concretion and therefore he chooses himself in continuity. This concretion is the individual's actuality, but since he chooses it according to his freedom, it may also be said that it is his possibility or, in order not to use such an aesthetic expression it is his task. In other words, the person who lives aesthetically sees only possibilities everywhere; for him these make up the content of future time, whereas the person who lives ethically sees tasks everywhere. Then the individual sees this, his actual concretion as his task, as goal, as objective. But in seeing his possibility as his task, the individual expresses precisely his sovereignty over himself, something he never surrenders, even though on the other hand he does not relish the very unconstrained sovereignty that a king without a country always has.[50]

To choose oneself in continuity with oneself is to see one's natural and social givenness not merely as facts to be acknowledged but as "material" to be developed. The Judge, in fact, will speak of the self who chooses himself

---

in terms of the masculine. This is, in part, because his letters are addressed to the Aesthete, but is also because, more significantly, the fullness of human selfhood, for the Judge, is reserved for man.

48. As Mooney says, "Finally, the outcome of self-choice for the Judge is the achievement of full and *self-responsible* personhood." See his *Selves*, 17. Quoted in Mehl, *Thinking through Kierkegaard*, 18

49. Rudd, *Kierkegaard and the Limits*, 75.

50. Kierkegaard, *Either/Or*, Part II, 251.

PART TWO—Kierkegaard and Love's Promise

as an editor who works with the raw material of his given being—who takes on the development of this material as his primary task.[51]

> The person who has ethically chosen and found himself possesses himself defined in his entire concretion. He then possesses himself as an individual who has these capacities, these passions, these inclinations, these habits, who is subject to these external influences, who is influenced in one direction thus and in another thus. Here he then possesses himself as a task in such a way that it is chiefly to order, shape, temper, inflame, control—in short, to produce an evenness in the soul, a harmony, which is the fruit of the personal virtues. Here the objective for his activity is himself, but nevertheless not arbitrarily determined, for he possesses himself as a task that has been assigned him, even though it became his by his own choosing.[52]

To choose oneself is to accept one's given self as essential to who one is, yet it is also to acknowledge that this given self is not the end of the story, for the immediate must be taken up in an intentional way. I must make decisions about which skills should be developed and which left to languish, which desires should be acted upon and which left unattended, and which aspects of my personal history cultivated and which left fallow. "[T]he ethical task is to integrate the various aspects of human existence into a stable and coherent personality. This is what the aesthete lacks; his life falls apart into a series of disconnected moments. . . . The ethicist, on the contrary, chooses to . . . integrate his various capacities, to acquire a stability and constancy of disposition."[53]

In her discussion of the transition from the aesthetic to the ethical, and in her consideration of the moment of self-choice in *Either/Or*, Part II, Ferreira cautions against seeing the backward and forward-looking moments of self-choice in terms of too strong a contrast. She observes that Judge William speaks of the transition from the aesthetic to the ethical in terms of a person becoming "transparent to himself." Thus Ferreira argues: "The decisive transition which constitutes becoming oneself, repenting oneself, choosing oneself absolutely is *the penetration of one's concreteness with consciousness*, i.e., seeing oneself truly."[54] Here, Ferreira acknowledges, "choosing oneself" actually is a matter of "knowing oneself," yet she

---

51. Ibid., 260.
52. Ibid., 262.
53. Rudd, *Kierkegaard and the Limits*, 75.
54. Ferreira, *Transforming Vision*, 65. Italics added.

argues that this is not merely an objective and uninterested knowing but a knowing that is "self-involving and efficacious."⁵⁵ That is, "the demand for transparency is not . . . a demand for the static revelation of what is already there so much as it is a demand for transforming what is there."⁵⁶ To know oneself in the sense that Ferreira is speaking of it is both to perceive what one has been immediately and to be open to what one might become—thus, the transition from the aesthetic to the ethical is precisely in imaginative self-reflection.⁵⁷ She summarizes: "The transitional choice [of oneself] is effectively an imaginative penetration or imaginative gathering together, the achievement of a clear vision which *itself transforms*. The activity of penetrating one's concreteness with consciousness just is the activity of choosing self, transforming self—it constitutes the transition."⁵⁸

In terms of the process of becoming a self, then, the rearward-looking aspect of self-choice (receiving what has been) and the forward-looking aspect of self-choice (imaginatively anticipating what one might become) are not distinct "moments" in the process of human becoming. Rather, precisely in receiving myself as this particular being, and in penetrating my concreteness with consciousness, I know myself as the person I have been and imaginatively reconsider who I might become. In seeing myself truly, I see both what I have been and what I might become. Of course, this raises the complex question of the place of the will in the moment of choice, since according to this interpretation, choice cannot be a matter of standing before two equivalent options and then, by force of will, pursuing one as opposed to the other.⁵⁹ Choice, rather, is a matter of an *active seeing*.⁶⁰ As a self who transcends the finite and immediate, I perceive myself in my finitude and precisely in this perception become aware

---

55. Ibid., 66.

56. Ibid., 65.

57. Judge William writes: "The ethical individual knows himself, but this knowing is not simply contemplation, for then the individual comes to be defined according to his necessity. It is a collecting of oneself, which itself is an action, and this is why I have with aforethought used the expression 'to choose oneself' instead of 'to know oneself.' When the individual knows himself, he is not finished; but this knowing is very productive, and from this knowing emerges the authentic individual." See Kierkegaard, *Either/Or*, Part II, 258.

58. Ferreira, *Transforming Vision*, 66. Italics added.

59. The question of how the will functions in the moment of choice is an important one. Ferreira offers an answer that goes firmly against that of MacIntyre. For a full discussion of this question see Ferreira's *Transforming Vision*. See, also, Rudd, "Reason in Ethics," 131–50, and Davenport, "Meaning," 75–112.

60. Ferreira, *Transforming Vision*, 67.

PART TWO—Kierkegaard and Love's Promise

of (and imaginatively explore) what it means that the finite and immediate do not have the last word or who I am as a self. The will is involved, here, not in a "bare choice" of myself but in desire—the self is attracted to, and interested in, what it is and what it might become.[61]

According to Ferreira, then, the transition from the aesthetic to the ethical is in large measure a question of seeing oneself in a new and different way—a seeing that is oriented toward possibilities that could not be seen or embraced within the merely aesthetic framework. As we continue to explore the Judge's account of human becoming, we briefly extend our consideration of imagination before turning finally to consider the relation between the human self and duty. In the context of his discussion of self-choice as a kind of self-knowledge, Judge William writes: "Through the individuals' intercourse with himself the individual is made pregnant by himself and gives birth to himself. The self the individual knows is simultaneously the actual self and the ideal self, which the individual has outside himself as the image in whose likeness he is to form himself, and which on the other hand he has within himself, since it is he himself."[62] (See Figure 2)

---

61. The question of how one might arrive at this point of imaginative transformation is, obviously, not an uncomplicated one. Along with Rudd, however, we notice that the Judge's writings are not merely abstract philosophical essays but personal letters from the Judge to a friend. The Judge seeks to engage with his friend in such a way that the Aesthete might see his own life-view as despair and might become interested in his self in a way that opens up toward new possibilities of selfhood. See Rudd, "Reason in Ethics," 137–38.

62. Kierkegaard, *Either/Or*, Part II, 259.

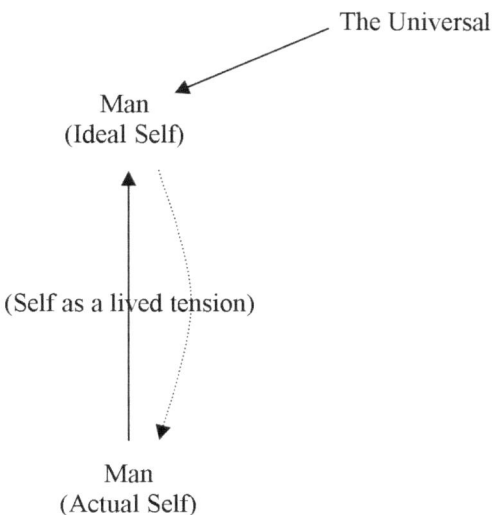

Figure 2. Judge William on human becoming

Being and becoming a self, here, is a dialectical process by which one lives as an actual self and moves outward toward a "projected" ideal self, an ideal self that owes its content to the actual self.

But the ideal self is not the actual self, and the imagination comes into its own in Judge William's thought precisely as the self "prophetically envisions" an ideal self that a person is to become in continuity with the actual self. The Judge writes: "Meanwhile the exemplary self is an imperfect self, for it is only a prophecy and thus is not the actual self. But it escorts him at all times; yet the more he actualizes it, the more it vanishes within him, until at last, instead of appearing before him, it is behind him as a faded possibility."[63] As Gouwens puts it then, "the ideal self of possibility is engendered by imaginative reflection on the actual self and so gives an 'inward infinity' ... [and] the actual self conditions the ideal self and opens up possibilities."[64] Thus, the imagination is in some sense restricted by the limit that the actual self represents for a person, and the person who relates to the synthesis that he is must walk a fine line between the Scylla of infinitude's despair (allowing one's imagination to disconnect from actual-

63. Ibid.
64. Gouwens, "Kierkegaard on the Imagination," 204–20.

PART TWO—Kierkegaard and Love's Promise

ity) and the Charybdis of finitude's despair (failing to exercise imagination in becoming oneself—becoming instead, just another number 1+1+1+1, just another human being).

In her account of the self's imaginative becoming, Ferreira argues that the ideal self toward which a person orients him or herself in the process of becoming should "not be thought of as a static presentation or 'image.'"[65] This is in part because the activity of the self in becoming a self is "an active picturing of the actual and ideal self together, at the same time, in tension. The 'picture' to which [a person] refers is not a passively viewed separate possibility, but a maintained tension . . ."[66] There is a constant dialectical movement, and tension, between the actual self and the ideal self, and imagination is the holding together of these two poles in their tension. Less paradoxically, of course, the imagination should be seen as the process by which the self reflects on the possibilities inherent in the actual self and by which it envisages the self (the ideal self) that might come to fruition through the actualization of various possibilities. However, this does not diminish the fact that imagination is the skilful (although imagination is a "skill" possessed by all) holding together of the actual and ideal self in paradox and tension. The ideal self, then, is not a fixed goal but is an always tentative possibility toward which one moves, all the while keeping one's dialectical eye on the actual self and the possibilities inherent therein.

Interpreting Judge William's description of self-choice in terms of an imaginative holding together of the actual and ideal in paradox and tension does not imply that very concrete decisions and actions are excluded from consideration. Indeed, the Judge's account of self-choice, and his whole ethical vision, is tightly bound up with a commitment to a traditional view of the self in relation to family, religion, and society. It is in view of this, we should say, that Ferreira's account of self-choice as imaginative and interested self-knowledge requires qualification. This becomes evident when we attend to the Judge's insistence that every man has an obligation to marry—or, as Hall puts it, "that no man is free not to marry."[67] Marriage is, for the Judge, the paradigmatic institution of the ethical life, and the self's imaginative capacities are in some sense restricted by (or

65. Ferreira, *Transforming Vision*, 62.
66. Ibid.
67. Hall, *Human Embrace*, 73. We are reminded, however, that the Judge does not think it sinful for a person not to marry, "except insofar as he himself is responsible for it, because then he trespasses against the universally human." See Kierkegaard, *Either/Or*, Part II, 302.

function within) the social structures within which a person is, and must be, situated. That is, self-choice is bound up with the choice for marriage. As we turn to consider briefly the Judge's requirement of marriage, we explore also the relationship between particular and universal, as well as the notion of duty.

Running parallel to Judge William's dialectical account of the actual and the ideal self is his account of the relationship between particular and universal. From the Judge's point of view, the goal of ethical existence is to embrace and transform the particular and aesthetic (drives, inclinations, affections, skills) within the universal. Thus, the Judge insists that "the universal can very well continue in and with the specific without consuming it; it is like that fire that burned without consuming the bush."[68] Just as the ethical preserves the aesthetic, so does the universal preserve the particular—in fact, these are simply two sides of the same coin, since the aesthetic is the particular and the ethical is the universal. According to the Judge, however, the universal is not outside of the self—if it were outside the self, there could be "only one possible method, and that is to take off my entire concretion."[69] The universal is the essential nature of the self—the universal is the structure of the self that is common to human persons, and is the process of becoming that is followed by every human person. This is not to deny the importance of the particular, but is to say that to live in the immediate/particular is to be less than a self, less than a human person. To say more about the relation between the particular and the universal, it is helpful to explore the notion of duty. After all, "Duty is the universal . . ."[70]

Concerning duty Judge William argues: "[D]uty is not something laid upon [*Paalæg*] but something that lies upon [*paaligge*]. When duty is regarded in this way, it is a sign that the individual is oriented within himself."[71] With these words the Judge rejects duty as a multiplicity of particular rules brought to bear, heteronomously, on the life and being of a particular person (duty as laid upon). The mistake in this supposedly ethical life-view, according to Judge William, is that "the individual and duty stand outside each other."[72] Judge William writes: "Of course, a life of duty such as that is very unlovely and boring, and if the ethical did not

---

68. Kierkegaard, *Either/Or*, Part II, 261.
69. Ibid., 263.
70. Ibid.
71. Ibid., 254.
72. Ibid.

have a much deeper connection with the personality it would always be very difficult to champion it against the aesthetic."[73]

The Judge insists that duty is intimately related to the self that I am, both in terms of the *universal* requirement of self choice (everyone has a duty to choose himself) and in terms of *particular* choices a person makes (I have a duty to actualize possibilities inherent in *my* actual self). If I feel myself compelled to actualize a particular aspect of my being—compelled to cultivate a particular skill and to exercise it over the long-term—this is only because the very nature of the self compels this cultivation and this commitment for the long term. As Peter Mehl puts it: "One's duty as the Judge refers to it, appears not simply as the requirements of practical reason or as something required that is ultimately alien to us as human beings. Rather our duty is the fulfillment of our being as creatures who have an interest in how our lives are going and who can critically evaluate and shape our lives, who are predisposed toward the freedom of personhood."[74] A failure to evaluate and actualize particular possibilities inherent in my actual being, and to discipline myself in the actualization of these possibilities—which is a failure to do my duty—is despair, is precisely not to be a self. The answer to the Aesthete's despair, then, is the dialectical and imaginative process of self choice, and a concomitant embrace of duty as the need to become myself (as universal and particular). The Judge concludes: "Therefore, the truly ethical person has an inner serenity and sense of security, for he does not have duty outside himself but within himself. The more deeply a man has structured his life ethically, the less he will feel compelled to talk about duty every moment, to worry every moment whether he is performing it, every moment to seek the advice of others about what his duty is."[75] As Louise Mackey puts it: "The principle of duty can be stated in a form applicable to every man without exception: Thou shalt become thyself."[76]

In order to pull together some of the various threads of Judge William's ethical thought, we do well to consider what is the paradigmatic form of the ethical life for him, namely, marriage. Marriage, for the Judge, is a universal social institution and is, therefore, a duty for every person—thus, the particularity of the person, or his uniqueness in becoming, does

---

73. Ibid.
74. Mehl, *Thinking through Kierkegaard*, 24.
75. Kierkegaard, *Either/Or*, Part II, 254–55.
76. Mackey, *Kierkegaard*, 55.

Judge William

not imply freedom not to marry.[77] While the Judge will insist that as a particular person I will be drawn toward some persons and not toward others, this insistence on particularity does not translate into a choice as to whether or not I will marry.[78] There is a tension here, however, since it could legitimately be asked whether every person will be able find someone (or, the right person) to marry—yet the Judge assumes that, in general, each man will be able to find a woman, in love.[79] If circumstances, however, do not unfold in such a way that a person is able to realize the universal (that is, he is unable to marry) then this individual is able to express the importance and primacy of the universal by mourning over its non-accomplishment. Such a person "will rejoice over the others to whom it is granted to consummate it; Perhaps he will perceive even better than they how beautiful it is, but he himself will grieve, not cravenly and dejectedly, but deeply and openly. . . . And this grief is beautiful, is itself an expression of the universally human, an emotion of its heart within him, and will reconcile him with it."[80] In the case of marriage, then, we cannot speak only of *my* duty—we must also speak of a *universal* duty to marry. Nevertheless, Judge William might suggest that one can still speak of *my* duty to marry inasmuch as I am responsible to seek out, or discover, the particular circumstances of my own marriage.

But again, this duty to marry is not merely something "laid upon" every human person—it is a duty that "lies upon" every person, which is to say marriage is a necessary expression of the human. There is, we might say, a *need* in every human person to marry, inasmuch as the fulfillment of the human, and of each human person, is bound up with marriage—those who fail to marry fail also to fulfill the human and the universal. The important question, of course, is *why* it is necessary for every person to marry, and the Judge offers a number of possible answers to this question. A first reason is that marriage alone leads to the fulfillment of the aesthetic, to the fulfillment of romantic and erotic love—which is to say that if a person wants to retain the aesthetic nature of love, marriage becomes a requirement. But of course, this logic does not support a universal demand for

---

77. As the Judge puts it: "Ethics tells [a man] that he should marry, it does not say whom." *Either/Or*, Part II, 305.

78. Thus the Judge suggests that his aesthetic friend will require another friend, of equal aesthetic skill, to help him decide who he might marry. *Either/Or*, Part II, 302.

79. We are reminded of the Judge's insistence that there is, really, only one reason to marry—and that is because one is in love with a particular woman. *Either/Or*, Part II, 63; 72.

80. Kierkegaard, *Either/Or*, Part II, 330.

PART TWO—Kierkegaard and Love's Promise

marriage, since it only applies to those who have experienced "first love" and who would, therefore, seek its historical fulfillment in marriage.

It is precisely on the question of "why marriage," however, that our whole discussion of Judge William's thought comes full circle, since it is in response to the question of the universality and necessity of marriage that we find the Judge advising the Aesthete:

> One may be ever so intelligent, ever so industrious, ever so enthusiastic for an idea, but there nevertheless come moments when time drags. You often flout the opposite sex, and I have warned you often enough to desist. Look upon a young girl as an imperfect creature as much as you wish, but I would like to say to you: My wise fellow, go to the ant and become wise; learn from a girl how to make time go by, for in that she is a natural virtuoso. She may not have the conception of rigorous and sustained work that a man has, but she is never idle, is always busy; time never drags for her. I am able to speak about this from experience.[81]

We come full circle, here, because it is precisely in his defence of marriage as a universal institution (as a duty of every man) that the Judge points to woman's virtuosity in explaining the natural and the finite. Whatever the strengths of a particular man (however industrious or strong or intelligent he is), there will always be something fundamental lacking in him if he does not become implicated in marriage since it is only through a resolute commitment to marriage (and to a particular woman) that he is brought into a necessary relationship with the temporal and natural. Thus, Judge William's account of the need to imaginatively choose oneself, and of the need of each man to fulfill the universal (to do his duty), culminates in a defence of marriage as that institution alone in which man might become himself—uniting temporal and eternal. Without woman his becoming will be stunted since he will lack the necessary connection to temporality and nature that woman provides. In this, we remember, the Judge proposes that woman is not to be conceived as the weaker party—rather, her strength is in her difference, and the fulfillment of the human requires that she inhabit her difference unreflectively (how else could she do it?).

But there is something of a tension at play in Judge William's thought, here, for as much as he insists that man can only be appropriately related to the finite and natural through *his relation to woman* in marriage, he will also argue that a man can be related to the temporal through *the*

81. Ibid., 305–6.

commitments and promise that constitute marriage. This suggests the possibility that man's access to temporality and the finite can be conceived, in the Judge's thought, without reference to the Judge's essentialist and complementarian account of sexual difference.

Judge William, it should be noted, argues that first love, even in its merely immediate form, unites the temporal and eternal. "First love" is temporal inasmuch as it is the "first" experience of love, and it is eternal inasmuch as those who experience it have a profound sense of its atemporality. Regarding the eternal nature of aesthetic, first love, the Judge writes: "Like everything eternal, [first love] has implicit the duplexity of positing itself backward into all eternity and forward into all eternity. This is the truth in what poets so frequently have celebrated—that to lovers, even the very first moment they see each other, it seems as if they have already loved each other for a long time."[82] Yet the Judge will also argue that without a resolute decision in and for marriage, the unity of the temporal and the eternal in first love will collapse, since without such a decision first love necessarily becomes nothing more than "a perishing instant that ever disintegrates into a specious present and an equally specious 'forever.'"[83] It is precisely marriage, then, that takes "first love" up into a higher concentricity so that its temporal and eternal aspects are not only preserved but actually come into their own. More specifically, it is the *commitment* of each spouse to the other, before the eternal (God), that secures the eternal aspect of "first love;" and it is the resolute *promise* of each to the other that secures the historical aspect of "first love."

In affirming the temporal dimension of marital love, the Judge points out that the adjectives used to describe love require us to conceive of a historical and temporal unfolding of love. He reminds his reader that love is described as faithful, constant, humble, patient, long-suffering, tolerant, honest, content with little, alert, persevering, willing, and happy. He adds: "All these virtues have the characteristic that they are qualifications within the individual. The individual is not fighting against external enemies but is struggling with himself, struggling to bring his love out of himself. And these virtues *have the qualification of time*, for their veracity consists not in this, that they are once for all, but that *they are continually.*"[84] Although

---

82. Ibid., 43. As Mackey reminds us, first love is also eternal since within itself the whole of love (past, present, and future) is contained. "This accounts, to the Judge's satisfaction, for the all-engrossing power of romantic love which makes the lovers oblivious to the world around them." See Mackey, *Kierkegaard*, 72.

83. Ibid., 75–76.

84. Kierkegaard, *Either/Or*, Part II, 139. Italics added.

the essential struggle of marriage is an inner struggle (a struggle with or against the self in its lethargy and/or weakness), it is a struggle that takes place in the course of time—thus, the virtues that correspond to marriage are developed in time. Whereas romantic love *in itself* cannot gain a history, romantic love can gain a history as it is taken up into the promise and commitment of a man and woman to each other.

All of this implies, again, that the Judge is conflicted in his description of the unity of the temporal and the eternal in marriage. On the one hand, he insists that sexual difference (a man's relation to a woman) allows a man to unite the temporal and the eternal, the finite and the infinite. But, on the other hand, he will insist that the resolute promises of marriage (before the eternal) allow man to unite these aspects of life and self. In the latter case, man finds his place within temporal existence (and is at home in the finite), not in virtue of woman's virtuosity with respect to the temporal/finite (and in virtue of his relation to her), but as he exercises the virtues essential to marriage, through time. He lives the unity of the temporal and the eternal as he struggles to live rightly in marriage, rightly in relation to his wife, to whom he has made promises of love and faithfulness.

The Limits of the Ethical—*Works of Love*[85]

Having provided an outline of Judge William's account of human being and becoming, we turn to consider the relationship between Judge William's thought and that of Kierkegaard himself—particularly as this is represented in the non-pseudonymous *Works of Love* and the pseudonymous *Sickness unto Death*. This is particularly important since we are on our way to articulating a Kierkegaardian theory of sexual difference and, following on from that, a Kierkegaardian ethics of sexual difference—in this we will rely on both *Either/Or* and *Works of Love*. Thus, if Judge William and Kierkegaard are found to be at odds with each other, our whole project is in jeopardy. The dilemma is particularly pressing since within Kierkegaard's wider corpus (and, indeed, within the covers of *Either/Or*, Part II itself) the writings and thought of Judge William are subject to substantial critique. In this third section of the chapter, then, we take up this critique and the important discontinuity that exists between Judge William and Søren Kierkegaard.

---

85. The title of this third section traces its origin to Rudd's work: *Limits of the Ethical*.

We will conclude that, particularly on religious or theological questions, there is an important divide between Judge William and Kierkegaard. At the same time, in reaching toward this conclusion it will be helpful to begin with a consideration of those who argue that there is, rather, a decisive *continuity* between them on religious and theological questions. George B. Connell, for example, argues that Judge William's God is in large measure the God of the Christian tradition, inasmuch as God gives the self as a gift and task and is an authoritative guarantor of the ethical life. In this regard, Connell points to the Judge's contention that "the unbounded self, the self that knows no higher authority than itself, is subject to its own whims and moods."[86] Here, God is the Archimedean point around whom the self revolves and without whom the self lack substance and direction.[87] According to Connell's interpretation of Judge William's religious vision, God is conceived of as a divine being who creates the self, who gives the self to the self as task, and who holds the self responsible in its choice of self. With this interpretation of Judge William's God in mind, it is possible to conceive a confluence between the Judge's letters and *Works of Love*, since the latter assumes God as creator of the self, as one in relation to whom each person is a bondservant, and as one who judges how each person should live. In this vein, also, it is not surprising to find *the Judge* exploring the logic of God as the middle term. Connell's exploration of this logic, in fact, resonates to some degree with the ethical vision we have presented in the previous chapter, for Judge William envisages an intersubjectivity in which each person is set free from his own sinful tendencies and is prevented from smothering the other in their shared life.[88] The possibility of continuity between *Works of Love* and *Either/Or*, then, on the nature of the divine and on the question of an ethical intersubjectivity, seems strong.[89]

---

86. Connell, "Theonomous Ethics," 63, quoted in Mehl, *Thinking through Kierkegaard*, 36.

87. Connell, "Theonomous Ethics," 65–66. We are reminded here of Judge William's insistence that to choose oneself is not to create oneself. See Kierkegaard, *Either/Or*, Part II, 215.

88. Connell, "Theonomous Ethics," 63. The Judge will speak of God as a divine being also when he speaks of the love that God claims from each person. Judge William argues that God does not claim our love in such a way that we must love God more than father or mother. God, he says, "is not that selfish." See Kierkegaard, *Either/Or*, Part II, 245.

89. For a broad discussion of the Judge's theological views, and his relation to Christianity, see Watkin, "Judge William," 113–24.

PART TWO—Kierkegaard and Love's Promise

Notwithstanding seeming parallels, however, we observe that Judge William's God is largely peripheral to the process of becoming that constitutes life in the ethical sphere. As our own description of self-choice has made apparent, the individual himself, in his eternal validity, is conceived by Judge William as a bulwark against the fluctuation and despair that necessarily attend life in time. Furthermore, self-choice is such that no eternal guarantor is required since self-choice is implied in the very structure of the self. Here God might somehow stand in the background of self-choice, but God is by no means necessary as a motivational or authoritative backdrop for the ethical life. As Peter Mehl rightly argues, the Judge "does not need a higher authority to keep him engaged, he is no longer subject to whims and moods, he is secure in himself by virtue of his firm and absolute point of departure: personhood has its *telos* in itself."[90] Even if God is not *utterly* peripheral to ethical existence, God remains very much in the background as Louis Mackey points out (when describing the ethical need to unite immediacy with reflection):

> Judge Wilhelm's God, like the God of Immanuel Kant, is a supersensible guarantor of the validity of his moral position and its invisible harmony with the seemingly independent domain of natural desire. Though the point of reference is transcendent, the act of referral (resolution or faith) is the immanent act of human will, and the import of the act and its object lies wholly within the sphere of worldly ethical activity. Religion, for Judge Wilhelm, is not a distinct way of life, but a dimension of the ethical life, essential if the strength of resolution is to be equal to the task of redeeming its (also essential) dimension of immediacy.[91]

If God has any place in the ethical life it is merely in the background, as an abstract guarantor of the possibility of selfhood, of the possibility of embracing the immediate/aesthetic within ethical/universal existence. As Rudd puts it, memorably: Judge William's religion "is a sort of metaphysical epiphenomenon of his ethics—a halo on its head, but no part of its body."[92]

Beyond the fact that God seems peripheral to the Judge's ethical vision, the letters of *Either/Or, Part II* also hint at God as an impersonal

90. Mehl, *Thinking through Kierkegaard*, 36.

91. Mackey, *Kierkegaard*, 61.

92. Rudd, *Limits of the Ethical*, 141. As Rudd goes on to say: "Even when he uses religious phrases, it turns out that what he means by them is not essentially religious at all."

Judge William

power that pervades the universe (a panentheistic vision), rather than as a Creator before whom one stands responsible. We find a hint of this theological framework in the Judge's assertion that when a man chooses himself, "with all the inwardness of his personality, his inner being is purified and he himself is brought into an immediate relationship with *the eternal power that omnipresently pervades all existence*."[93] In arguing that his view is essentially panentheistic, many interpreters point to that remarkable passage in which the Judge describes the moment of self-choice: "When around one everything has become silent, solemn as a clear starlit night, when the soul comes to be alone in the whole world, then before one appears, not an extraordinary human being, but the eternal power itself, then the heavens seem to open, and the I chooses itself or, more correctly, receives itself. Then the soul has seen the highest, which no mortal eye can see and which can never be forgotten; then the personality receives the accolade of knighthood that enables it for an eternity."[94] As Mehl will argue, Judge William's God seems to be the God described by Climacus in *Concluding Unscientific Postscript*: "[God] is in creation, everywhere in the creation, but he is not there directly, and only when the single individual turns inward into himself (consequently only in the inwardness of self-activity) does he become aware and capable of seeing God."[95] Here, again, God is not a divine being who creates the world and who gives the self as gift and task, a divine being to whom one might relate in adoration and obedience, but God is a "divine power" that pervades the universe and is perceived by the individual in the very moment he becomes aware that he might choose himself in his eternal validity.

The opposition between the religious vision of Judge William and Kierkegaard (in *Works of Love*) can be illuminated by attending to the christological and soteriological assumptions at work in *Works of Love*. We have pointed out, above, that the God of *Works of Love* is the Triune God of the classical Christian tradition, and have observed that we need go no further than the opening prayer for this to become apparent. God is Father, Son, and Holy Spirit. In terms of the second person of the Trinity, specifically, Kierkegaard's prayer unfolds as follows: "How could one speak properly about love if you were forgotten, you who revealed what love is, you our Savior and Redeemer, who gave yourself in order to save all."[96]

---

93. Kierkegaard, *Either/Or*, Part II, 167. Italics added.
94. Ibid., 177.
95. Kierkegaard, *Concluding Unscientific*, 35.
96. Kierkegaard, *Works of Love*, 3.

Furthermore, in language that parallels this early identification of Jesus as savior and redeemer, Kierkegaard affirms that Jesus Christ himself is love and, therefore, that "he knew in his innermost being and in responsibility before God that it was the sacrifice of Atonement that he was bringing, that he truly loved the disciples, loved the whole human race, or in any case everyone who would allow himself to be saved!"[97] Within the context of *Works of Love*, then, Jesus Christ is conceived of as the divine-man who is both savior and redeemer—he is the one through whom human beings might be saved from the sin that had separated them from God. While Kierkegaard does not engage in extensive reflection on christological themes in *Works of Love*, it is evident that he assumes the truth of classical Christian dogma concerning the person and work of Jesus Christ. But in terms of the theological visions of *Either/Or*, Part II and *Works of Love*, respectively, what matters is not simply that Kierkegaard makes orthodox-sounding noises while Judge William does not, since the Judge can certainly pay lip service to orthodoxy.[98] Rather, of primary importance are Kierkegaard's christological and soteriological assumptions for his wider religious and ethical vision.

In *Works of Love*, the logic of Christ as savior and redeemer corresponds with Kierkegaard's insistence on the sinful nature of humans and on the fundamental inability of humans to save themselves or transform their existence—Kierkegaard is profoundly aware of the many ways in which we fail to love according to the pattern of Jesus Christ. In our decisions, actions, and judgments we invariably fail to love ourselves, God, or our neighbor, which is to say that our lives are perpetually marked by a failure to meet the requirements of God's law (and the law of love). Unlike Jesus Christ, who is himself the embodiment of love and the fulfillment of the law, human beings are unable to meet the requirements of the law or to love others according to the pattern of Jesus Christ. It is for precisely this reason that humans require a savior and redeemer—one who will atone for sin and effect reconciliation with God. Only by way of union with God ("one who loves is what he is only by being in [God]"[99]), and by taking

---

97. Ibid., 111–12.

98. In his first letter to the Aesthete, we find Judge William affirming the Christological assertions of Philippians 2: "And Christ did not regard it robbery to be equal with God but humbled himself, and you want to regard the intellectual gifts bestowed upon you as a robbery." See Kierkegaard, *Either/Or*, Part II, 16. In this case, it seems evident that Judge William's appeal to the example of Christ is simply a convenient way to bolster his own argument—a way to add rhetorical flair to his point.

99. From the opening prayer of *Works of Love*, again.

Judge William

Jesus Christ as the prototype, might we understand and live love as that which builds up, hopes all things, believes all things, and does not seek its own.[100] This by no means reduces the demand of Kierkegaard's ethical vision in *Works of Love*—it does not mitigate the strenuousness of the like for like that pervades the whole of that work.[101] Nevertheless, as Gouwens rightly notes (over-against Barth) there is no assumption in Kierkegaard that through a life of love (through *works* of love) a person can make himself right in relation to the divine.[102]

It is precisely this insistence on the sinfulness of the human, and on the inability of humans to save themselves or transform their own existence, that is foreign to the ethical vision of Judge William. While the Judge will insist that the spiritual transformation of the person is something that "befalls" him only when "around one everything has become silent," his account of self-choice displays a profound confidence in the capacity of the human person to effect self-choice and thereby transform his existence. It is for this reason that repentance, for Judge William, is not a matter of acknowledging one's failure before God or of seeking forgiveness but is, rather, the process by which a person freely accepts his given nature and history as integral to his identity. Repentance, we should point out, can be redefined in this way (contrary to its classical Christian meaning) only within a theological system that no longer takes seriously the rigorous requirements of God's law and the inability of the human person to either understand or meet those requirements.[103] Within the ethical framework of Judge William, there is no conception of a profound or constitutional flaw within the human person that prevents him from freely taking responsibility for who he is and from engaging in the process of becoming as we have described it.

On the contrary, as Louis Mackey puts it: "Judge Wilhelm thinks that a man can get behind his whole history and push. He claims to do by means of repentance what he finds the aesthete unable to do by means of imagination: to overtake himself and take himself over completely."[104] In view of

---

100. Paul Müller writes, speaking of the prayer that opens *Works of Love*: "Without salvation and redemption by the Son, love, therefore, cannot be in the lover, since the lover is only loving through being in God." See Müller's *Kierkegaard's* Works of Love, 8.

101. See Ferreira's discussion of the like for like in *Love's Grateful Striving*, 244–48.

102. Gouwens, *Kierkegaard as Religious Thinker*, 190.

103. Where repentance is spoken of explicitly in *Works of Love*, it is conceived precisely in terms of a person's acknowledgement of sin/failure and willingness to live differently. See Kierkegaard, *Works of Love*, 93.

104. Mackey, *Kierkegaard*, 90.

PART TWO—Kierkegaard and Love's Promise

Judge William's insistence that "through the individual's intercourse with himself the individual is made pregnant by himself and gives birth to himself," Amy Laura Hall takes an equally critical tack when she suggests that the Judge "makes of God a mere accessory to self-birth."[105] Judge William's confidence in the freedom and ability of the human person to transform/become himself and to live ethically is, in the light of Kierkegaard's theological and ethical vision in *Works of Love*, almost breathtaking. God, for the Judge, is essentially a second thought. Sin is a minor and surmountable stumbling block in the path to self-realization.

Already within the covers of *Either/Or*, Part II, there is evidence that Judge William's ethical and religious vision will not stand up under scrutiny.[106] While Judge William suggests that the despair of temporal and finite existence can only be ameliorated through a choice of oneself in one's eternal validity, the Jylland Pastor, in a sermon appended to the Judge's letters, raises the possibility that the self is not such that it can provide this protection against despair. The pastor explores this point by way of a critique of the common sentiment that "one does what one can." To rest one's life on the sentiment that "one does what one can," he argues, is to rest upon a shifting and unstable foundation, since honest reflection invariably brings a person to the realization that he has *not*, in fact, done what he could. The Jylland Pastor writes:

> So every more earnest doubt, every deeper care is not calmed by the words: One does what one can. If a person is sometimes in the right, sometimes in the wrong, to some degree in the right, to some degree in the wrong, who, then is the one who makes the decision except the person himself, but in the decision may he not again be to some degree in the right and to some degree in the wrong? Or is he a different person when he judges his act than when he acts? Is doubt to rule, then, continually to discover new difficulties, and is care to accompany the anguished soul and drum past experiences into it? Or would we prefer continually to be in the right in the way that irrational creatures are?[107]

From this perspective, a person's capacity for self choice and his resolute pursuit of ethical existence is fraught with tension, inasmuch as the person

---

105. Hall, *Kierkegaard and the Treachery of Love*, 125.

106. Although it is the Judge himself who includes the sermon with his letters to the Aesthete, this does not require, as many have observed, that the Judge fully understands the implications of the sermon for his own life-view.

107. Kierkegaard, *Either/Or*, Part II, 347.

cannot be certain that he has in fact fulfilled the requirements of ethical existence.[108] Furthermore, how is one to know that the social institutions of one's own culture are not implicated in a denial of ethical existence? There is always the possibility, then, that a person has chosen the wrong path, has made the wrong decision, has contravened the law, and has not, in fact, "done what he can." Contrary to the Judge's argument, to despair absolutely is not to overcome the despair of the finite but is to mistakenly find rest and comfort in that which simply cannot provide rest and comfort—namely, in the self.

The Pastor insists, over against the Judge, that the only way to secure oneself against the despair and change of temporal existence is to rest in the infinite, to rest in God we might say. Thus, the Pastor encourages us to freely embrace the assumption that "before God we are always in the wrong," since this thought alone is an upbuilding thought—this thought alone might provide a bulwark against the despair that accompanies life in the finite world.[109] As David Law argues, while the Judge "seems to view the problem faced by the exception to the ethical as being due to an awkward particularity that will not permit itself to be taken up into the universal [for example: the person who does not, cannot marry], the Pastor has won through to the insight that *'wrongness' is determinative of the totality of human existence.*"[110] Over-against the soothing and reassuring (and finally dishonest) sentiment that "one does what one can," the truth that in relation to God we are always in the wrong becomes for the Pastor a

---

108. Mark Taylor makes a similar point, differently: "The more earnestly one struggles, the deeper the disparity becomes, until at last the self acknowledges a persistent conflict between the opposites it ought to synthesize. The awareness of this failure to fulfill the ethical task brings with it a sense of the self's guilt. Kierkegaard's ethical stage does not culminate in beautiful souls contemplating their own divinity but in the guilty individual painfully conscious of his separation from and opposition to the absolute." See Taylor, *Journeys to Selfhood*, 251.

109. The use of the word "freely" in this sentence is not unintentional. The Pastor argues that a person's acceptance of the truth that he is "always in the wrong before God" on the basis of calculation and deliberation (which implies necessity) cannot become upbuilding for him; only when he loves God, when his soul is turned toward the infinite, does he freely discover the truth that is upbuilding for him, that he is always in the wrong before God. The embrace of this truth, in love, says the Pastor, is a person's adoration, his devotion, his piety. It is an adoration, devotion and piety freely given. See Kierkegaard, *Either/Or*, Part II, 350.

110. Law, "Place, Role, and Function," 253. Italics added. We observed that the Judge believes that one's failure to give universal expression to the particular can be remedied through a mourning after this failure. That is, through mourning a person gives expression to his conviction that the universal is the highest.

PART TWO—Kierkegaard and Love's Promise

source of confidence and encouragement: "Only in an infinite relationship with God could the doubt be calmed; only in an infinitely free relationship with God could his cares be turned to joy. He is in an infinite relationship with God when he acknowledges that God is always right; he is in an infinitely free relationship with God when he acknowledges that he is always wrong."[111] Only the relationship to the infinite can overcome the doubt and despair that characterize human existence in the world, and this relationship requires acknowledgment that one is always in the wrong.

Johannes Climacus similarly points to the limitations of the ethical life-view when he writes: "The discrepancy is that the ethical self is supposed to be found immanently in despair, that by enduring the despair the individual would win himself . . . But this does not help. In despairing, I use myself to despair, and therefore I can indeed despair of everything by myself, but if I do this I cannot come back by myself. It is in this moment of decision that the individual needs divine assistance.[112] To despair absolutely is, if one is merely cast back upon one's own resources, to remain in despair—if one is to overcome despair it is precisely in this moment that one must rely upon the *divinum auxilium*.[113] As Hall puts it, "Rather than ignoring his predicament, depending on 'woman' to save him from it, or ethically willing himself free, [the man living in the ethical sphere] must find himself indicted, infinitely, before God."[114] Only as he accepts himself, in faith, as so-indicted, might he truly despair of temporal existence and find the security of the infinite.[115] Thus, the pastor writes: "Therefore this thought, that in relation to God we are always in the wrong, is an upbuilding thought; it is upbuilding that we are in the wrong, upbuilding that we are always in the wrong. It manifests its upbuilding power in two ways, partly by putting an end to doubt and calming the cares of doubt, partly by animating to action."[116] The one who is always in the wrong is set free to live faithfully.[117]

111. Kierkegaard, *Either/Or*, Part II, 352.
112. Kierkegaard, *Concluding Unscientific Postscript*, 258.
113. This latter phrase is used by Mackey in, *Kierkegaard*, 92.
114. Hall, *Kierkegaard and Treachery*, 131–32.
115. Thus, as David Law rightly observes, the sermon that concludes *Either/Or* is in fact an assertion that "the ethical is not the definitive mode of existence for the human being, but must itself be replaced by something higher." See Law, "Place, Role, and Function," 251. Perkins argues more explicitly that the sermon in fact introduces the religious sphere. See Perkins, "Either/Or/Or," 208.
116. Kierkegaard, *Either/Or*, Part II, 351.
117. David Gouwens writes, of Religiousness A (of which we take the Jylland

Judge William

Within *Works of Love* we find an echo of the argument of the Jylland Pastor, and a parallel refusal of the Judge's over-confident conception of the self. In our earlier discussion of human bond service we noted Kierkegaard's insistence that we are infinitely indebted to God—that, no matter our success in following the love command of Jesus, we are still infinitely indebted to the God who has loved us first. Developing this thought, in the context of his argument that human persons are unable to fulfill the law of God, Kierkegaard writes:

> In earthly affairs we usually speak of the lamentable circumstance that one must go into debt in order to start an enterprise; in relation to God, every person begins with an infinite debt, even if we forget what the debt amounts to daily after the beginning. All too often this is forgotten in life, and why, indeed, if it is not because God also is forgotten. Then one person compares himself with another, and the one who has understood somewhat more than others congratulates himself on being something. Would that he himself might understand that before God he is nothing.[118]

According to *Kierkegaard's* logic of indebtedness to God, every action of love is finally a gift of God and has its source in God—we are not, independently, sources of love or goodness. According to the *Pastor's* logic, similarly, we cannot reconcile the particular and the universal, the temporal and the eternal, and must throw ourselves upon the infinite ("before God we are always in the wrong!") in order to be set free from the doubt and despair that attend life in the temporal sphere. In each case (that of Kierkegaard and of the Pastor) it is only by way of the infinite (of God), and by way of an acknowledgment of our own incapacities, that we are set free both to live and act confidently in the world. Not to acknowledge God (one's indebtedness to God—that one is in the wrong before God) is to mistakenly find oneself as the source of love and is to mistakenly find within oneself the resources for the fulfillment and completion of oneself. Not to acknowledge God is to be in despair. What the Pastor and Søren Kierkegaard invite us to, then, is a profound hermeneutic of self-suspicion whereby we acknowledge that we can neither fully understand the life to

---

pastor to be an example): "One's nothingness in the God-relationship is not absorption into God, but a recognition of one's radical dependence at every moment upon God. ... Apart from God, one is nothing; with God, one is indeed something, in radical dependence." Gouwens, *Kierkegaard as Religious Thinker*, 113.

118. Kierkegaard, *Works of Love*, 102.

PART TWO—Kierkegaard and Love's Promise

which we are called nor faithfully live it. It is this radical need of grace that Judge William never succeeds in apprehending.

In considering tensions and continuities between Judge William (*Either/Or*, Part II) and Kierkegaard (*Works of Love*), it is helpful also to explore marriage, which Judge William takes to be the paradigmatic institution of ethical existence. From the perspective of *Works of Love*, the Judge's confidence in marriage as an expression of the universal, and of ethical existence, is as misplaced as his confidence in the capacity of the human person to simply "get behind his whole history and push." What we find in the Judge, in fact, is a conviction that the social institutions of his culture give expression to the universal—or are the universal—and that ethical existence requires an acceptance of these institutions. As Perkins puts it, however, in this the Judge has radically reversed "the fundamental value structure of the theological tradition, changing the transcendent God of Luther into a God who is the handmaid of socially approved historical and cultural modes . ."[119] That is, Judge William essentially provides religious and ethical legitimization for the institutions of his cultural context: God, here, justifies "our private or provincial social arrangements: marriage, civil society, state, and international relations—to appropriate Hegel's scheme of human relations."[120] This is not to say, as Watkins rightly notes, that Judge William is incapable of submitting social institutions and conventions to deep scrutiny but it is to say that his ethical framework seems to accept key features of his social context merely as given.[121] It is perhaps not speaking too strongly to say: "[T]he judge is . . . a bourgeois Lutheran Protestant whose God confirms the world."[122]

Thinking back to *Works of Love*, it quickly becomes apparent that while Søren Kierkegaard and Judge William agree on the basic features of marriage, they are worlds apart in the esteem they grant to marriage. For Kierkegaard the easy matrimony of Judge William (his matrimony is easy both personally and theoretically) represents a failure to understand the extent to which marriage constitutes a distraction (at best!) from the life to which each person is called as a disciple of Jesus Christ. In his naïve adherence to the social conventions and institutions of his time, the Judge has

119. Perkins, "Either/Or/Or," 220.

120. Ibid., 225.

121. Watkins, "Judge William," 134.

122. Perkins, "Either/Or/Or," 208. We note that Perkins quickly adds that this God "is not a pussy cat who purrs when stroked." Most specifically, Perkins suggests that this is the case because of the degree of responsibility that this God requires with reference to the ethical life we are called to live.

become incapable of recognizing that these conventions and institutions are in fact particulars that cannot bear the weight of the "universal"—he cannot see that these particulars, when construed as the universal, function to undermine the love command of Jesus. While Kierkegaard does not view marriage as inappropriate for those who would follow the love command of Jesus, he does argue that his contemporaries have failed to understand marriage in a truly Christian way—their view of marriage is essentially baptized paganism. When marriage is subjected to the scrutiny of the love command of Jesus (to the requirement of neighbor-love), Kierkegaard suggests, we realize that marriage as it is generally understood and lived is in fact a barrier to the ethical and religious life.

Thus, while Judge William will insist that the fullness of ethical existence is found in marriage and that becoming a self is bound up with entry into the marital estate, Kierkegaard will argue that focusing on marriage in this way reflects confusion about why Christianity has come into the world. Christianity, he argues, has not come into the world in order to baptize erotic love and friendship (and then to add a nice word about love for neighbor) but in order to cast erotic love and friendship down from the throne of our lives and imaginations—in order that neighbor-love might be set up in their place. While Kierkegaard will not object to the Judge's argument that marriage represents the fulfillment of erotic love, he would suggest that Judge William's preoccupation with erotic love and marriage represents a failure to understand the significance of the love command.[123] Kierkegaard has argued, for example, that marital love as lived in his cultural context has invariably become a stumbling block on the way to love of neighbor (both the neighbor that the spouse is, and the neighbor who is a third party to the marital relationship). For Kierkegaard in *Works of Love*, if marriage is universal it is so only historically, which is to say that marriage is a particular that has mistakenly been elevated to the status of universal and, as such, has become a distraction from the life of neighbor-love to which each disciple is called.

Continuity

If there is such a clear discontinuity in the relationship between Judge William and Kierkegaard, then what of our wider intention to develop a Kierkegaardian theory and ethics of sexual difference—and one that relies

---

123. If anything, the fulfillment of erotic love in marriage is conceived of, within the context of *Works of Love*, as a relatively insignificant aspect of the Christian message.

PART TWO—Kierkegaard and Love's Promise

on both *Either/Or* and *Works of Love*? The answer is that this clear and important discontinuity between them is neither final nor decisive, in view of our specific purpose. No doubt we must continue to take this discontinuity into consideration, yet the final word in terms of the relationship between them, for our purposes, is *continuity*. Most importantly, Judge William's account of human being and becoming is, in large measure, embraced and incorporated within Kierkegaard's own thought, and particularly within *Works of Love*. To demonstrate how this is so, we begin with the logic of the "stages" or "spheres."

For both Judge William and Kierkegaard, the aesthetic is taken up into the higher concentricity of the ethical and religious. In each there is a logic of retention and of transformation—in which the aesthetic is retained but also transformed within the higher stage or sphere. In the discourse "Love Builds Up," within *Works of Love*, we discover an explicit indication that the logic of retention and transformation is also at play within *Works of Love*. In that discourse, as we have already observed, Kierkegaard argues that a human person does not become conscious of himself as spirit until later in life and that this person, therefore, "has sensately-psychically acted out a certain part of his life prior to [becoming conscious of himself as spirit]. But this first portion is not to be cast aside when the spirit awakens any more than the awakening of the spirit in contrast to the sensate-psychical announces itself in a sensate-psychical way. . . . The person in whom the spirit has awakened does not as a consequence abandon the visible world."[124] For both Judge William and Kierkegaard (in *Works of Love*) the sensate-psychical is embraced and transformed within the higher ethical/religious sphere of existence. Thus, we are not prevented from embracing fundamental aspects of the Judge's theory of becoming within the framework of *Works of Love*.

In the secondary literature that addresses the relationship between *Either/Or*, Part II, and *Works of Love*, we find opinions that concur with the judgment we have rendered. According to Robert Perkins, for example, Judge William's understanding of the self, and his original account of self-choice, are points never subsequently rejected (though they are extensively modified) in Kierkegaard's authorship.[125] Peter Mehl makes the same point when he argues that "a strong case can be made . . . that much of the Judge's convictions carry through to Kierkegaard's later writings such as *Works of Love* and *The Sickness unto Death*. . . . They share a similar

124. Kierkegaard, *Works of Love*, 209.
125. Perkins, "Either/Or/Or," 220.

understanding of the structure and dynamics of human existence and (to a lesser extent) of the perils of despair and the possibilities for existential identity."[126] It is for this reason, for example, that we have discerned a fundamental continuity between Judge William and Anti-Climacus (in *The Sickness unto Death*) on the nature of the self as a synthesis of the finite/infinite, the temporal/eternal, and of freedom/necessity. Each conceives of despair in terms of the despair of infinitude (which is to lack finitude) and the despair of finitude (which is to lack infinitude).

Furthermore, each author argues that becoming a self is precisely a matter of imaginatively holding together the synthesis that constitutes the self—the self strives, in continuity with the given, to become that which it is not. As David Gouwens argues, the task of both ethical and religious life is "to become a self in subjective passion oriented to the imagined ideal, striving for a repetition which incorporates imagination and will in realizing a harmony of the actual and the ideal in the concrete life."[127] Of course, a key difference between *Either/Or* and *The Sickness unto Death* is the source of the ideal toward which a person strives. In the religious sphere, as Gouwnes writes, "Christ presents himself to the ethical imagination not as a glorious internally-generated ideal, but as the suffering God-man who atones for sin—an offense to the self-reliance of the imagination as well as reason."[128] Thus, between the early pseudonym Judge William, and the later pseudonym Anti-Climacus, there is a fundamental continuity in the conception of the self and in the process of becoming that makes the self what it is, even if the ideal is construed differently by each author.

In this vein, we do well to attend to Westphal's insistence that *Works of Love* and *Practice in Christianity* represent a teleological suspension of Religiousness B (with its emphasis on Christ as the paradox to be *believed*) in Religiousness C (with its emphasis on Christ as the Pattern, Prototype, and Paradigm to be *imitated*). Westphal argues: "In the movement from Religiousness B to Religiousness C and the corresponding movement from offense B to offense C, we move from *credo quia absurdum est* to *imitatio Christi*. Climacus complained in *Postscript* that the Hegelian system had no ethics. Now, in effect, Anti-Climacus acknowledges that Religiousness B as presented in *Postscript* has no ethics. Metaphysical orthodoxy needs to be completed with an ethics of neighbor love. Christian belief

---

126. Mehl, *Thinking through Kierkegaard*, 78.
127. Gouwens, "Kierkegaard on the Ethical Imagination," 216.
128. Ibid., 217.

PART TWO—Kierkegaard and Love's Promise

calls for a corresponding Christian behaviour."[129] In view of Westphal's argument, we are reminded that *Works of Love* sets up Jesus Christ as the ideal, prototype, and pattern after whom a person is to model himself in his becoming. Not only is Jesus Christ the paradox to be believed but, within *Works of Love* Jesus Christ is the one who (as the embodiment of love, and as the fulfillment of God's law) is to be imitated/followed. Although the love command and example of Jesus Christ do not provide a substantive answer to every question as to *how* we are to love, Kierkegaard is convinced that the love command is not thereby opaque or inadequate. Indeed, the whole of *Works of Love* represents precisely an exploration, on the basis of the Apostolic word, of the nature of those works of love to which the disciple is commanded and invited—while his ethical vision is in many ways formal, the substantive is not neglected.

It is possible to conclude, then, that Judge William's account of human becoming, of the relation between actual and ideal, can be preserved within the context of *Works of Love*, though with important caveats. For Kierkegaard in *Works of Love*, the self can be construed as being in a process of becoming, as existing in a dialectical and imaginative tension between the actual self (my immediately given self, with *this* physiological make-up, *this* social history, and *these* drives, inclinations, and abilities) and the ideal self. That is, the ideal self is fundamentally in continuity with the actual self, as Judge Williams has suggested. However, given that the self is neither the source of itself nor a bulwark against the despair of temporal existence, and given that the self is constitutionally incapable of projecting or attaining an ideal self that correlates with genuine fulfillment of the self, the ideal self must be conceived in relation to, and under the guidance of, Jesus Christ the prototype. Furthermore, since Kierkegaard provides only a formal account of the nature of love, the self can project an ideal self that owes to the particularity of the person yet is under the constraint and discipline of Jesus Christ as savior and prototype. Thus, while the ideal self is in continuity with the actual self (the actual is nowhere denied or refused in *Works of Love*), the individual person is acknowledged as incapable of projecting (on his own) an ideal that might give expression to the fullness of the human. This fullness might only be expressed when the actual and ideal are together under the constraint of Jesus Christ, when they are taken up in to the higher concentricity of neighbor-love.

---

129. Westphal, "Kierkegaard's Religiousness C," 536.

PART THREE

Between Irigaray and Kierkegaard

5

Sexual Difference

> The command of God will find man and woman as what they are in themselves. It will disclose to them the male or female being to which they have to remain faithful.... In all this it may perhaps coincide at various points with what we may think we know concerning the differentiation of male and female. But it may not always do this. It may manifest the distinction in new and surprising ways. The summons to both man and woman to be true to themselves may take completely unforeseen forms right outside the systems in which we like to think.
>
> —KARL BARTH, *CHURCH DOGMATICS*

ON THE WAY TOWARD a constructive, Kierkegaardian ethics of sexual difference, we have spent time exploring the writings of Luce Irigaray and have subsequently delved into the pseudonymous and non-pseudonymous writings of Søren Kierkegaard. With that work behind us, the moment has arrived to break each writer out of the "silo" of his and her own thought in order to stage a conversation between them. The goal is, as stated from the outset, to demonstrate that Kierkegaard's theocentric ethics of intersubjectivity correlates with, and can accommodate, important aspects of Irigaray's ethics of sexual difference. Otherwise put, our intention is to demonstrate that a Kierkegaardian ethics of sexual difference is conceivable.

PART THREE—Between Irigaray and Kierkegaard

On the way to such a Kierkegaardian *ethics* of sexual difference, however, it will first be necessary to seek a foundation for this ethics in a Kierkegaardian *theory* of sexual difference. That is, if a Kierkegaardian *ethics* of sexual difference is to be more than tentative and provisional in nature, a foundation for this ethics must be provided by way of a Kierkegaardian account of the distinct beings (if not Beings) of man and woman—a Kierkegaardian *theory* of sexual difference. The goal of the present chapter is to outline just such a theory.

Some will no doubt argue that the caveats we must place around our Kierkegaardian theory or account of sexual difference are such that the confluence we perceive between Irigaray and Kierkegaard is no confluence at all. While there is some validity to this argument, we nevertheless insist that our Kierkegaardian theory of the becoming of man and woman in difference approximates to that of Irigaray; our alternative theory embraces key features of her account of the human as two. In any case, it is not our intention to answer every doubt whether a final alignment between Irigaray and Kierkegaard is possible on these questions. Our intention, rather, is to demonstrate that the limitations of Kierkegaard's own thought (the patriarchal assumptions that shape his writings) can be ameliorated by way of engagement with Irigaray. Success, here, is determined by whether Irigaray's thought approximates closely enough to that of Kierkegaard that she can inform and correct his theological and ethical vision on the way to a theological ethics of sexual difference.

In mediating between Irigaray and Kierkegaard, it is clear that we have not taken up some position of neutrality between them, as if neither one has priority for us. Rather, in setting up the discussion between Irigaray and Kierkegaard as one in which Irigaray informs Kierkegaard, we have aligned ourselves with Kierkegaard's theological vision. As an apologetic for this approach, we would suggest that the conversation between Irigaray and Kierkegaard only becomes interesting and profitable when a clear position is staked out on the significant theological issues that divide them.

Redistributing the Nature/Culture Poles

As observed, Luce Irigaray's reformulation of the negative requires a *redistribution* of the nature and culture poles so that man and woman are each implicated in both nature and culture. According to this redistribution, man is no longer identified with culture while woman is assimilated

Sexual Difference

to nature. While previous steps need not be fully retraced here, we recall Irigaray's contention that a genuine human culture becomes possible only in the recognition of nature—which is two. Thus, as man and woman recognize this twoness in nature (and recognize that neither, by itself, constitutes the human) they together take a step into a genuinely human culture. Conversely, where recognition of this two-fold nature is lacking, a genuinely human culture remains impossible—here "culture" will necessarily be anti-natural in its basic orientation and woman will be prevented from attaining subjectivity in her own right. According to Irigaray, then, there is a nature/culture that corresponds to woman and a nature/culture that corresponds to man. Importantly, this redistribution applies not only to the nature/culture poles, but to various other binaries that have invariably been mapped onto sexual difference (caressed/caresser; passive/active; home/civil society; immediacy/reflection).

Beyond this redistribution, however, Irigaray will insist on a refusal of the binary logic itself—there is an *undoing* of the binary logic. Thus, rather than seeing each pole in opposition to the other, Irigaray conceives the poles as mutually implicated—they are, therefore, not "poles" in the way that binary logic would suggest. Not only do man and woman each gain access to both nature and culture, these "poles" are conceived in continuity with each other rather than in opposition. From Irigaray's perspective, at the same moment that the binary poles are redistributed within each genre, the binary logic is undone.

The question arises whether Judge William's account of human becoming allows for a similar *redistribution* of binary poles and a parallel *undoing* of the binary logic. As observed, Judge William's explicit account of sexual difference is subject to Irigarayan critique since he distributes the nature and culture poles in the same way they have been distributed throughout patriarchal thought and culture. We recall his argument: "Woman explains the finite; man pursues the infinite. This is the way it must be, and everyone has his pain, for woman bears children in pain, but man conceives ideas in pain. . . ."[1] Parallel to this, we have found Judge William arguing that woman is a virtuoso when it comes to explaining the natural and the finite while man has an affinity with the spiritual and infinite. In order to conceive/develop a Kierkegaardian theory of sexual difference, then, it will be necessary to simply acknowledge *and refuse* the Judge's patriarchal mapping of the nature/culture poles onto the identities of woman and man. While it will inevitably be asked whether the

---

1. Kierkegaard, *Either/Or*, Part II, 311.

PART THREE—Between Irigaray and Kierkegaard

Judge's theory of human becoming (which we accept and develop) can be disjoined from his patriarchal account of sexual difference, we will both assume and demonstrate this possibility.

In Judge William's thought, we should perhaps add, there is a subtle if inadequate move away from this traditional mapping of the nature/culture poles onto the identities of woman and man. We have observed a tension in Judge Williams thought on the relationship of man to the natural and finite inasmuch as he both insists that man must gain access to finitude in virtue of his relationship to woman (who embodies finitude) *and* that man gains access to finitude in virtue of the promises and commitments, before God, that constitute marriage. But if the latter argument is true, then man can be conceived as gaining access to finitude (and thus as living the continuity between finitude and infinitude) without reference to woman as representative of finitude. Here we have both a redistribution of the poles and, in the same moment, a step toward the undoing of the binary logic itself.[2] That the binary logic is undone is revealed in the Judge's insistence that man lives the unity of the temporal and eternal, the finite and the infinite, in the institution of marriage, before God. Indeed, our wider argument will bear this out since Judge William's account of human becoming requires precisely that we conceive a continuity between nature and culture, the physical and spiritual, the finite and infinite, and the temporal and eternal (at least at the level of the human person).

Of course, that Judge William seems to undo the binary logic that marks much of Western philosophy and culture, or that he suggests man can live the continuity between finitude and infinitude or between the temporal and the eternal (without reference to woman as representative of the finite or temporal), does not mean that the judge has not defined woman precisely in terms of nature, finitude, and temporality (he does not redistribute the poles). It does mean, however, that a key aspect of Irigaray's own theory of sexual difference (the undoing of the binary opposition) finds resonance in Judge William's account of human becoming and self-choice.

The undoing of the binary logic comes to expression, in the Judge's writings, also, as he explores the idea that becoming a self requires an avoidance of the despair of infinitude. The despair of infinitude is that form of despair in which a person is led fantastically "out into the infinite in such a way that it only leads him away from himself and thereby

---

2. We will return to this question, below.

Sexual Difference

prevents him from coming back to himself."³ It is a form of despair in which a person loses touch with the physical, concrete, finite self/world and finds himself lost in an imaginative and fantastic reverie. According to the Judge's account of human becoming, this form of despair must be resisted in being and becoming a self, since to lose touch with the physical, concrete, and finite self/world is to lose touch with a fundamental aspect of one's humanity.

We find in Irigaray's objection to Hegel's negative an echo of Judge William's criticism of the despair of infinitude. She argues that since Hegel conceives of spiritual work as "the activity by which the rational subject negates, sublates and transcends natural facticity," he does not allow a person be "led back to himself," and does not allow the person a return to the finite/natural/temporal aspect of his being.⁴ Within Hegel's thought, says Irigaray, man is lost in a fantastic reverie. Thus we discern something of Irigaray's critique of Hegel in the following words of Judge William (where he takes aim at a person who, having been confronted with the infinite/eternal aspect of his being, allows himself to be carried away in this infinitude):

> When the individual has grasped himself in his eternal validity, this overwhelms him in his fullness. Temporality vanishes for him. At the first moment, this fills him with an indescribable bliss and gives him an absolute security. If he now begins to stare at it one-sidedly, the temporal asserts its claims. These are rejected. What temporality is able to give, the more or less that appears here, is so very insignificant to him compared to what he possesses eternally. Everything comes to a standstill for him; he has, so to speak, arrived in eternity ahead of time. He sinks into contemplation, stares fixedly at himself, but this staring cannot fill up time. Then it appears to him that time, temporality is his ruination.⁵

For both Judge William and Luce Irigaray, becoming a self requires treading the line between the Scylla of infinitude's despair and the Charybdis of finitude's despair—being and becoming a self requires that a person live the continuity and tension between the finite and the infinite. For each, the binary logic is undone.

---

3. Kierkegaard, *The Sickness unto Death*, 31.
4. Cheah and Grosz, "Of Being-Two," 8.
5. Kierkegaard, *Either/Or*, Part II, 231.

153

PART THREE—Between Irigaray and Kierkegaard

This continuity between Irigaray and Judge William on the refusal of infinitude's despair is confirmed when one attends to the Judge's account of self-choice. The Judge argues that self-choice is not merely a question of choosing oneself in one's eternal validity; rather in choosing oneself in one's eternal validity a person simultaneously *chooses or embraces himself as a finite being*.[6] Indeed, a failure to choose oneself in one's particularity, as a finite being, is precisely a failure to choose oneself—it is to be implicated in the despair of infinitude. Here again the confluence between Irigaray and Judge William is significant since each argues that the natural and immediate aspect of a person's being is more than peripheral to his or her becoming a self—indeed, it is central and vital to identity and becoming.[7]

As should be apparent, there is an important difference between Irigaray and Judge William on how one makes the transition from mere nature into culture. For her part Irigaray insists on acknowledgment of sexual difference (acknowledgment of two-fold nature of the human) as the beginning of culture, while for his part the Judge focuses on self-choice as the moment in which a person becomes more than a merely aesthetic being. But even here an alignment between Irigaray and the Judge is evident. For each, an intentional acceptance of the natural is integral to the movement beyond mere nature into culture. Irigaray argues: "If man and woman respect each other as those two halves of the universe that they represent, then by recognizing the other they have overcome their immediate instincts and drives. They are spiritual persons from the fact of recognizing that they do not represent the whole of the person."[8] To embrace nature (to embrace sexual difference) is to enter culture. Likewise for Judge William, to choose the natural, finite self is a necessary and primary moment on the path to spiritual existence—without such a choice, there

---

6. Judge William's account of the possibilities inherent in the self is limited in nature and he demonstrates little imagination in conceiving possibilities beyond those already present in his society. Irigaray, on the other hand, sees the sexuate self as representing a potentiality beyond articulation in terms of our present categories of understanding, our present way of living the human. Here, then, we must push the logic of Judge William's own thought well beyond his own limited sense of possibility.

7. We could appropriately borrow language here from Elisabeth Grosz who articulates the relation between nature and culture as follows: "Nature is the ground, the condition or field in which culture erupts or emerges as a supervening quality not contained in nature but derived from it." See Grosz, *Time Travel*, 44.

8. Irigaray, *I Love to You*, 51. As Cheah and Grosz, again, put it: "Sexual difference undoes the binary opposition between nature and spirit because it is nothing other than the internal natural means by which nature becomes spiritualized." See "Of Being-Two," 9.

Sexual Difference

is no truly spiritual existence. Thus, for both Irigaray and Judge William, the choice or acknowledgment of the natural is in some sense coterminous with (or at least necessary for) the movement into cultural and spiritual existence—the choice or acknowledgment of the natural and finite is in some sense constitutive of the human as more than natural/immediate.

To demonstrate a further confluence between Judge William and Irigaray on the nature of the self, we also focus on the Judge's concept of imagination. Imagination, we recall, is the human capacity *instar omnium* (according to Anti-Climacus) and is the medium for infinitizing. Imagination is the "rendition of the self as the self's possibility."[9] Thinking through the logic of imagination we discover a twofold confluence between Judge William and Luce Irigaray on human becoming. In the first instance, in continuity with what has been shown, the imagination implies an undoing of binary logic as applied to the self. Imagination, as the rendition of the self as the self's possibility, is the self's capacity to project an ideal after which a man or woman might aspire, toward which a person might progress. This ideal, however, gives expression to, and is in continuity with, the actual or real. The self, in fact, is this process of becoming between actual and ideal. We have diagrammed Judged William's account of the self in its becoming in Figure 2.

Here there is no opposition between actual and ideal—the actual is the basis of the ideal, though the ideal is not a mere repetition of the actual.[10] As Eldrod expresses it (though he is pushing toward Anti-Climacus's more developed account of the self): "The self is . . . a dialectical relationship in which the physical and psychical events of the synthesis are constituted as a synthesis by a positive third element, viz., spirit."[11] Spiritual or cultural existence, here, is not antithetical to the finite and natural aspect of the self but is precisely a living out of the self as a synthesis—binary opposition is undone. Thus a profound sympathy between Irigaray and Kierkegaard is in evidence since they share a conviction that the self is not constituted in a flight away from the natural and finite aspect of the self but is an imaginative living out of this reality in the cultural and infinite.

---

9. Kierkegaard, *The Sickness unto Death*, Part 1, 31.
10. For Kierkegaard, of course, there is never a *mere* repetition.
11. Elrod, *Being and Existence*, 39.

PART THREE—Between Irigaray and Kierkegaard

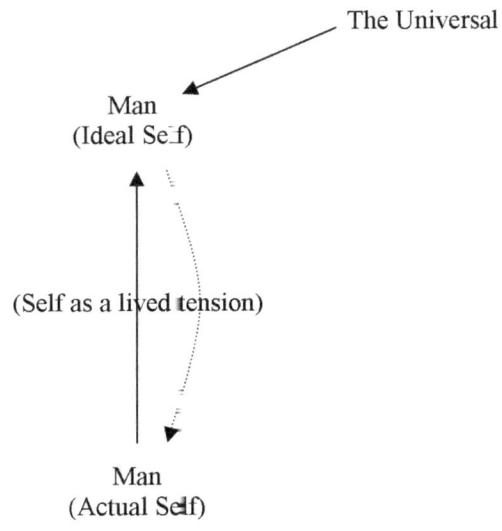

Figure 2. Judge William on human becoming

Judge William's account of the imagination points to a second important agreement between him and Irigaray inasmuch as this account implies that the identity of a particular self is not fixed—it can never be grasped. As Ferreira has compellingly argued, the Judge's ideal self should not be thought of as "a static presentation or 'image.'"[12] Imagination, rather, is a holding together of actual and ideal *in tension*—living imaginatively is a matter of dwelling in the paradoxical space of what is (of necessity) and what might be (of possibility), which is to say that the self cannot be pinned down or described in essentialist terms. To highlight the confluence between Judge William and Irigaray here, we point to the latter's insistence that the God of masculine religion is nothing more than the projection of a fixed ego-ideal after whom he aspires, and toward whom he progresses. And we recall that Irigaray does not consider this projection of a fixed ego-ideal benign. As Deutscher points out, Irigaray argues that man's relationship "to an idealized masculine-paternal God produces a fragile structure for masculine identity" and "provokes a compensatory displacement of devalued qualities onto the feminine."[13] As a result, over-

12. Ferreira, *Transforming Vision*, 62.
13. Deutscher, *Politics*, 93.

Sexual Difference

against the divine as a fixed ego-ideal, Irigaray sets an alternative vision of the divine, and one that finds certain resonance with the ideal self as conceived by Judge William.

Deutscher's summary of Irigaray's account of the divine gives a sense of this confluence:

> What if women had their own divine, a feminine divine? It should not occupy the same structural role as the masculine-paternal God. It should not be an ideal that is radically exterior to the individual, from which one is severed but with which one identifies. Irigaray probes the possibility of a relationship between the feminine and the divine where women and men might have a "perception of a divine that was not opposed to them, perhaps? That was not even distinct from them." Men would need an alternative relationship to divinity also. Irigaray has diagnosed as problematic the representation schism between man and God. For this reason men, like women, would need a new relationship to divinity as that with which they are interconnected, rather that that from which they are severed.[14]

These words echo Judge William's description of the ideal self, which he conceives as an *active picturing* of future possibilities, possibilities that owe something fundamental to the substance of the actual/given self. The ideal self is not, for the Judge or Irigaray, a fixed ego-ideal. Here we are free to apply Irigaray's description of the female divine—it is a horizon, some shadowy perception of achievement, toward which woman moves—to Judge William's ideal self.[15] Judge William's ideal is Irigaray's divine.

Before summarizing the argument of this section, we briefly attend to the ontological presuppositions that seem to govern Kierkegaard's account of the self, as articulated by Judge William. We ask, more specifically, whether Kierkegaard's view of the self implies a thoroughgoing anti-essentialism—whether it implies that the self simply is a "fluid" becoming detached from any essentialist presuppositions. On this question Richard Colledge reminds us that the pseudonymous writings invariably assume a "basic ontological structure of the human person: the—albeit minimalist and dynamic—'essence' or common factors involved in all human being; the definitively human *way of being*."[16] Thus, Judge William (together with Anti-Climacus) suggests that the human self is both soul

---

14. Ibid., 94. Here Deutscher quotes Irigaray, *Marine Lover*, 173.
15. Irigaray, "Divine Women," 63–64.
16. Colledge, "Kierkegaard's Subjective Ontology," 8.

and body, finite and infinite, temporal and eternal, and that becoming a self entails an imaginative embrace of the synthesis that the human person is (universally!). While this essentialist vision is not subject to straightforward explication, a fundamental ontological structure remains in place.

At the same time, however, Colledge points out that "Kierkegaard's universals *do not statically define the meaning of the individual's existence* but rather are general categories for organizing the individual's reflection upon its existence in all its unique richness; they provide a horizon within which this reflection may take place, without detailing what must lie within that horizon."[17] Thus Colledge refers to Kierkegaard's ontology as a subjective ontology, as an ontology that opens up space for the existing individual to both comprehend and live his or her life. Whether at the level of the given/actual self, or at the level of the ideal self, Kierkegaard does not offer a thick (essentialist) description of the identity of the self. Although Kierkegaard affirms that the human person is a particular, finite, physical being, a full or thick description of this given/actual self is not possible—rather, possibilities are necessarily left open. To describe the becoming of the self in terms of the projection of an ideal self, as Judge William does, is not to foreclose on possibilities but is to open up possibilities for becoming. Thus, while there is an essentialist ontology at the heart of Kierkegaard's description of the self, it is, as Colledge rightly suggests, a limited or thin essentialism that opens up space for the existing individual to pursue and comprehend his or her being and becoming.

In a parallel manner, Irigaray's thought, while essentialist in nature, is so in only a thin way. That is, while Irigaray requires that we conceive a fundamental difference between man and woman (thus locating the site of mystery ahead of time), this does not imply that the identity of man or woman can be finally or fully pinned down. We can say something about what it is to be man or woman, yet this "something" does not foreclose on the possibilities for becoming that are open and available to those who belong to each genre. Thus, while Irigaray herself insists that her later account of sexual difference is not essentialist in nature, there is nevertheless a "thin" essentialism at work in her later writings. The fact that man and woman take up particular subject positions depending on their difference/non-difference in relation to the mother, and that this relation of difference/non-difference is expressed in particular uses of language and particular approaches to intersubjectivity, does not imply that we have said everything, or much at all, about the identity of man and woman. When

17. Ibid. Italics added.

Sexual Difference

this account of the alternative subject positions of man and woman is considered against the backdrop of Irigaray's metaphysical realism, it becomes clear that, rather than foreclosing on possibilities for becoming, Irigaray's thought is intended to resist simplistic or full descriptions of the identity of man or woman.

Between Luce Irigaray and Judge William, then, there is a fundamental agreement on the nature of the human inasmuch as they share a universal, formal account of the self in its becoming.[18] The self for each is precisely an imaginative and lived tension between actual and ideal. The self is engaged in becoming as it accepts its given nature and, in accepting this given nature, lives in continuity with the natural/given in a cultural and spiritual existence. While the self cannot be understood or accounted for without reference to the finite, natural, and temporal aspect, to describe the self only with reference to these is not to describe the self. The self embraces and accepts its actual/given self and on the basis of this imaginatively progresses toward some future iteration of itself which owes to that nature but is not limited to it. The self takes itself on as a task, in freedom—the self is defined in/by becoming.

In the development of a Kierkegaardian theory or account of sexual difference we have made some progress. Yet a question that could derail the whole project must now be answered. Specifically, we must attend to the fact that Judge William conceives the human as *one*. We must attend to the fact that while Irigaray is able to provide a positive and constructive account of the difference between man and woman, the Judge's only explicit description of the difference between man and woman is mired in the patriarchal logic of the same. Thus, our consideration of the possibility of a Kierkegaardian theory of sexual difference now takes a further step— that of discerning whether and how Judge William's account of human becoming might be conceived as an account of the human *as two*.

JUDGE WILLIAM, HUMAN BECOMING, SEXUAL DIFFERENCE

Judge William and Luce Irigaray disagree on the fundamental question whether the human is one or two. Judge William, in fact, is implicated in the logic of the same, according to which woman is defined in terms of the needs and identity of man—more specifically, she is assimilated to

---

18. Irigaray herself would be most dissatisfied with our insistence that her thought allows us to describe human becoming in universal terms. Nevertheless, it is difficult to see how this is incompatible with her wider thought.

PART THREE—Between Irigaray and Kierkegaard

nature/finitude while he accedes to cultural existence and to infinitude. Notwithstanding this denial of sexual difference, however, and notwithstanding his elision of woman as subject, his account of human becoming does not itself require a denial of sexual difference and of woman as subject. His thought opens up beyond the limited and patriarchal vision of sexual difference that he articulates. In view of this, we turn to ask whether Irigaray's description of the human as two (her substantive account of the nature of the difference between man and woman) might be embraced within the terms of this generous reading of the Judge's vision of human becoming.

In our exposition of Irigaray's thought, two overlapping yet distinct descriptions of the difference between man and woman were offered. In the first instance she argues that the difference between man and woman owes to the difference (boy) or non-difference (girl) of a child in relation to the mother. In the second instance, she roots sexual difference in an ontological vision according to which the human is defined in terms of the fluid and bipolar nature of the cosmos itself. Neither of these conceptualizations makes an appearance in the writings of either Judge William or Søren Kierkegaard, yet we ask whether one or both might be embraced within the framework of human becoming developed by the Judge. First, concerning sexual difference as owing to the difference/non-difference of the child in relation to the mother, we recall Irigaray's observation that to be born a girl of a woman, someone belonging to the same gender, and with the ability to engender like her, or to be born a boy of a woman, someone of a different gender, and with whom subjective relations will be complex, notably because it will be impossible for him to engender as she does, entails a different structuring of subjectivity.[19] Irigaray suggests, then, that while biological and anatomical differences reflect the truth of sexual difference, they do not constitute sexual difference. As she puts it, biological and anatomical differences "lead to [other differences]: in constructing subjectivity, in connecting to the world, in relating."[20] Leaving aside the important question whether this account of the difference between man and woman sustains Irigaray's contention that sexual difference is both universal and primary and the question whether this account is finally defensible, we ask whether it can be embraced within Judge William's framework of human becoming.

19. Irigaray, "Towards a Sharing," 87.
20. Irigaray, *Why Different?* 96.

Sexual Difference

To answer this question we attend first to the Judge's conviction that self-choice is, in part, a matter of choosing oneself as a *social* being—a being in some sense defined by the relationships within which he or she is or has been implicated. Judge William speaks of this social dimension of the self in terms of a person's history, and argues that in his or her particular history a person "stands in relation to other individuals in the race and to the whole race, and this history contains painful things, and yet is the person he is only through this history. . . . He repents himself back into himself, back into the family, back into the race . . ."[21] Self-choice and repentance, here, entails acceptance of one's self and identity as necessarily bound up with one's relationships to other people—these relationships, to some extent, constitute him or her as *this* person. Importantly, we add, the Judge argues that to choose this social history (and to take it up into the higher concentricity of spiritual existence) relativizes it. These relationships define me as *this* person, but do not define me in such a way that I am unable to be other than I have been.

The question is whether Irigaray's description of the differing subject positions of boys/men and girls/women can be conceived as part of the social history that, according to Judge William, constitutes a person in *this* way, rather than *that*. If so, the embrace of one's social history would represent an acknowledgment of one's difference/non-difference in relation to the mother and an embrace of oneself as inhabiting a subject position that is fundamentally determined by this relationship of difference/non-difference.

Here we recall Irigaray's argument that these alternative subjectivities are ours unconsciously, apart from reflection, which is to say that a person is necessarily and immediately implicated in either a masculine or feminine subject position. We also recall, however, that for Irigaray we can become aware of and "embrace" this necessary and immediate aspect of our identity. Irigaray's insistence on the transparency of language differences between boys and girls, and on the transparency of their differing approaches to intersubjectivity, only confirms her conviction that we can become aware of the ways in which we are differently constituted as subjects. Indeed, her insistence that we must develop a culture of sexual difference builds on the twin assumptions (i) that sexual difference exists and (ii) that becoming aware of sexual difference represents the first step into a cultural or spiritual existence. With reference to the thought of

---

21. Kierkegaard, *Either/Or*, Part II, 216. We note that the language of "the race" gives voice to the Judge's implication in the logic of the universal, neuter subject.

PART THREE—Between Irigaray and Kierkegaard

Judge William, then, we might say that to repent oneself into history, and into the relationships that constitute oneself as *this* person, would be to embrace oneself as constituted by one's difference or non-difference in relation to the mother. To repent oneself back into the family, furthermore, would be to acknowledge all of the complexities this implies for language use and intersubjectivity (as articulated by Irigaray).

Both Judge William and Luce Irigaray, we note, assume that being/becoming a self entails the attainment of a vantage point from which a person can perceive and embrace what he or she was/is in immediacy. Further, they agree that in the attainment of this vantage point the significance of the given and immediate is relativized, so that one's social history is no longer determinative to the same degree. Expressed differently: While a person's social history determines his or her identity in important ways, cultural influences and personal intentions/decisions can mitigate the negative aspects of a person's social history. Thus Irigaray's conviction that a culture of sexual difference might become the basis upon which man's anti-natural and anti-woman mode of existence might be overcome. There is no reason to think that this conviction of Irigaray's cannot be embraced within a Kierkegaardian theory and ethics of sexual difference.

Moving beyond Irigaray's first account of sexual difference, we consider the Irigarayan view (put forward by Alison Stone) that sexual difference is rooted in the bipolar and fluid nature of the universe in which men and women live and have their respective Being. According to Irigaray's ontology, we recall, there are two fundamental rhythms or principles at work in the cosmos (or, which constitute the cosmos) and, correspondingly, two instances of the human. Each human person is shaped by one of the two rhythms that mark/define the cosmos and therefore also has a particular fluid constitution. Returning to Judge William, we recall that becoming a self requires an embrace of one's given nature—it entails living in the imaginative tension between actual and ideal. If we conceive of this given nature in terms of the twofold, rhythmic nature of the cosmos (in terms of Irigaray's metaphysical realism), then to choose the self is to embrace the rhythm in which one is necessarily and immediately implicated. In this framework, although there are myriad differences between human beings, sexual difference is fundamental and primary. Whatever other differences (in drives, inclinations, skills, relations) mark individuals, each person is first and necessarily determined by a particular rhythm and belongs to a particular genre. This implies, as above, that culture is also fundamentally two, since the ideal that is projected owes its content to the given/real. While the ideal is not merely the real, the ideal cannot be

Sexual Difference

conceived without reference to the real, which is twofold. A man is born a man and must become the man he is; a woman is born a woman and must become the woman she is.

There remain important differences that divide Luce Irigaray and Judge William. To take one example, while Irigaray refuses any account of "the universal" (since the universal represents a denial of the two, and of woman), Judge William places the universal at the heart of his ethical theory. Although Irigaray might appreciate the Judge's insistence that law lies upon, rather than being laid upon (the universal is conceived teleologically, as arising out of the human, rather than deontologically, as set over-against the human), she will not accept his insistence that the institutions of society give expression to the fullness of the human. Indeed, she will argue that the Judge's universals are constructed according to the logic of the same and entail an elision of woman's subjectivity. Notwithstanding the important differences between Luce Irigaray and Judge William, however, it is clear that basic features of Irigaray's theory of sexual difference cam be embraced within the context of his theory of human becoming. His account of the self in its becoming, in fact, can fairly be described as entailing the existence of a twofold nature/culture—that of man and that of woman. In concluding this section of the chapter, a summary description of a Kierkegaardian theory or account of sexual difference (as it has unfolded thus far) is offered.

A Kierkegaardian theory of sexual difference requires that a man or woman choose or embrace of his/her genre and particular subjectivity and rhythm. For example, since woman is necessarily and immediately implicated in a particular subject position, and is necessarily and immediately shaped by a particular rhythm, her becoming cannot be cut off either from this subject position or this rhythm—these represent the given/actual for her. Becoming a self (or spiritual being) for woman requires that she choose or embrace this particular subjectivity and this particular rhythm. Becoming a self, furthermore, requires that she live in an imaginative tension between this actual/given and the ideal that she projects in continuity with the actual. Thinking beyond the individual person it is evident that since a woman's given nature is shared with other women, her becoming cannot be cut off from that of other women. Or, at least, her becoming is in profound continuity with that of other women—the ideal or horizon toward which they move (recall, it is a shadowy horizon) is in some sense a shared horizon (in a way that woman does not share a common horizon with man), given that the real or actual from which they proceed is shared.

163

PART THREE—Between Irigaray and Kierkegaard

All of this applies also to man. In his becoming, however, he is irreducible to woman since he is shaped by a rhythm and subjectivity particular to him as man. Since he is irreducible to her in his actual/given self, he is also irreducible to her in his projection of an ideal self. Thus, our previous diagram of human being/becoming is amended to produce Figure 3.

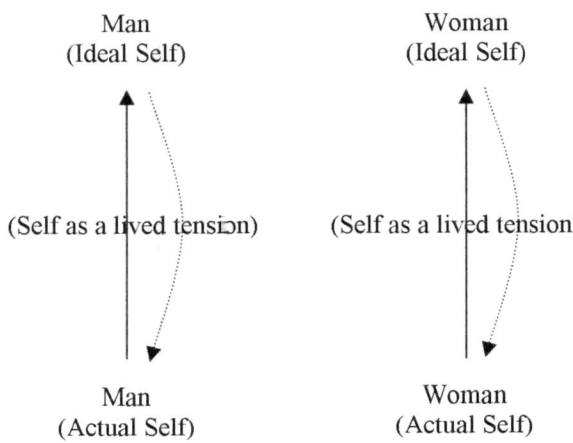

Figure 3. A Kierkegaardian theory of sexual difference

But perhaps this leaves us wishing for a more concrete description of what it means to be man or woman, for a fuller account of the implications of man and woman's respective subjectivities and rhythms for their becoming. The theory and ethics of sexual difference toward which we are working, however, requires precisely a refusal to answer these questions since we have offered only a "thin" account of what it means that man is man and that woman is woman, and since the account of intersubjectivity toward which we work is rooted in wonder—in a refusal to circumscribe or name or define the one who differs from me sexually. In fact, we do well to recall that Irigaray's ultimate defense of her theory of sexual difference is that it leads to more ethical and happy relations between man and woman (hers is at some level a eudaimonistic theory)—it undoes woman's elision as subject and undoes man's anti-natural mode of existence as these have been perpetuated under patriarchy.

Sexual Difference

CAVEATS—DIVINITY AND DIFFERENCE

In filling out our Kierkegaardian account of sexual difference we push beyond Judge William to engage with Kierkegaard himself, recalling that the Judge and Kierkegaard disagree on the nature of the divine and on the implications of the divine for ethical and religious existence. Notwithstanding these differences between Judge William and Kierkegaard, however, we have insisted that the Judge's account of human becoming (of the self as a lived and imaginative tension between actual and ideal) can be embraced within the context of Kierkegaard's *Works of Love*. More specifically, and most importantly, *Works of Love* requires that the ideal be conceived under the constraint and discipline of Jesus Christ as the prototype. The ideal self, as a feature of the Judge's theory of human becoming, is under the constraint and discipline of a theological framework in which Jesus Christ is the one who fulfills the law and embodies love; is the one in relation to whom men and women might become other, and more, than they are and have been.

In view of this challenge to Judge William's thought, it is important to augment the sketch of human becoming and sexual difference offered thus far since it is our intention to consider the relation and disjunction between Irigaray and *Kierkegaard* (and not merely between Irigaray and Judge William). We need not repeat every aspect of our earlier sketch here—rather, we come immediately to the point at which Judge William's account of human becoming requires augmentation, from the perspective of *Works of Love*.

In *Works of Love*, Kierkegaard insists that Jesus Christ came into the world "to become the prototype, to draw human beings to himself so that they might be like him and truly become his own . . ."[22] In view of this theological conviction, which is central to *Works of Love*, we augment our Kierkegaardian account of sexual difference by acknowledging that a man or woman's imaginative projection of an ideal must be informed or constrained by the one who is prototype and who would draw all men and women to himself. Notwithstanding important differences between human persons at the level of the actual (sexual difference and myriad other differences), and therefore also at the level of the ideal, to become a self in the full sense is to become *like Jesus Christ* and is to become *in rela-*

---

22. Kierkegaard, *Works of Love*, 264. Here it becomes apparent that Jesus Christ does not represent a merely abstract form of life after which we model ourselves— rather, in drawing the believer to himself Christ allows that the individual follower would be conformed to him.

PART THREE—Between Irigaray and Kierkegaard

tion to him. In view of the fact that Jesus Christ is the embodiment of love, and that it is Christ's intention to draw each person to himself, the becoming of the self (and the projection of the ideal self that this becoming requires) cannot be abstracted from engagement with the person of Jesus Christ. Here we offer a diagram (Figure 4) that incorporates this aspect of Kierkegaard's thought into our Kierkegaardian account of sexual difference:

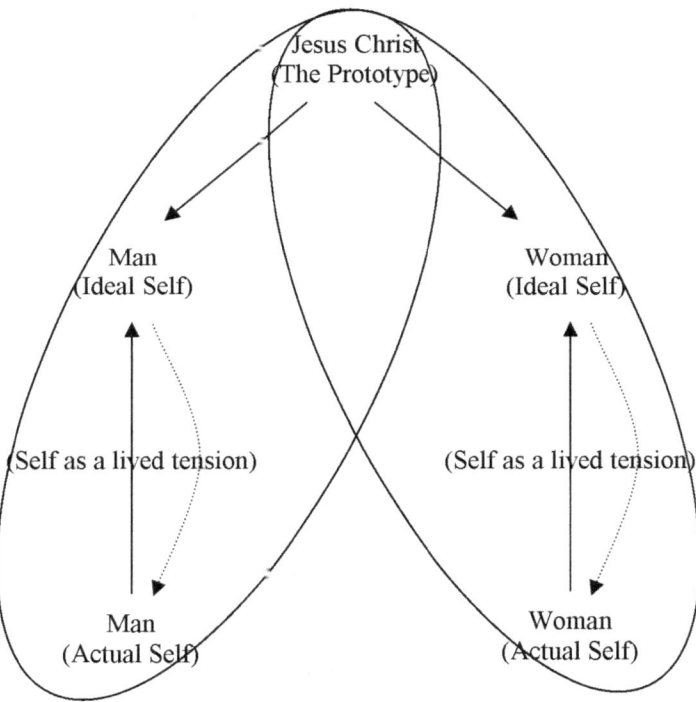

Figure 4. An augmented Kierkegaardian theory of sexual difference

This diagram makes it apparent that our Kierkegaardian account or theory of sexual difference requires that the ideal self is consistent with the actual/given (sexuate) self but also that the ideal self is informed or constrained by the identity of, and the relation to, Jesus Christ. That is, insistence on Christ as prototype does not undermine the significance of the actual/given for the self. In an important sense, a person can only be and become what he or she is—I cannot exercise or develop skills I do not possess, act upon inclinations that are not present to me, or embrace a (sexuate) nature that is not mine. At the same time, however, the projection of an ideal is not left to my own wisdom or the collective wisdom of my genre or culture. Rather, a man or woman, in becoming, owes fidelity to the prototype, who is also a person.

The question that arises is whether our insistence on Jesus Christ as the prototype undermines difference. Hasn't a third (middle) term been set up which undermines the sexuate nature of human persons—don't we end up, here, with a neuter, universal subject? In response to this question it should be acknowledged that insistence on Jesus Christ as prototype, and on God as the middle term, *does* undermine Irigaray's *thoroughgoing* account of sexual difference. According to Irigaray, the human is fundamentally two—there is a logic, a divinity, and a subjectivity corresponding to each. What Irigaray means is clarified by returning to her notion of wonder. In engagement with Descartes, Irigaray insists that the first of all the passions is wonder, and that the first locus of wonder is sexual difference. "To wonder at one who differs from me sexually is to recognize that I will never occupy her place and that she will never occupy mine, which is to say that the woman I encounter is forever new to me. I am perpetually surprised in this encounter, for she is different from what I knew or thought she would be."[23] Woman is essentially a mystery to man, and man to woman: "The other is moving within a horizon, and constructing a world, that lie beyond us."[24] Wonder, then, gives expression to Irigaray's insistence that the human is two—and it gives a sense of Irigaray's parallel insistence that there is a divinity, a logic, and a subjectivity that corresponds to each instance of the human. It is apparent that Irigaray's is a *thoroughgoing* account of difference.

Admittedly, there is something of a tension in our argument that Irigaray's is a "thoroughgoing" account of sexual difference, since her insistence on the irreducibility of the genres to each other does not imply that their respective worlds are utterly cut off from each other. Thus it is helpful to locate Irigaray on a continuum of possible accounts of sexual difference. On one extreme of this continuum would be *radical* sexual difference, where man and woman are constitutionally incapable of communication and of intersubjectivity. On the other extreme would be a *refusal of*

23. Irigaray, *Ethics*, 74.
24. Ibid., 7.

sexual difference, according to which man and woman are defined by their shared humanity, according to which their respective sexuate natures are irrelevant to their being and becoming. If Irigaray is appropriately located toward the radical end of this continuum, our Kierkegaardian account of sexual difference would be located somewhat toward the other end. While this way of characterizing their respective positions tells us little of substance regarding these accounts of difference, it nevertheless helps us realize that the language of "thoroughgoing" is not intended to definitively locate Irigaray on this continuum. Rather, our intent is simply to locate her account of difference in relation to our Kierkegaardian account. Thus, the term "thoroughgoing" is a relative one.

Coming back to the conversation between Irigaray and Kierkegaard, we recognize that Kierkegaard's insistence on Jesus Christ as the prototype, and on God as the middle term, requires a refusal of Irigaray's "thoroughgoing" account of sexual difference. Expressed differently, Irigaray herself would object that our Kierkegaardian account of sexual difference is not, finally, an account of sexual difference at all. According to our Kierkegaardian account, Jesus Christ is the prototype, which is to say that there is *one* standard that governs the becoming of both man and woman (recall Figure 4, above). Beyond this, there is also *one* person to whom both man and woman must relate in the process of becoming fully man and fully woman. Jesus Christ represents the fullness of the human in the sense that every human person (whether man or woman) can enter into the process of becoming fully human only by accepting him as the prototype and by entering into a meaningful relationship with him. Accordingly, there is necessarily a substantial "point of contact" between man and woman in becoming, a point that we can designate under the concept "the human" and which finds expression in Jesus Christ, the one who is the fulfillment of the human (by virtue of his fulfillment of the love command). Irigaray's construal of man and woman's irreducibility to each other, and her description of the ontological difference between man and woman, is undermined by Kierkegaard's insistence that those who actually practice works of love are able to do so only by being *in God*. Whichever language is used (that of *belonging to Christ*, or of *being in God*), a similar refusal of Irigaray's thoroughgoing account of sexual difference is implied.

This refusal of Irigaray's thoroughgoing account of difference can be clarified by pointing out that Kierkegaard's *Works of Love* requires the possibility of communication between man and woman concerning the one in whom the human is fulfilled, namely Jesus Christ. In raising this point we move onto the difficult terrain of Kierkegaard's theory of

Sexual Difference

communication and of his epistemological assumptions, yet it will be helpful to highlight Kierkegaard's conviction (expressed in and through *Works of Love*) that it is both possible and necessary to communicate something decisive concerning Jesus Christ, the one who fulfills the law and who gives full expression to love. Of course, to say that Kierkegaard assumes that all humans may share knowledge of Jesus Christ is not to suggest that objective knowledge of Jesus Christ is adequate for spiritual life or to suggest that direct communication concerning life in Christ is possible.[25] Nevertheless, Kierkegaard's *Works of Love* assumes the capacity of men and women to communicate with each other about the person and identity of Jesus Christ, and also concerning the love that is embodied in him and required of them.[26] We could add that the very existence of *Works of Love* as a text (a non-pseudonymous one, at that), and as a series of deliberations that would "awaken and provoke people and sharpen thought," implies that Kierkegaard embraces the possibility of meaningful communication concerning the ideal of love embodied in Jesus Christ.[27] This implies a profound discontinuity between Irigaray and Kierkegaard inasmuch as Irigaray will not allow that there is one prototype or that knowledge of such could be communicated between two. To suggest that man and woman share a world to the extent that they can communicate meaningfully concerning the identity of the prototype is, from her perspective, precisely to undermine difference.[28]

---

25. As C. Stephen Evans argues, commenting on Kierkegaard's *Postscript*: "The task of the believer . . . [is] to bear witness. He will proclaim, 'I believe that the God has appeared . . .' By proclaiming the news of God's appearance he may become the occasion for another person to encounter the God for himself. This witness, however, provides only the occasion; if the recipient of the communication does not receive the condition, which is faith, from the God himself, he does not and cannot believe." See his *Kierkegaard's "Fragments" and "Postscript,"* 109. We also should not neglect to mention the role of the Holy Spirit in bringing a person to a conviction that the Scriptures faithfully reveal Jesus Christ as the one in whom God's love is revealed and fulfilled. On this question see Frawley, "Essential Role," 93–104.

26. We may appropriately ascribe Climacus's view of the knowledge of Christianity to Kierkegaard in *Works of Love*. In describing the epistemologial framework assumed by Climacus in the *Postscript*, Evans says that "though he says one can understand what Christianity is without being a Christian, [Climacus] claims one cannot understand what it is to *be* a Christian without being one." See Evans, *Kierkegaard's "Fragments" and "Postscript,"* 100.

27. See Ferreira's discussion of the status of *Works of Love* as a deliberation in the form of a discourse. Ferreira, *Love's Grateful Striving*, 13–17.

28. We will say more, shortly, concerning the nature of their communication of this truth.

PART THREE—Between Irigaray and Kierkegaard

This disjunction between Irigaray and Kierkegaard does not, however, imply the impossibility of a Kierkegaardian theory of sexual difference. Indeed, Kierkegaard's insistence on Christ as the prototype and on God as the middle term does not imply a full or substantial denial of difference. This becomes evident when we recall that for Kierkegaard the love command is decidedly formal in nature—that is, the love command leaves open myriad possibilities for becoming. For example, Kierkegaard leaves open the question whether or not a person will marry and suggests that neighbor-love can come to expression both outside of the marital relationship and within it. This already implies that one's projection of an ideal self allows for some variability. While this leaving open of the question of marriage represents only a limited expression of openness toward new possibilities in human becoming, it is nevertheless emblematic of the wider openness implied in *Works of Love*. The love command—which finds expression in the faithfulness of the lover, in a willingness to serve others, in an intention to seek the other's own, and in the effort to build the other up in love—does not require a particular, substantive account of what it is to be a fulfilled human person. This account of love leaves (relatively) open the identity, life, and projects a person might imaginatively conceive.[29]

This does not imply, however, a disjunction between form and content—as if a formal love command has no bearing on the form of life a man or woman might imaginatively conceive. That is, we are not suggesting that *any* form of life, *any* imaginative projection of an ideal self, or *any* set of life projects can be embraced and pursued in conjunction with the love command of Christ. Rather, the love command is such that it represents a constraint on human becoming, and against any form of life, ideal self, or life project, that is in opposition to the vision of intersubjectivity implied

29. In his discussion of the relationship between neighbor love and marital love, Evans illuminates, though indirectly, the point we are making. He writes: "Individuals must attempt to work out what the obligation [to love the neighbor] means for them in the absence of algorithmic procedures." See his *Kierkegaard's Ethic of Love*, 207. Evans's point is that there is no straightforward or formulaic way in which the requirements of the love command can be brought to bear in particular circumstances—a degree of wisdom and imagination is required in bringing the love command to bear in a person's life and circumstances. This affirms the formal nature of the love command and points to the fact that the love command does not itself imply a one-size-fits-all form of life for man or woman. For Kierkegaard, the way in which the love command might find expression in particular circumstances cannot be pre-determined, and an obvious correlate of this realization is the fact that the love command can be brought to bear in a wide variety of circumstances. Thus we can insist, again, that the love command is not such that it requires us to adopt a particular substantive account of what the life and becoming of man or woman must look like.

Sexual Difference

in the love command. Thus, while the love command is formal in nature, it only leaves the process of human becoming *relatively* wide open—the love command will rule out certain ways of being, certain paths of becoming. Furthermore, it should be clarified that Kierkegaard's appeal to the love command does not imply that he conceives of the love command as the only constraint upon human becoming. While the love command of Jesus Christ is in some sense decisive for those who would live a truly human existence, Kierkegaard's deference to the apostolic word implies deference also to other scriptural arguments that might bear on the substantive nature of the self in its becoming.

Knowing the Neighbor

A consideration of the discourse "Love Believes All Things—and Yet is Never Deceived" (from *Works of Love*) will demonstrate a further confluence between Irigaray and Kierkegaard—particularly on the status of the other as a mystery. In this discourse, Kierkegaard argues that knowledge of the motivation and meaning of another person's actions or words is not available to us—that is, to hear a word or observe an action does not allow us to determine whether those words or actions are intended for, or motivated by, good or ill. For Kierkegaard, this inability to know leads to the realization that what matters is whether we will become a cynical person or a loving person. When the *cynical* person hears a word or observes an action, she chooses not to believe that it is rooted in love. Rather, on the basis of her awareness that there are many possible interpretations that could attach to this word or action, and out of an unwillingness to be deceived, the cynical person determines not to believe that love is present in the other. In language that Kierkegaard prefers, *she does not believe all things*. On the other hand, when the *loving* person hears a word or observes an action, she chooses to believe that it is rooted in love. She too realizes that there are many possible interpretations that could attach to this word or action, but chooses to believe that love is present in the other.[30] Again using language preferred by Kierkegaard, *she believes all things*. Kierkegaard adds: Since the greatest deception lies in the refusal to love, it is the cynical person who is deceived, rather than the loving person. Here

---

30. Thus, the loving person is not merely naïve. Rudd writes: "The lover differs from the naïve or inexperienced person in that he or she is fully aware of all the possible interpretations that could be placed on anyone's actions. Faced with this objective uncertainty, the lover chooses to believe . . ." See his "Believing All Things," 123.

PART THREE—Between Irigaray and Kierkegaard

the tables are turned, for the person who wished to protect herself against deception is deceived—and in the same moment s/he reveals her/himself to be unloving.

In the next chapter we will attend to some of the implications of this discourse for intersubjectivity between man and woman. Here, however, we consider the epistemological assumptions at play. For Kierkegaard, knowledge of the other is only ever a matter of possibilities: "As far as judging another person is concerned, knowledge at best leads to the equilibrium of the opposite possibilities..."[31] Or, as he puts it earlier: "Knowledge is the infinite art of equivocation, or infinite equivocation; at most it is simply a placing of opposite possibilities in equilibrium."[32] The person with knowledge is the person who hears a word or observes an action and understands that this word or action is open to a multitude of possible interpretations. For Kierkegaard, this implies that knowledge is at a remove from actuality, but since human life is lived in actuality, knowledge cannot be the decisive category for personal identity or for intersubjectivity.[33] The decisive factor for human being and intersubjectivity is, rather, decision—the decision whether to believe all things.[34] The decisive factor is whether a person will *love*. The importance of this theme for Kierkegaard cannot be denied, and as early as the first discourse of *Works of Love* we find him insisting that belief, rather than knowledge, is the decisive category when it comes to the question of love, to the question of intersubjectivity between persons.[35]

Kierkegaard's insistence that knowledge cannot be the decisive category for human identity and intersubjectivity owes, in part, to his insistence that each human being is created by God, and created in *distinctiveness*. Remaining with the discourse "Love Believes All Things," we note that Kierkegaard's deployment of an anonymous person's words demonstrates the link between human distinctiveness and the mystery that the neighbor represents.[36] The anonymous person writes: "How much that is hidden may still reside in a person, or how much may still reside hidden! How

31. Ibid., 233.

32. Ibid., 231.

33. As Kierkegaard puts it: "There is no decision in knowledge; the decision, the determination, and the firmness of personality are first in the 'ergo,' in belief." See ibid., 233.

34. Ibid.

35. Ibid., 16.

36. This person is, in effect, an unnamed pseudonym. See Rudd, "'Believing All Things,'" 132.

inventive is hidden inwardness in hiding itself and in deceiving or evading others, the hidden inwardness that preferred that no one would suspect its existence, modestly afraid of being seen and mortally afraid of being entirely disclosed. *Is it not so that the one person never completely understands the other?*"[37] Later in the same passage, Kierkegaard reveals the connection between the mystery of the other's being (the fact that the outer does not transparently reveal the inner) and their creation by God as a distinctive being since, following immediately on from his insistence that the superiority of the human consists in the distinctiveness that attaches to each person, he writes: "Indeed, if it were not so that one human being, honest, upright, respectable, God-fearing, can under the same circumstances do the very opposite of what another human being does who is also honest, upright, respectable, God-fearing, then the God-relationship would not essentially exist, would not exist in its deepest meaning. If we were able with unconditioned truth to judge every human being according to a universally given criterion, then the God relationship would be essentially abolished . . ."[38] Each person relates to God independently of the other, and the relationship of each person to God is not transparent to any other—it is essentially a secret, says Kierkegaard. Thus, any insistence that I know the other person, or am rightly judging the other person's intentions and motivations, represents a refusal of the (secret, inner) relationship to God. Again, this insistence on the secret, inner nature of the God-relationship translates into recognition that the outer does not transparently reveal the inner.[39] The other, to state it simply, in his or her being and becoming, is essentially a mystery to me.

In this vein, our Kierkegaardian theory of sexual difference can be developed and illuminated by turning briefly to Johannes Climacus and his *Concluding Unscientific Postscript to Philosophical Fragment*. There (specifically, in the short section entitled "Possible and Actual Theses by Lessing") Climacus offers a discussion of knowledge that runs parallel to the argument of Kierkegaard in "Love Believes All Things."[40] In the sec-

37. Ibid., 228–29. Italics added.
38. Ibid., 230.
39. However, the inner must manifest itself outwardly. Kierkegaard explores this complex dialectic in the first discourse of *Works of Love*, "Love's Hidden Life and Its Recognizability by Its Fruits."
40. In its own right, Climacus's *Postscript* offers a wealth of resources in the development of a possible Kierkegaardian account of human becoming in difference. We focus here, however, only on a point of overlap between *Postscript* and *Works of Love* and on the way in which *Postscript* thereby illuminates Kierkegaard's point in *Works of Love*.

ond of the four "possible and actual theses by Lessing," Climacus offers an answer to the question "What is the thinker's relation to the truth" and, in doing so, takes aim at what he refers to as "the positive."[41] He takes aim, more specifically, at those who are convinced that one can attain certainty and truth in the domain of the senses, of historical knowledge, or of speculative reflection. Climacus replies, rather pointedly: "Sensate certainty is a delusion (see Greek skepticism and the entire presentation in modern philosophy, from which a great deal can be learned); historical knowledge is an illusion (since it is approximation-knowledge); and speculative result is a phantom." Continuing on, a few lines later, he writes: "In historical knowledge, [the subject] comes to know much about the world, nothing about himself; he is continually moving in the sphere of approximation-knowledge, while with his presumed positivity he fancies himself to have a certainty that can be had only in infinitude, in which, however, he cannot be as an existing person but at which he is continually arriving. Nothing historical can become infinitely certain to me except this: that I exist."[42] Since certainty is only available from the perspective of the infinite, and since human existence is lived in a tension between the finite and infinite, Climacus concludes that certain knowledge is not available to existing human beings—or, rather, that the only certainty I have is my own subjectivity.[43] The search for certainty by way of sense perception, historical knowledge, or speculative thought (which Kierkegaard labels "the positive") represents a refusal of human existence—it is a flight away from the tension in which human life is inevitably lived.

In opposition to the positive (sense certainty, historical knowledge, and speculative thought) Climacus sees *negativity* operating at the heart of human subjectivity, a negativity which owes to the fact that a human person is a synthesis of the finite and the infinite, the temporal and the eternal, the physical and the spiritual: "The negativity that is in existence, or rather the negativity of the existing subject (which his thinking must render essentially in an adequate form), is grounded in the subject's synthesis, in his being an existing infinite spirit. The infinite and the eternal are the only certainty, but since it is in the subject, it is in existence, and

41. Westphal, *Becoming a Self*, 67.

42. Kierkegaard, *Postscript*, 81.

43. Regarding the self's certainty in its own subjectivity, Mehl writes: "This sounds like Descartes' cogito, but it is really more than consciousness; it is the self-constituting power of spirit. The inward relationship I can sustain to the content of my thought by decisively identifying with it, this I can know with certainty. This is my ethical actuality or myself from the subjective perspective."

Sexual Difference

the first expression for it is its illusiveness and the prodigious contradiction that the eternal becomes, that it comes into existence."[44] As Westphal argues, in focusing on the negative Climacus is not suggesting that nothingness defines human existence in the sense that death has the final word (though Climacus argues that the illusiveness of the infinite is that the possibility of death is present at every moment), since the positive has its place in Climacus's thought.[45] Westphal writes:

> Hegelian complacency requires that one never seriously consider the implications of the fact that the thinker is one who may die at any moment. The equal but opposite complacency of secular postmodernism resides in the confidence that death is the ultimate fact of life. But what if it is not? What if, as Climacus and Socrates suppose, this self, who will surely die, nevertheless has a destiny beyond death? What if our inability as existing selves to transcend the cave does not mean that there is no life in the sunshine toward which we are ordered?[46]

Human existence is marked by the negative in the sense that certainty, truth, and unity are not available to the human subject/person in time—life is a perpetual and lived tension between the finite and the infinite. Yet positivity shapes human existence to the extent that there is a goal of integration and certainty and truth toward which each person might move.[47]

In terms of our Kierkegaardian theory or account of sexual difference, what is most important is Climacus's conviction that the existing individual is perpetually in a process of becoming. Since life is a constant striving toward integration and certainty—a constant striving after the unity of the finite and infinite—existence must be described as a continual process of becoming. "That the existing subjective thinker is continually striving does not mean, however, that in a finite sense he has a goal toward which he is striving, where he would be finished when he reached it. No, he is striving infinitely, is continually in the process of becoming,

---

44. Ibid., 82.

45. Ibid. The reality of death, that is, points to the tension in which life is constituted, to the truth that the perspective and life of infinity is finally beyond our grasp in temporal existence.

46. Westphal, *Becoming a Self*, 68.

47. Peter Mehl objects that Climacus mistakenly (contrary to his own epistemological assumptions) assumes that the self is transparent to itself, and therefore aspires to a degree of certainty that he otherwise rightly dismisses as impossible to attain. For this important engagement with Climacus, see Mehl's *Thinking through Kierkegaard*, 41–77.

something that is safeguarded by his being just as negative as positive. ... The process of becoming is the thinker's very existence, from which he can indeed thoughtlessly abstract and become objective."[48] Elsewhere Climacus makes the same argument, pointedly: "What is existence? It is that child who is begotten by the infinite and the finite, the eternal and the temporal, and is therefore continually striving."[49] The self as a synthesis of the finite and the infinite, the temporal and the eternal, and lives in a perpetual tension as it strives to unify existence yet remains perpetually unable to do so—perpetually unable to bring together the actual and the ideal in a comfortable or static relationship. The contrast between Johannes Climacus and Judge William is apparent. Climacus's insistence that life is a never-finished process flies in the face of the Judge's easy confidence that he has unified the temporal and the eternal, the natural and the cultural—it flies in the face of his easy confidence that his comfortable marital relationship is emblematic of the unity and integrity of his self. According to Climacus, again, "I can never fully get myself fully together but must always be striving to unify."[50]

We have drawn Climacus into the conversation because these reflections serve as an important point of contact between Judge William and Søren Kierkegaard and because they help in filling out the Kierkegaardian theory or account of sexual difference we are developing—specifically, on the profound gap that separates person from person. For Kierkegaard in *Works of Love*, human subjectivity and the God relationship are such that knowledge of the other person's inner life, intentions, and motivations are concealed from our sight. Climacus concurs with Kierkegaard's judgment and points out that certain knowledge, in any case, simply isn't available to those who live in the tension between the finite and the infinite. And Climacus contributes further to our Kierkegaardian theory of sexual difference (and the account of human subjectivity it implies) when he reminds us that human life is a constant striving—a realization that contributes to a

---

48. Kierkegaard, *Postscript*, 90. Later in *Postscript*, Climacus puts it thus: "It is not forgotten that the subject is existing, and that existing is a becoming, and that truth as the identity of thought and being is therefore a chimera of abstraction and truly only a longing of creation, not because truth is not an identity, but because the knower is an existing person, and thus truth cannot be an identity for him as long as he exists." (Ibid., 196.)

49. Ibid., 92.

50. Mehl, *Thinking through Kierkegaard*, 43.

Sexual Difference

conclusion that full or decisive knowledge of the other isn't available since the other can never be identified or pinned down in one moment.[51]

The gap between persons, to summarize, is an existential, epistemological, God-defined, gap. In terms of our Kierkegaardian theory or account of sexual difference, then, as in Irigaray's own theory of difference, the other is, in a profound sense, at a remove from me. The other person relates secretly to the divine; she lives in a creative and imaginative tension between actual and ideal; she is in perpetual process of becoming and striving; and she relates to (and is under the discipline of) Jesus Christ the prototype in becoming a self. This cumulative account entails the conclusion that the other is, by definition, a mystery to me.

In working toward a conclusion to this chapter, we must acknowledge again that Kierkegaard and Climacus are not preoccupied with the twofold becoming of the human but with the individual in his becoming. That is, Kierkegaard's preoccupation is with the mystery and difference that lies at the heart of human subjectivity—and not with the mystery of sexual difference. Here, then, we come up against an issue raised above, when we highlighted Penelope Deutscher's question whether the primary locus of difference is human subjectivity itself (as Deutscher would have it) or between man and woman in sexuate difference. With respect to Irigaray's thought, it was observed that there is an insistence both on the difference that lies at the heart of the human but also on sexual difference as the first difference in the human. Thus we found Irigaray acknowledging: "Of course, no one can be reduced to anyone else, but the most fundamental locus of irreducibility is between man and woman."[52] In the becoming of the human, and in the formation of a genuine human culture, according to Irigaray, the starting point must be an acknowledgment that there are two instances of the human and that each is irreducible to the other. To begin elsewhere than with the twoness of the human, elsewhere than with sexual difference, will be to re-inscribe the logic of a singular, neuter, and universal subject—this subject, according to Irigaray, will inevitably be male.

To some extent, our Kierkegaardian theory of sexual differences comes down on the side of Deutscher, concluding that human mystery is

---

51. Earlier in "Possible/Actual Theses by Lessing," Climacus argues: "Wherever the subjective is of importance knowledge and appropriation is therefore the main point, communication is a work of art; it is double reflected, and its first form is the subtlety that the *subjective individuals must be held devoutly apart from one another and must not run coagulatingly together in objectivity*. This is objectivity's farewell to subjectivity." Kierkegaard, *Postscript*, 79.

52. Irigaray, *I Love to You*, 139.

PART THREE—Between Irigaray and Kierkegaard

defined first by the nature of human subjectivity rather than first by sexual difference. In order to push toward some alignment between Irigaray and Kierkegaard, however, we could consider whether Kierkegaard's notion of distinctiveness is broad enough to encompass sexual difference—in which case sexual difference, and the wonder implied by sexual difference, retains its force for human (inter)subjectivity. When Kierkegaard insists that within the species each individual is essentially different or distinctive, we can insist that sexual difference is a first and fundamental aspect of this difference and distinctiveness. Though the human is defined by variety, the first expression of this variety is sexual difference—and it could be argued that acknowledgment of sexual difference can become the acknowledgment of other differences in the human. Thus, while human subjectivity is such that there is an existential, epistemological, and God-defined gap between any two persons, the gap between man and woman must also take into account the reality and nature of sexual difference.

SUMMARY—WOMAN BECOMING

In coming to a conclusion, then, and in order to give some clear statement of our Kierkegaardian theory of sexual difference, we offer again a sketch of the becoming of woman. Woman, within our revised theory of sexual difference, is necessarily and immediately implicated in a particular subject position and is necessarily and immediately shaped by one of the two rhythms that define the human. These represent the given/actual for her. This is not to deny that there are other differences that set her apart from both other women and other men, yet her being and becoming is determined, in a fundamental sense, by her implication in, and embrace of, her particular subjectivity and rhythm. Becoming a self, furthermore, requires that she live in an imaginative tension between the actual self and the ideal self that she projects in continuity with the actual (which includes, decisively, her sexuate identity). To refuse the actual is to fail to be and become a self or subject—it is to fail in the task of becoming human, and of becoming the woman she is, and is to fall into the despair of infinitude. Beyond a woman's individual becoming, we should acknowledge that since her given/actual nature is shared with other women her becoming cannot be cut off from that of other women. Or, at least, that her becoming is in profound continuity with that of other women—the ideal or horizon toward which they move is in some sense a shared horizon (in a way that woman does not share a common horizon with man), given that the real or actual from which they proceed is shared.

Sexual Difference

But our description of woman's being and becoming is only complete when we attend to the reality of her indebtedness to God and to the reality of Jesus Christ—the one who is prototype and who would draw her to himself. That Jesus Christ is the source and embodiment of the love command does not entail a denial of woman's identity as woman—no, her being as woman remains the basis of her projection of an ideal in becoming who she is and will be. At the same time, however, her imaginative becoming between actual and ideal is constrained by the person and command of Christ. In her becoming woman owes fidelity to the love command of Christ, even if the precise implications of the love command for her becoming cannot be defined ahead of time. According to the ethical vision articulated within *Works of Love* as a whole, Christ's command is brought to bear in a woman's life. It is a command to love the neighbor, to love the self, to believe all things, to respect the distinctiveness of the other, to seek the interest of the other, to remain faithful in love, to praise love by loving others, etc. This is not to say that teleology is without place in woman's becoming, since the love command actually gives expression to the fullness of human life—the command gives voice to the *telos* of human existence in Love, in God. As Evans suggests, "we do not have to think that the commands God makes are divorced from our human need to actualize our true selves, for what God asks of us is precisely to become the self that he intends us to become."[53] Woman becomes the woman she is, here, in faithfulness to her given/actual identity as woman, and also in faithfulness to the form of life embodied in the one who fulfilled and fulfills human existence.

Our Kierkegaardian theory of sexual difference, then, cannot abide Irigaray's insistence on a fundamental, ontological difference between man and woman—cannot abide the capital "B" in her account of the Being of man and the Being of woman. Again, the difference between Irigaray and our Kierkegaardian theory of sexual difference can only be articulated loosely, or imperfectly, yet on the question of the divine and of Christ as prototype their opposition to each other's thought becomes more than apparent. However, this difference between Irigaray and Kierkegaard is not a decisive stumbling block in fulfilling the task we have set ourselves,

---

53. Evans, *Kierkegaard's Ethic of Love*, 21. As a whole, we should point out, Evans's work explores the question and implications of the unity of the teleological (ethical) and the deontological (moral) in Kierkegaard's *Works of Love*. For two other possible answers to the question of the relationship between ethics (teleology) and morality (deontology) see O'Donovan, *Resurrection and Moral Order*, 121–39 and Ricoeur, *Oneself as Another*, 140–296.

PART THREE—Between Irigaray and Kierkegaard

for we have demonstrated a sufficient confluence between Irigaray and Kierkegaard to proceed now to the development of a Kierkegaardian *ethics* of sexual difference. The possibility of such an ethics is rooted in their shared conviction that being and becoming a self entails living between actual and ideal, that becoming a self is a never-closed process, and that the other person in his or her becoming is fundamentally a mystery to me. Furthermore, although there are myriad differences in the human, sexual difference remains the first, and a definitive, difference in the human from the perspective of our Kierkegaardian theory of sexual difference—the becoming of the human is a becoming as two.

6

Intersubjectivity

> All love is tinged with the anthropophagic urge. All lovers want to smother, extirpate and cleanse the vexing, the irritating alterity that separates them from the beloved; separation from the beloved is the lover's most gruesome fear, and many a lover would go to any lengths to stave off the spectre of leave-taking once for all. What better way to reach that goal than making the beloved an undetachable part of the lover? Wherever I go, you go; whatever I do, you do; whatever I accept, you accept; whatever I resent, you resent. If you are not and cannot be my Siamese twin, be my clone!
>
> —Zygmunt Bauman, *Liquid Love*

What does/should the relationship between woman and man, respecting their difference, look like? This is the question that has been in the back of our minds (sometimes at the fore, also) as we have worked our way through the writings of Irigaray and Kierkegaard and have begun to stage a conversation between them. From the outset, in fact, the proffering of a *theological* answer to this question has been our goal. As is apparent, such a theological ethics of sexual difference can neither be pulled from thin air nor established as an act of sheer will—thus, we have laid the foundation for a theological and Kierkegaardian ethics of sexual difference by developing a tentative Kierkegaardian *theory* of sexual difference.

In what follows we will push the conversation between Irigaray and Kierkegaard one step further—reprising as little as possible what has been

PART THREE—Between Irigaray and Kierkegaard

defended, argued, and concluded above. In these final two chapters we will simply sketch out a Kierkegaardian ethics of sexual difference. In terms of the cumulative diagram developed through the previous chapters, the discussion in these chapters focus on the encounter and interaction of man and woman in difference.[1] What follows, in fact, nothing less than an exposition of Figure 6.

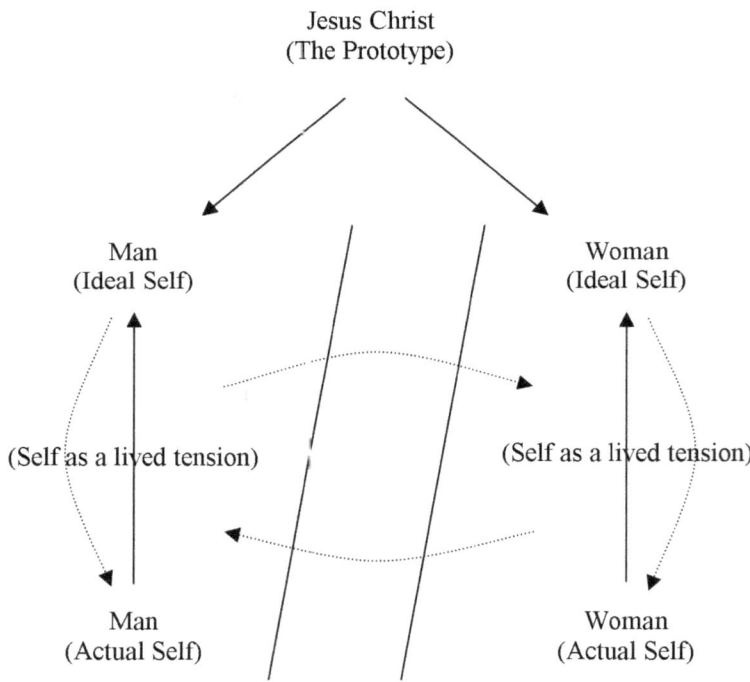

Figure 5. A Kierkegaardian ethics of sexual difference

---

1. Here we have left out the ovals which, in an earlier diagram, gave expression to the union of man and woman, respectively, with Jesus Christ (thus signifying that Christ is not only the prototype but also the one who would draw all people to himself)—they are left out only because they clutter the diagram at this point.

DISTINCTIVENESS AND SEXUAL DIFFERENCE

According to Kierkegaard, love entails a refusal to look out for one's own best interest—love, rather, requires loving the other's own, which is a requirement to love the other in his or her *distinctiveness*. Each human person is created as a particular individual and, as a *distinctive* being, is secretly and personally related to God. To have distinctiveness (to acknowledge one's own distinctiveness) is simultaneously to believe in the distinctiveness of everyone else, "because distinctiveness is not mine but is God's gift by which he gives being to me, and he indeed gives to all, gives being to all."[2] We have argued that distinctiveness should not be construed only in terms of the individual's particular and secret relationship to God but in terms of a person's sensate-psychical particularity. Indeed, in view of Judge William's account of human becoming and self-choice, it is difficult to conceive how the actual/given could not be a part of a person's distinctiveness since a person's skills, inclinations, desires, and physiological makeup are fundamental to his or her being and becoming. Here Andic's words are illuminating: "[W]e should love each human being as he or she actually is, and may authentically become as an ethical subject before God, boundlessly different and irreplaceable and valuable."[3] Love of the other is therefore love of the distinctiveness that marks him or her in every dimension of his or her being.

The question to be asked is whether a confluence exists between Irigaray's account of sexual difference and Kierkegaard's notion of distinctiveness. Already we have seen that a Kierkegaardian *theory* of sexual difference allows for an embrace of Irigaray's account of the twoness of the human. Yet we push further, here, to ask concerning Kierkegaard's *ethical* vision. We are asking whether sexuate identity (or, sexual difference) can be construed as a fundamental aspect of the neighbor's distinctiveness, which we are to acknowledge and affirm. To this question a simple answer of "yes" is offered. Since the natural and given (the sensate-psychical) is an aspect of a person's distinctiveness, since sexual difference is an aspect of the natural and given, and since one's spiritual being is bound up with the natural and given, then sexual difference is vital to a person's distinctiveness. As a result, to love the other's own is to love the other in her sexuate identity—it is to encourage and support her in the process of becoming

---

2. Kierkegaard, *Works of Love*, 271.
3. Andic, "Love of Neighbor," 119.

between an actual and ideal that is irreducible to my own, and which I cannot fully comprehend.

Here it is helpful to recall the two examples Kierkegaard gives of those who fail to love the other's own—who fail to love the other in his or her distinctiveness. On the one hand, there is the rigid and domineering person who "lacks flexibility, lacks the pliability to comprehend others; he demands his own from everyone, wants everyone to be transformed in his image, to be trimmed according to his pattern for human beings."[4] Kierkegaard suggests that "if the rigid and domineering person cannot ever create, he wants at least to transform—that is, he seeks his own so that wherever he points he can say: See, it is my image, it is my idea, it is my will."[5] On the other hand, there is the small-minded person, who has never had the courage to become a distinct self before God. This person does not believe in his own distinctiveness and so cannot believe in the distinctiveness of the neighbor. In either case—that of the domineering person or the small-minded person—the result is the same. The distinctiveness or particularity of the neighbor is diminished or denied.

Here a further confluence between Irigaray and Kierkegaard can be conceived on what an ethical intersubjectivity looks like (or better, perhaps, what it *does not* look like). Irigaray's ethics of sexual difference invites/commands man and woman to respect the distinct nature/culture represented in the other—this ethics implies resistance to any attempt to define the other in terms of oneself, to circumscribe the other, or to appropriate the other for oneself. One can almost hear Irigaray's voice when Kierkegaard describes the rigid and domineering person who "wants everyone to be transformed to his image, to be trimmed according to his pattern for human beings," or when he suggests that the small-minded person can only love his own specific shape and form. In the same way we can almost hear Kierkegaard's voice when Irigaray argues: "It is impossible in a way to describe who I am, who the other is—an energy makes it so that a subject, still living, is ungraspable and, moreover, changes all the time. If it is possible to contemplate a subject, it is not possible to represent (to oneself) who this subject is—the subject has already escaped from this fixed form, from this sort of naming what it is. Unless the subject accepts being taken, imprisoned, annihilated there."[6] While Kierkegaard's intent (in his discussion of distinctiveness) is not to argue for our constitutional

---

4. Kierkegaard, *Works of Love*, 270.
5. Ibid.
6. Irigaray, *The Way of Love*, 84.

inability to know the other (though he argues this elsewhere), he and Irigaray share an awareness of our tendency to think we have full or decisive knowledge of the other—a tendency to circumscribe and name the other. They share an awareness of our constant tendency, as Kierkegaard puts it elsewhere, to substitute for the other "an imaginary idea of how we think or wish that this person should be."[7] Irigaray and Kierkegaard each insist, more positively, that an ethical intersubjectivity entails recognition of distinctiveness/difference—it entails support and encouragement for the other in his or her imaginative becoming between actual and ideal.

On the basis of Irigaray's account of the caress, we briefly extend this consideration of an overlap between the notions of difference and distinctiveness. Irigaray has argued that the caress represents "the lifting of all schemas by which the other is defined. Made graspable by this definition."[8] The caress, as an interruption of (inter)subjectivity as it has been lived, represents the possible emergence of an alternative (inter)subjectivity, in which the tendency to grasp and name and define is refused—it represents the possibility of an acknowledgment of the mystery and distinctiveness of the other. The caress, the erotic encounter, is a means by which the boundaries between man and woman are affirmed and their irreducibility to one another is preserved. The caress, further, invites each subject to abide by the outlines of the other and is the means by which a man or woman is provided with a sense of his or her own integrity and identity. It is evident that Kierkegaard's argument concerning distinctiveness is, at least metaphorically speaking, a commitment both to abide by the outlines of the other and to assist her as she embraces her own life and distinctiveness in relation to Jesus Christ, the prototype—thus, his affirmation of distinctiveness finds resonance in Irigaray's account of the caress. But is there any reason that this must be a merely metaphorical account of the caress? Is there any reason that a Kierkegaardian ethics of sexual difference should not embrace the caress as a means by which man and woman respect the other's being and becoming (both physically and spiritually[9]) and as that by which the other might find herself?[10]

---

7. Kierkegaard, *Works of Love*, 164.

8. Irigaray, *Ethics*, 186.

9. Recalling that Irigaray's sensible transcendental is at play in her account of the caress.

10. Russell insists that Kierkegaard is inattentive to human nature as embodied, but does not explore the ways in which his thought is open to human nature as physical and embodied. See her *Multiplicity and Internal Relationality*, 210.

PART THREE—Between Irigaray and Kierkegaard

While Kierkegaard does not explore in an extensive way the reality of human embodiment, and does not explore the nature of physical interaction between those who are in process of becoming, his account of the human opens toward an embrace of the human person as an embodied, physical being. Indeed, within our Kierkegaardian theory of sexual difference we have insisted that the sensate and psychical aspects of the human person are essential to the self in its becoming, which is to say that there is room for the caress within a Kierkegaardian ethics of sexual difference. Given the overlap we have conceived between Irigaray's logic of difference and Kierkegaard's logic of distinctiveness, love of the other's own (distinctiveness) can be conceived according to the logic of the caress. Along these lines, Irigaray's words find resonance within a Kierkegaardian ethics of sexual difference: "Bringing me back to life more intimately than any regenerative nourishment, the other's hands, these palms with which he approaches without going through me, gives me back the borders of my body."[11] The other's hands affirm my distinctiveness and the difference that persists between us. The other's hands affirm that though we find ourselves in relation to one another, my being and becoming are irreducible to that of the sexuate other. I receive myself from the other, through and in the caress.

Importantly, of course, Kierkegaard cannot abide Irigaray's insistence that the erotic encounter between man and woman, woman and man, is foundational to human (spiritual) fecundity since he will not elevate the erotic relationship above other relational encounters. For Kierkegaard, genuine fecundity owes to the dynamic relation between each person and God and owes to the expression of love in human relations generally. At the same time, however, it is evident that Kierkegaard makes room for romantic, preferential relationships within his account of an ethical intersubjectivity between persons (though such relationships are under the discipline of neighbor-love). But this means that the romantic, preferential relationship is allowed to stand, which implies that the caress (the erotic encounter) might become a means by which the other's distinctiveness in becoming is both acknowledged and affirmed.[12] The caress might become an expression of neighbor-love. In a Kierkegaardian ethics of sexual difference, the caress is not a gesture that claims the other as my own pos-

11. Irigaray, *Ethics*, 187.

12. An expanded account of the caress (toward which Irigaray's own thought pushes) could be developed in which the "erotic" is either displaced or significantly redefined so that in various relationships touch becomes a means of both acknowledging the other and of receiving oneself.

session, as mine to grasp—rather, it acknowledges the other's mystery and subjectivity and gives her back (or acknowledges) the boundaries of her self. Woman is a distinctive being (at the level of the natural and cultural, the physical and spiritual, and the finite and infinite) and the caress gives voice to this truth. Through the caress I acknowledge the boundary of her being—a boundary at once physical and spiritual—and remind her of the locus (and independence) of her own becoming in relation to God. She might offer me the same gift as she reminds me of my own distinctiveness and reminds me that I am not "nothing."

Coming back momentarily to Kierkegaard's insistence on the *equality* of human beings—and to his concomitant insistence that we love the other in virtue of this equality—we ask concerning the relation between equality or universality on the one hand and distinctiveness or difference on the other. As above, Kierkegaard insists that every person is the neighbor since every person has been created by God and shares in the universal divine likeness. Kierkegaard writes: "The neighbor is the utterly unrecognizable dissimilarity between persons or is the eternal equality before God—the enemy, too, has this equality."[13] This insistence on the universal divine likeness, and on eternal equality before God, is the basis of Kierkegaard's conviction that there is not one person who can be excluded from the scope of our love. In view of this we ask concerning the relationship between the universal divine likeness and the insistence that we love the other in his or her difference and distinctiveness. Here, in fact, the parallel we have conceived between Irigaray and Judge William on the universal nature of the self (the self exists in imaginative process of becoming between actual and ideal) becomes important, since this universal account of the self points toward a logic of equality and universality. In this vein we recall Stone's suggestion that Irigaray holds to a theory of equality or universality, even if only an "equality in the ability to realize oneself culturally as a sexually specific being."[14]

Within Irigaray's thought, then, and within our Kierkegaardian ethics of sexual difference, equality/universality is affirmed, yet this equality/universality is considered inadequate for describing the fullness of human culture and intersubjectivity. Indeed, to remain only within the universal is to lapse into the despair of infinitude. As Kierkegaard might also have put it (in the context of his argument in *Two Ages*), to remain with the universal in describing the human is to engage in a process of leveling that

13. Ibid., 68.
14. Stone, "The Sex of Nature," 74.

PART THREE—Between Irigaray and Kierkegaard

fails to account for the individual in his or her subjectivity and distinctiveness.[15] Thus, for both Irigaray and Kierkegaard the equality of human beings must be held together with an insistence on the twoness of the human and on the freedom of man and woman to become (in their distinctiveness and difference). Equality cannot by itself become the basis for a development of human culture and spirituality—rather, equality, hand in hand with irreducible sexual difference/distinctiveness, represents the fullness of human life and culture. A man or woman is never merely a being in becoming between actual and ideal—he or she is *this* being in becoming. Distinctiveness is vital to him or her.

∾

We are by no means strangers.[16] *Years of a shared life form a thick and complex backdrop to our everyday conversations and encounters. Between us, the invitation to a caress is a summons to a privileged and private intimacy. And even if this invitation and encounter is marked by a degree of ambiguity or uncertainty, nevertheless a shared history of trust and care mean that the caress may be given, and received, in freedom. Risk remains, certainly—but who could or would mitigate every risk.*

This one I caress—open palms of my hands moving in arcs of intimacy—she is alive before me, a mystery pressed and pressing against my very being. Is it possible that this caress, this tenderness of touch, might be less about me and less about my desires than it is about her? Is it possible that this touching upon might be less a grasping after her (body) and more a simple

---

15. Kierkegaard, in *Two Ages*, writes: "Purely dialectically the relations are as follows, and let us think them through dialectically without considering any specific age. When individuals (each one individually) are essentially and passionately related to an idea and together are essentially related to the same idea, the relationship is optimal and normative. Individually the relation separates them (each one has himself for himself), and ideally it unites them. . . . Thus the individuals never come too close to each other in the herd sense, simply because they are united on the basis of an ideal distance." See Kierkegaard, *Two Ages*, 62–63, quoted in Westphal, "Kierkegaard's Sociology," 139. It is the capacity for, and reality of, the relation to the ideal that constitutes humans in equality, yet this equality does not give expression to the fullness of the human without reference to the passionate (subjective) relation each has to the idea(l). In substituting "Christ" for 'ideal," here, we are not far from our diagram of a Kierkegaardian ethics of sexual difference. For a helpful discussion, see Tuttle, *The Crowd is Untruth*.

16. In each of the three sections of this chapter, I have appended a first-person reflection on the theme of the particular section. The purpose of these reflections is to illuminate the ethics of sexual difference through listening to a first-person, masculine voice.

affirmation that she is beyond me—that she is becoming fully alive as the woman she is? I have known her these many years, but might this touching upon be a reminder that she is and will be more than I can know?

Ribs rise and fall beneath a hand gently placed—her hand, mine. She lives and breathes, alive beyond my knowing. She lives and breathes in a rhythm of body and spirit that is not mine.

She is alive in the Spirit. She is alive in the living Breath of the One who would draw all to himself in gentleness and service. Through Christ I am created and called—she is created and called.

Can this caress become a reminder for her, and for me, of the most intimate life she has in the Spirit? In this touching upon, am I able to fade imperceptibly into the background as she becomes the self she is?

LOVE OF SELF

Kierkegaard's exploration of distinctiveness takes place in the context of a consideration of the Apostle Paul's insistence, in 1 Corinthians 13:5, that love does not seek its own. Reflecting on these words, Kierkegaard writes: "*Love does not seek its own. The truly loving one does not love his own distinctiveness but, in contrast, loves every human being according to his distinctiveness; but 'his distinctiveness' is what for him is* **his own**; *that is, the loving one does not seek his own; quite the opposite, he loves what is the other's own*."[17] Since Kierkegaard insists that love of the other's own requires that a person not seek his or her own, the legitimacy of self-love seems to have been put in question here.[18] We are asking: What are the implications of Kierkegaard's suggestion that the truly loving one does not love his own distinctiveness?

Within Irigaray's theory and ethics of sexual difference, as observed, self-love is vital both for one's own becoming as man or woman and for an ethics of sexual difference. Indeed, unless the self can remain with itself, and can make a home with itself, the relationship to the other will inevitably become a relationship in which one of the two, man or woman (inevitably woman), is submitted to the logic and intention of the other. Unless a person becomes capable of self-affection, he or she will not become free to encounter the other in a way that respects the other's sexuate difference

---

17. Kierkegaard, *Works of Love*, 269. Bold and italics in the original. Underline added. Kierkegaard will go so far as to say that the life of one who loves is "squandered on existence, on the existence of others." See *Works of Love*, 279.

18. Ferreira, *Love's Grateful Striving*, 153.

PART THREE—Between Irigaray and Kierkegaard

and becoming. Irigaray writes: "Without a return into oneself, how still to approach the other? To respect the other in their mystery? As invisibility to be sure, but also as proximity with oneself which needs distance in order to touch oneself again, to find oneself again, to restore the integrity of intimacy with oneself."[19] In terms of our diagram of Irigaray's account of intersubjectivity, self-love is bound up with the vertical dimension of the diagram since a person's love of self is bound up with the spiritualization of his or her nature, is bound up with the relation to genre (those who share his or her given nature), and is bound up with an embrace of his or her distinctiveness (see Figure 6).

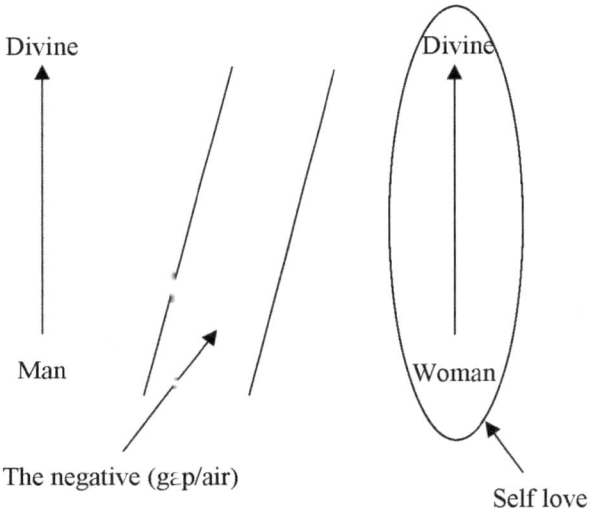

Figure 6. Self love in Irigaray

The prominence of self-love in the Irigarayan framework raises the question whether self-love can find a place within a Kierkegaardian ethics of sexual difference, whether (contrary to Kierkegaard's explicit statements) it is legitimate for a person to love and embrace his or her own distinctiveness.

Notwithstanding his insistence that the truly loving one does not love his own (distinctiveness), we have noted that Kierkegaard gives place

19. Irigaray, *The Way of Love*, 150.

to the notion and reality of self-love elsewhere in *Works of Love*. Commenting on the love command of Jesus in Matthew 22:39, Kierkegaard points out that if the love command had excluded the phrase *as yourself*, and was simply rendered "You shall love your neighbor," then the question of self-love would have been held in abeyance. As it stands, however, the love command includes the *as yourself*—thus it both presupposes self-love and seeks to root out the selfishness in our self-love. Kierkegaard's intention, then, is not to dismiss self-love as illegitimate for those who would follow the love command of Christ but to discipline self-love.

In applying this account of self-love to the question of distinctiveness, it becomes evident that Kierkegaard's insistence on "love for the other's own" is intended to overcome our preoccupation with our own distinctiveness. According to Kierkegaard, our problem as human beings is not that we demonstrate an inadequate level of self-concern but that we tend to live out the attitudes of the small-minded or the domineering person. Invariably we refuse the distinctiveness of the other, just as we invariably love ourselves more than we love others. Either we are inadequately confident in our own distinctiveness (inadequate self-love) or are consumed with our own distinctiveness (exaggerated self-love)—in either case the distinctiveness of the other comes to us as a threat. But this is precisely to say that proper self-love is consistent with, and necessary for, an acknowledgment of the other's distinctiveness. Without an appropriate sense of myself in relation to the God who creates me as a particular being and individual, I become incapable of honoring the distinctiveness of the sexuate other.

Returning to Kierkegaard's consideration of those who do not manifest love of self, we note his argument: "Whoever has any knowledge of people will certainly admit that just as he has often wished to be able to move them to relinquish self-love, he has also had to wish that it were possible to teach them to love themselves."[20] Kierkegaard goes on to give examples of those in whom self-love needs to find expression. "When the bustler wastes his time and powers in the service of futile, inconsequential pursuits, is this not because he has not learned to love himself? When the light-minded person throws himself almost like a nonentity into the folly of the moment and makes nothing of it, is this not because he does not know how to love himself rightly? . . . When someone self-tormentingly thinks to do God a service by torturing himself, what is his sin except

---

20. Kierkegaard, *Works of Love*, 23.

not willing to love himself in the right way?"[21] Kierkegaard, then, would rein in a self-love that is rooted in selfishness and self-preoccupation, but would encourage a self-love that corresponds with one's status as a creature of Love (of God's love)—one's status, in fact, as a distinctive being.[22] To lack such self-affection is to be less than human, is to be less than what God would have a man or woman be/become. Between Irigaray and Kierkegaard, there is profound agreement that self-love is a necessary dimension of an ethical intersubjectivity, and that alongside the recognition and affirmation of the other in his or her distinctiveness/difference must lie a concomitant recognition and affirmation of the myself in my distinctiveness/difference.

This agreement or alignment between Irigaray and Kierkegaard on self-love can be further illuminated by returning to Kierkegaard's argument that "the concept of the neighbor is actually a redoubling of your own self." For Kierkegaard, as shown, the notion of the neighbor as a redoubling of your own self implies that every person is a self in becoming decisively related to God—every person is a synthesis that relates itself to itself and is invited to rest transparently in God. Thus, *Works of Love* suggests self-love and neighbor love are together rooted in the fact that every human being is a self in relation to God. To love oneself is to recognize the self as gift and task given by God and is to live in a dynamic relationship with God—always acknowledging that the neighbor is a redoubling of oneself. For both Irigaray and Kierkegaard, it might be said, self-love is implicated in the vertical dimension of the intersubjective framework. Thus, self-love in our Kierkegaardian ethics of sexual difference is located or situated as in Figure 7.

---

21. Ibid.

22. Anti-Climacus's discussion of feminine and masculine despair in *The Sickness unto Death* is instructive here. As Walsh reminds us, Anti-Climacus suggests that woman's despair lies in not willing to be herself and therefore in not having any separate or independent self-identity. Man's despair on the other hand is unwarranted self-assertion. In terms of our discussion of self-love, woman loses herself in the object of her devotion (and thus lacks self-love) while man is implicated in a self-awareness and self-assertion that loses sight of God and other. As Walsh points out, however, this account of feminine and masculine despair is not required by Anti-Climacus' account of the self—it is culturally determined. Which is to say that Anti-Climacus' account of feminine and masculine despair is an account of self-love as it has found expression (or not!) under the culture of patriarchy. See Walsh, "On 'Feminine' and 'Masculine,'" 203–16.

Intersubjectivity

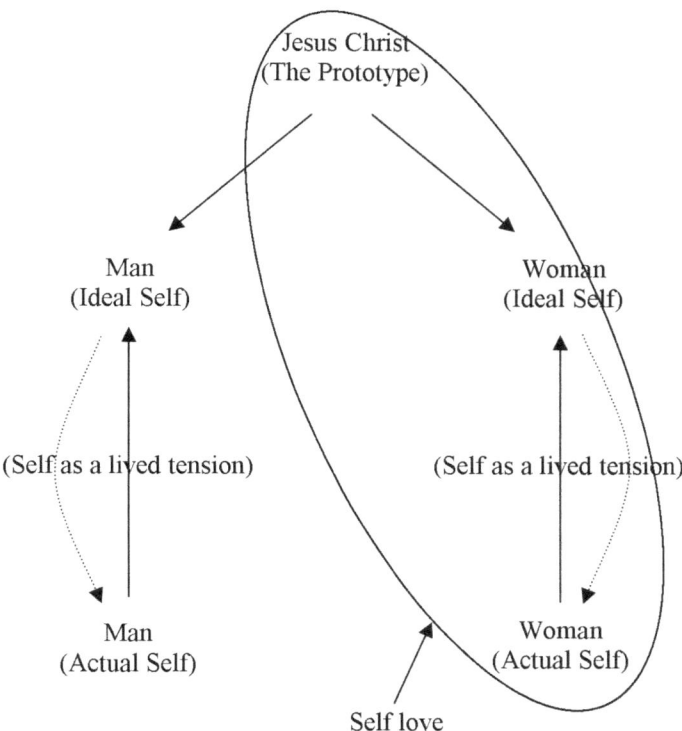

Figure 7. Self love in a Kierkegaardian ethics of sexual difference

The oval that previously represented union with Christ (see Figure 4), here has come to represent self-love, which is simply a reminder that self love is bound up with the vertical—with one's relation to the divine. For both Irigaray and Kierkegaard, and thus for a Kierkegaardian ethics of sexual difference, love of self is a necessary feature of the self and thus of an ethical intersubjectivity. One cannot become fully human—one cannot become man or woman—or relate to the other in love, without loving oneself.

To extend this discussion somewhat, it is helpful to recall Irigaray's argument that, within the culture of the same, self-love on the part of man and woman has been impossible. Self-love for man has taken the form of

PART THREE—Between Irigaray and Kierkegaard

nostalgia for the maternal-feminine that has been forever lost, a nostalgia that Whitford defines in terms of the concomitant denial/refusal of woman's subjectivity: "Everyone is born into dereliction through the loss of their original home but men palliate the loss at woman's expense. One will always find in this imaginary a nostalgia for the original home, an attempt to keep it for himself, own it and control it, in order to be able to return to it in phantasy . . ."[23] Man's self-love imprisons woman through his demand that she provide a home, dwelling, or space for himself. In terms of woman's self-love, on the other hand, we have observed that "woman is meant to assimilate love to herself as her preserve, without any return for her, without any love of her which might offer her access to a space-time of her own."[24] A whole history, as we have seen Irigaray argue, separates woman from love of self.

Given the confluence that has been traced between Irigaray and Kierkegaard, and keeping Irigaray's analysis of the failure of self-love in mind, a Kierkegaardian ethics of sexual difference will insist that man's love of self can no longer be built upon his need of woman to provide a home, a dwelling, or a space in which he might live. A Kierkegaardian framework requires a refusal of Judge William's comfortable dwelling at home with his wife—she who has an innate sense of time and nature, and who gives expression to this in her keeping of (his) home. His self-love must be his own.[25] Here again the question of self-control is pertinent since it will require self-control on the part of man to allow woman a self-love that is in service to her own becoming in relation to God (rather than in service to his own becoming).

For her part, we note, woman is also set free for self-love or self-affection, for she is conceived as free to love self without reference to man's presumed need of her. She may embrace her own existence and becoming, between actual and ideal, in relation to Jesus Christ, without reference to man's own expression and experience of self-love—she stands, again,

23. Whitford, *Luce Irigaray*, 153.

24. Irigaray, *Ethics*, 71.

25. This also means, to return to an earlier theme, that he must accept his own death, and not project death and darkness onto woman. It is worth repeating the following quotation from Canters and Jantzen: "It is indeed true that in giving birth to man, woman has also given him death, since death is the condition of all life. But man has been preoccupied with struggling against death, trying to overcome his mortality; and since he has identified woman with death he struggles also against her. But until he acknowledges both his origin and his mortality, he will be alienated from himself and unable to accept either his own subject position or that of woman." See Jantzen and Canters, *Forever Fluid*, 73.

independently in relation to God who gives her the gift of self and the task of becoming a self. This does not imply that God in Christ does not invite woman to "works of love" (and to works that are necessarily self-sacrificial in nature, since she too is invited to seek "the other's own") but this invitation and command to "works of love" is held in dialectical tension with the freedom she has to love herself in becoming (as is the case for man), the freedom she has to stand in her own right.

∽

To be alive in the world is, invariably, to find myself at a loss—to find myself displaced and exiled. And very often I have searched for a rescuer, for someone to palliate my experience of homelessness and exile. Too often, I have required her/woman to provide that sense of home and security and belonging.

I have put her in service of my self-love. I have defined her in terms of my need—someone to comfort, and caress, and provide, and nurture. But defining her in this way, putting her in service of my self-love in this way, has cut her off from her own becoming as woman and human. Who is she? I do not know. She is there, for me.

To set her free in her becoming requires that I confront and dwell with my own displacement and exile. This is not to cut myself off from the community of those who love and support me—but it is to acknowledge that a denial of her independent being and becoming is a denial of her and of the human. As long as she serves my self-love, and is not free in her own self-love, I deny the human that I am, too.

Where to root this self-love that would set me free, and would set her free, too? In the one who would draw all people (including me) to himself—the one who gives me being and to whom I am infinitely indebted. This Christ sets me free to become the one I am—in him I acknowledge who I am and have been, and become free to imagine new possibilities for who I might become. In him I find myself at home.

She and I may come close in greeting and encounter—might go so far as to make a home together—but she is never a home for me. Any such nostalgia must be relinquished, for her sake and mine. Our covenant-making must be ever dynamic, never final or settled. We are each in quest of the self, in relation to the one who draws us to himself—we will only ever be at home with him, and find our Life in him.

PART THREE—Between Irigaray and Kierkegaard

Sexual Difference and "Being in Relation"

The Kierkegaardian ethics of sexual difference developed in this chapter has placed particular emphasis on the vertical dimension of our cumulative relational diagram. The question that arises then, is whether these two will ever meet? Can a meaningful unity may be conceived between them? In attempting to answer this question we turn first to Irigaray, recalling that while she insists that man and woman are set at a profound remove from each other, she also argues that the human can, in some sense, be described as a being-in-relation. That is, the human is defined not only by the two who are irreducible to each other but also by the *encounter* of these two in difference, an encounter that opens up toward a fecundity that cannot be fully anticipated or described.

According to Irigaray, while being-in-relation has generally been thought in terms of "a link of or between parts in the unity of a whole," sexual difference requires that being-in-relation be thought first in terms of the irreducibility of man and woman to each other and secondly in terms of intersubjectivity between man and woman.[26] Here Irigaray's discussion of the unity of the human (A+B=1) becomes pertinent, a unity she describes in the following terms: "The unity of the relation between two subjects is a creation, a work of the two elaborated starting from the attraction, the desire which pushes the one toward the other without the relation being then already conceived as a 'with the other.'"[27] She adds: "The first gesture, the instinctive gesture, wants rather the satisfaction which takes the other as an instrument of pleasure, or even an appropriation that reduces or cancels the two in one of the parts. Which abolishes the relation as human."[28] For Irigaray, then, there is an attraction between man and woman (a drive toward sharing) and this attraction is constitutive of the human, is constitutive of the becoming of man and woman. Yet this attraction must be set free from mere instinct and desire (animal nature) and from the human tendency to allow attraction to find in the other an object that would satisfy my own desire for pleasure (an instrumental relation to the other). It should in fact be noted that Irigaray conceives of her

---

26. Irigaray, *The Way of Love*, 90. We recall her insistence that the real is three—the real is man, woman, and the encounter between these.

27. Ibid., 78.

28. Ibid.

authorship, from *I Love to You* forward, in terms of an effort to spiritualize or cultivate the attraction between man and woman.[29]

It is important to emphasize that Irigaray conceives of the unity of man and woman not as a static, ontological unity, but as a dynamic unity in intersubjectivity—thus it is, as she says, "a creation, a work of the two." As with human indentity in general, this unity is not something that can be pinned down ahead of time or described with any great assurance. Rather, the relation that is a unity is also a dynamic reality. Otherwise put, the unity of man and woman comes to expression in an ethical intersubjectivity, an intersubjectivity in which the interval of difference is acknowledged. Irigaray gives expression to this account of dynamic unity when she writes:

> Because I love you absolutely, I, myself, am no longer absolute. Recognizing you gives me measure. Because you are, you impose limits upon me. I am whole, perhaps, but not the whole. And if I receive myself from you, I receive myself as me. We are no longer one. Contemplating each other, we do not lose either the night or the light. Each can leave to the other his or her own life: sun, moon, stars. Being faithful to you requires being faithful to me. Does existing not mean offering you an opportunity to become yourself?[30]

While Irigaray insists, here, that man and woman cannot be conceived as one, the "oneness" she refuses is a oneness that sees man and woman as parts of a whole. At the same time however, this quotation gives voice to her dynamic account of the unity of man and woman—her words are a representation or re-definition of the unity of man and woman. Unity is in the dynamic intersubjectivity of subjects irreducible to each other, subjects who contemplate each other, who leave each other to their respective lives, and yet who impose limits on each other and who receive themselves from each other. Thus, an ethical intersubjectivity—love—is itself the unity of the human, this unity is a never-consummated, never-accomplished reality. It is always, by definition, a work in progress.

When it comes to a fuller, more concrete description of what the unity of the relationship between man and woman might, eventually, look like, or what it might issue in, Irigaray provides (as we should expect) almost nothing substantive. This is because a meaningful encounter or meeting between man and woman is forever future for her, even if she provides the

---

29. Irigaray, *To Be Two*, 37.
30. Ibid., 15.

PART THREE—Between Irigaray and Kierkegaard

example of her own relationship to Renzo Imbeni as a possible example of an ethical encounter in difference.[31] As she says of the human as two: "[W]hat the ultimate unity will be, we cannot anticipate."[32] Yet where she comes closest to describing what the meeting between man and woman will look like, and what fecundity between them consists of, she will speak of the capacity of each to give the other what is necessary for becoming.[33] Even this capacity remains opaque, but it is first and foremost that the mystery of *the other might become a light for my own becoming*:

> From the other irradiates a truth which we can receive without its source being visible. That from which the other elaborates meaning remains a mystery for us but we can indirectly perceive something of it. Such an operation transforms the subject, enlightens the subject in a way that is both visible and invisible. The light that then reaches us illuminates the world otherwise, and discloses to us the particularity of our point of view. It says nothing in a way, pronounces no word but makes clear the limits of a horizon, a site of thinking, of existing, of Being. . . . It keeps alive the astonishment, the questioning, the movement of thinking and of saying.[34]

This is an encounter in which attention to the mystery of the other might illuminate my own becoming—primarily by reminding me of the particularity and partiality of my own perspectives and being.[35] The negative determines the nature and shape of the relation, and the nature and shape of the relation is such that it drives man and woman back to the negative. The unity of man and woman, in relation, comes to expression in the fact that man and woman provide each other with a sense of themselves. Returning to the language of the caress, the other gives me a sense of the boundaries of myself (recalling that the sensible transcendental is in play

---

31. See Irigaray, *I Love to You*.

32. Irigaray, *The Way of Love*, 135.

33. Ibid., 93.

34. Ibid., 164. Irigaray adds: "Silencing what we already know is often more useful in order to let the other appear, and light ourselves up through this entry into presence irreducible to our knowledge." (Ibid., 165.)

35. It is also, then, an encounter that is not subject to capture. Irigaray writes: "Fidelity to oneself and to the other requires abandoning the lure of an immediate fullness in order to obtain sometimes another one, the fruit of an encounter that it would be fitting to celebrate and remember without wanting it to be permanent or at the disposal of one person alone." (Ibid., 157.)

here), returns me to myself. This wholeness in becoming is a gift of the two, and it constitutes the unity of the human.

At the conclusion of the discourse "Love Is a Matter of Conscience," Kierkegaard takes up the question of intimacy or confidence between persons and argues that if they (for our purposes, a man and woman) are to confide completely in each other (a confiding which implies trust and secrecy), they must first have a confidential relationship with God. As he makes this argument, Kierkegaard anticipates the objection that the presence of a third within the relationship (God) implies that the relationship between two is not a confidential relationship at all. Kierkegaard responds: "When two people completely confide in each other, is this completely confiding in each other if they first, each one separately, confide in a third person? Yet this is necessary if they are to confide completely in each other, even if in each individual's confidentiality with God there remains the inexpressible that is precisely the sign that the relationship with God is the most intimate, the most confidential."[36] With these words Kierkegaard comes back again to the secrecy of the God relationship, which cannot be communicated to another person (it is "inexpressible")—indeed, the God relationship is the most confidential and the most intimate relationship. To be in a confidential relationship with God is to know, love, and trust the God who gives the gift of life, who gives the gift of Jesus Christ the prototype (who draws all people to himself in love), and who teaches a man or woman concerning their identity as beloved of God and loving in God.[37] It is on the basis of this insistence that the God relationship defines the person in his or her being and becoming that Kierkegaard concludes: "With whom does a person have his most intimate relationship, with whom can one have the most intimate relationship?—is it not with God."[38]

Kierkegaard continues the argument: "But then all confidentiality between human beings ultimately becomes only confidentiality about confidentiality." The relationship of confidentiality (of knowledge, love

---

36. Kierkegaard, *Works of Love*, 152.

37. We recall our discussion, from Chapter 3, of the human response to the God who creates and loves and forgives each human person. It is a response of obedience and adoration. We recall a portion of the opening prayer of *Works of Love*: "How could one speak properly about love if you were forgotten, you God of love, source of all love in heaven and on earth; you who spared nothing but in love gave everything; you who are love, so that one who loves is what he is only by being in you. . . . O Eternal Love, you who are everywhere present and never without witness where you are called upon, be not without witness in what will be said here about love or about works of love . . ." (Ibid., 5.)

38. Ibid., 152.

PART THREE—Between Irigaray and Kierkegaard

and trust) between persons is derived from, or built upon, the confidential relationship to God. Kierkegaard explains this further when he acknowledges, again, that this insistence on the priority and primacy of confidentiality with God can be perceived as setting a wedge between persons: "Yes, it is like a separation, and yet it is eternity's confidentiality that is placed between them. Many, many times two people have become happy in the relationship of confidentiality with each other, *but never has anyone loved out of a sincere faith except through the separation's positing confidentiality with God, which in turn is indeed God's assent to the lover's confidentiality.* Only then, when it is a matter of conscience, is love out of a pure heart and a sincere faith."[39] In continuity with what we have already found in *Works of Love*, Kierkegaard's conviction is that intersubjectivity between persons is predicated on a profound gap or interval that separates them from each other—in this instance the gap is defined by each person's confidentiality with God. And yet the existence of this gap is such that it makes room for the confidentiality of persons with each other. Martin Andic provides a good summary of Kierkegaard's argument:

> Kierkegaard writes that complete confidence among human beings requires that each must confide first and above all in God: it is "the confidence of the eternal that is placed between them. . . . [A] separation through confidence with God, which again is God's consent to the lovers' confidence." We now see that this means that, truly to open and promise themselves in love to one another, they must open and promise themselves in love to God, *for only by loving him first does one come to know who one is and what one promises.* As only the love of God "forms the heart" that each is to open and give, so only confidence with God makes people individuals that as equals in spirit before him can truly face and speak with one another as *I* and *you*, speaking meaningfully and truthfully with and not merely about one another, open to one another because they are each inwardly open to God.[40]

If a person is to open herself to another in love, she must know who she is in love—and this she learns from God who gives her life and being and who walks with her in the path of becoming. If a person is to promise

---

39. Ibid. Italics added. Kierkegaard's reference to a pure heart and a sincere faith owes, of course, to the passage of Scripture upon which the reflections in this discourse are based: "But the sum of the commandment is love out of a pure heart and out of a good conscience and out of a sincere faith," 1 Timothy 1:5.

40. Andic, "Confidence as a Work," 177. Italics added in first italicized phrase.

Intersubjectivity

herself in love to another, she must know what it is to promise and what it is that she promises—and this she learns from Jesus Christ, in whom the love command finds expression. For Kierkegaard it is precisely confidentiality with God that makes confidentiality between persons possible and actual. To live in confidence with God is to be set free to confide in others, and also to encourage them in confidence with God. Just as our love is ever rooted in the God who is love, so is our confidence with others ever rooted in the God who is confidence.[41]

As has been the case throughout this conversation between Irigaray and Kierkegaard, on the question of unity and encounter between man and woman (on the question of being-in-relation) there is both agreement and disagreement. The disagreement, as from the outset, revolves around theological convictions—specifically, Irigaray's refusal of Kierkegaard's conviction that God is the middle term in every relationship. For Irigaray, this insistence on God as the middle term represents the insertion of a third term which she is convinced will inevitably be defined according to masculine (though purportedly neutral/neuter) parameters. The agreement between them, however, lies in their shared insistence that the unity between man and woman is a dynamic unity—it is defined by the ongoing encounter and relationship between them. While man and woman participate in, or are defined, by a shared humanity, this is simply to say that they find fullness by relating to each other, rather than by relating to some other species or some other natural reality—in some sense they are "made for each other." Yet this shared humanity does not define their unity or the nature of their encounter, for this shared humanity is merely formal in nature and does not give expression to the fullness of the human person. Unity, then, is something perpetually to be achieved—it is a relation to be pursued and deepened over time in relation to both God and the neighbor.

Is there anything that we might build together—she and I? Does the word "unity" have any meaning for those who cannot be reduced to each other, who are different from each other, and between whom a profound gap has been conceived?

Yes, there is something we may build if we are prepared to accept that it will never be realized—that it will remain perpetually a work in progress. For if I am never a static being, and she is never a static being (if neither of us may be defined as this *or* that*), then what we build together will always*

---

41. Kierkegaard, *Works of Love*, 152.

have a transitory or impermanent nature. What she and I build together is, in fact, the relationship itself. Intersubjectivity in a different register.

Our unity is in our attraction to each other, our desire for each other. Not a desire reduced to mere animality, though neither must physical desire be excluded. Not a desire reduced to the production of our child(ren), though children may be received as a gift. But a unity expressed in an unwillingness to become without the other. Apophaticism of intersubjectivity. I do not know who she is, or what our unity will be, but I will not be without her.

Our unity is in the illumination we receive from each other. My desires, my intentions, my preoccupations, my actions are illuminated when set against the backdrop of her life and becoming. I am challenged and corrected, moved and molded, on the way to a life that is more or different than it has been. "I moved in her light to see the light."[42]

In this becoming, together, we are united in sending each other back to the one who would draw us to himself. We do not have ourselves apart from our resting transparently in the one who gives us ourselves. And so we send each other back to this place of rest—this source that nourishes, directs, and sustains us. What we build together is not final or firm, for we are never this or that. We send each other back to Christ that we may become who we are called to be.

---

42. O'Siadhail, "Beyond," 14.

7

Communication

> I hail you; I thank you; I ask you; I offer you; I praise you; I celebrate you; I bless you etc.... These words generally involve two persons, and the participation of two in a relation, in reciprocity. Here the secret vector would always be
> *Who are you?*
>
> —Luce Irigaray, *I Love to You*

Irigaray and Kierkegaard are each preoccupied with the question of communication and each develops an account of intersubjective communication that corresponds with their account of human identity and subjectivity. The final question that arises for our study, then, is whether we may conceive a confluence between Irigaray and Kierkegaard on communication between man and woman—that is, whether there is a particular account of communication that might correspond with a Kierkegaardian ethics of sexual difference as we have developed it. In turning to explore this question, we begin with Irigaray and then return to Kierkegaard (and to Climacus with him), continuing the conversation between them in each case.

Irigarayan Indirection

At the outset it is helpful to recall Irigaray's argument that communication in the Western tradition has largely been a matter of passing on a closed truth. Responding to this, Irigaray argues that communication should not be "a question of transmitting an envelope in which a meaning would exist—speaking in a somewhat authoritarian manner, or at least a pedagogical or hierarchical one—unless it intends to annul the two in a supposedly common third, in the neuter, expropriating in this way the relation. It is instead a question of calling for an exchange by making already heard something of what is proposed in sharing, a question of opening some possibility or possibilities to sharing."[1] Thus, Irigaray resists communication modeled on a master-student paradigm in which a known truth is passed from one to the other. To communicate "directly" in this way between persons, or to insist that such "direct" communication is appropriate to intersubjectivity between man and woman, is to assume that what is essential to man or woman can be reduced to a neutral language, in which case difference is elided. Positively, Irigaray is suggesting that communication should be defined as the carving out of a space of encounter between two, a space that is not subject to any closed truth.

> Thus, not an a priori communication in an already constituted or coded meaning. But the opening and demarcating of a territory that is still always virgin with respect to meaning, where approach is possible, or not, according to whether the signs are perceived by the one to whom they are addressed, and whether they can move him, or her, on the path toward self and toward the other, such a step leading back to a deeper or more blossomed level of Being.[2]

Communication is an encounter in mystery—an encounter in which man and woman are not reduced to a neutral or third logic and in which neither one is finally or fully disclosed to the other.[3]

In *I Love to You*, Irigaray extends this discussion by considering the various ways in which communication patterns would necessarily be transformed if the irreducibility of man and woman to each other, and the mystery of each to the other, were instantiated intersubjectively. In the context of her discussion of indirection in speech, for example, she highlights those words and phrases that are better at respecting two subjects who come together, words and phrases that therefore make possible an

---

1. Irigaray, *The Way of Love*, 103-4.
2. Ibid., 16.
3. None of this is to say that Irigaray denies that direct communication about scientific or objective truth is possible. It is to say, however, that such an approach to language and communication should be restricted to its appropriate sphere.

encounter in difference: "I hail you; I praise you; I thank you; I celebrate you; I ask you; I bless you; I offer you; etc. These words generally involve two persons, and the participation of the two in a relation, in reciprocity. Here the secret vector would always be: *Who are you?*"[4] Rather than reserving mystery for God alone, mystery and wonder are re-situated between man and woman, which implies that encounter between the sexes is best exemplified by those patterns of speech which imply the question: "Who are you?"[5] This question expresses the truth that the other is forever a mystery to me—he or she is moving within a horizon, and constructing a world, that lies beyond me. I cannot simply meet her by way of the categories and language that have grown comfortable for me. As Graham Ward rightly observes, within Irigaray's thought "the addressing of the I to the other comes close at times to the quality of prayer."[6] A space of encounter, then, must be created, through language, a space of encounter that respects the mystery of the other and does not foreclose possibilities that might be actualized through this encounter.

Irigaray will also insist, to offer another example, that the insertion of the word "to" in the phrase "I love you" (giving "I love to you") might introduce a mode of indirection that emphasizes the distance between two and respects the interval of wonder between man and woman:

> The "to" is the site of non-reduction of the person to the object. I love you, I desire you, I take you, I seduce you, I order you, I instruct you, and so on, always risk annihilating the alterity of the other, of transforming him/her into my property, my object, of reducing him/her to what is mine, into mine, meaning what is already a part of my field of existential or material properties.
>
> The "to" is also a barrier against alienating the other's freedom in my subjectivity, my world, my language.[7]

According to Irigaray, the "to" of indirection might open up the possibility of genuine exchange between man and woman inasmuch as it recognizes

---

4. Irigaray, *I Love to You*, 138–39.

5. We are reminded of Irigaray's argument, in *The Ethics of Sexual Difference*: "The modalities of the utterances or sentences which imply or signify the act of a 'dialogue'— are they not used [by men] in the relation to God? In commands, prayers, appeals, graces, cries, dirges, glories, anger, and questions? Performatives, the means of gaining access to the presence of the other, to the relation to the other in and through language, as well across time, are habitually reserved for the relations between man and his God, and not for the exchange between men and women as others." See Irigaray, *Ethics*, 139.

6. Ward, "In the Name," 324.

7. Irigaray, *I Love to You*, 110.

PART THREE—Between Irigaray and Kierkegaard

the transcendence that persists between them and inasmuch as it recognizes that one Being is not free to circumscribe, or possess, or appropriate the other. This "to," she suggests, in a more positive vein, declares: "I hope to be attentive to you now and in the future, I ask you if I may stay with you, and I am faithful to you."[8] Here encounter becomes possibility. Here fecundity between man and woman is prior to and outside of any consideration of procreation—fecundity is precisely the unfolding of the human through the encounter of worlds and lives irreducible to each other.

In drawing Irigaray and Kierkegaard into conversation it should be observed that the overlap between their respective accounts of the gap that persists between persons permits an embrace of Irigaray's account of communication within a Kierkegaardian ethics of sexual difference. As argued in chapter 5, human subjects must be held at a remove from each other—they are separated from one another by an existential, epistemological, God-defined gap. And while neither Kierkegaard nor Climacus describes communication between persons in a way that mirrors Irigaray's account, her insistence on communication as the creation of a free space of encounter, and her insistence on indirection in speech, correlates with Kierkegaard's account of human subjectivity. As man and woman live in an imaginative tension between actual and ideal, in relation to Jesus Christ the Prototype, each must recognize that the other's identity and intentions are not transparent to him or her. Here it is evident that Irigaray's own words resonate with our Kierkegaardian account of human becoming: "It is impossible in a way to describe who I am, who the other is—an energy makes it so that a subject still living, is ungraspable and, moreover, changes all the time. If it is possible to contemplate a subject, it is not possible to represent (to oneself) who this subject is—the subject has already escaped from this fixed form, from this sort of naming of what it is. Unless the subject accepts being taken, imprisoned, annihilated there."[9] Since communication and intersubjectivity must correspond with the way things are (must correspond with human nature), communication and intersubjectivity within a Kierkegaardian ethics of sexual difference must be conceived and lived in a way that honors the difference and mystery of the other.

Expressed differently, as man and woman become in relation to the prototype they must acknowledge the existential, epistemological, God-defined gap that persists between them by deploying speech patterns that

8. Ibid.
9. Irigaray, *The Way of Love*, 84.

imply the question "Who are you?" Furthermore, they (must) acknowledge this gap through patterns of speech that hold the other at a remove—for example, "I love *to* you"—so that they do not run coagulatingly together in objectivity.[10] This approach to communication between persons honors the nature of the human as defined within our Kierkegaardian *theory* of sexual difference, formulated above. We are arguing, then, that Irigarayan indirection can be embraced within, or *constitutes part of*, a Kierkegaardian ethics of sexual difference. Man and woman, if they acknowledge their nature as beings in becoming, must employ patterns of communication that acknowledge the dynamic nature of the self, the subjective distance between persons, and the secret and dynamic relationship of each to God. Here it is possible to overcome patterns of communication that draw the other close in a relation of possession, appropriation, or denomination. Here the failure of communication between man and woman (his communication circles back to himself, hers aims at one who cannot respond[11]) might be mitigated as two subjects encounter each other for the first time.

We note that the reality of sexual difference has (once again) faded into the background as we have considered an embrace of Irigarayan indirection within the framework of Kierkegaard's thought. That is, while Irigaray builds her theory of indirection on the irreducibility of man and woman to each other, our embrace of her theory of indirection within a Kierkegaardian framework owes primarily not to sexual difference but to the nature of human subjectivity. Nevertheless, sexual difference is incorporated, here. In the first instance, as argued, a focus on the universal nature of human becoming does not preclude the fact of sexual difference—that is, since human becoming is between actual and ideal, and since the actual is two, sexual difference must remain in play. Even more, however, we might say that sexual difference is fundamental to a Kierkegaardian ethics of sexual difference inasmuch as the subjective distance between man and woman cannot be accounted for without reference to the irreducibly distinct worlds they inhabit. Sexual difference is a first and fundamental aspect of human distinctiveness, which is to say that the respective spiritual and cultural existence (the subjectivity) of man and woman sets them at a distance from one another in a way that men amongst themselves, or women amongst themselves, are not set at a distance from one another. They inhabit cultural worlds that are at a

---

10. This phrase, "run coagulatingly together in objectivity" is Climacus'—we will return to it shortly but deploy it anachronistically here.

11. See our discussion, above.

PART THREE—Between Irigaray and Kierkegaard

remove from each other, and in a Kierkegaardian ethics of sexual difference this remove may be acknowledged through communicative patterns that reflect and embrace Irigarayan indirection.

Kierkegaardian Indirection

It is one thing to acknowledge the mystery of the other, and to allow that communication entails the opening up of a free space of encounter between man and woman. It is quite another to ask whether/how a person might communicate substantively with another concerning his or her own identity. In exploring this question we move beyond Irigaray's account of indirection between man and woman in order to explore Climacus's account of indirect communication. In doing so it is important to note that while Kierkegaard does not develop his theory of communication in *Works of Love*, Climacus's theory is entirely in keeping with Kierkegaard's assumptions in *Works of Love*. Indeed, Kierkegaard's *Works of Love* was only completed and published, in 1847, after Kierkegaard took the decision to put aside a series of lectures he had been preparing on communication.[12] The lectures, for which Kierkegaard did a good deal of preliminary work, but which were never given or published, weave together the themes of direct and indirect communication (also taken up in *Postscript*, published in February, 1846) and the theme of the "dependent independence" of the other (developed in *Works of Love*, published in September, 1847). Thus, *Works of Love*, the lectures on communication, and Climacus's discussion of communication in the *Postscript* come meaningfully together in a discussion of Kierkegaardian indirection.

Returning to Climacus's "Possible and Actual Theses by Lessing," we note Climacus's argument that direct communication correlates with objective thinking and is therefore indifferent to subjectivity, inwardness, and appropriation.[13] In saying that direct communication is indifferent to subjectivity Climacus is not suggesting that direct communication and objective knowledge are utterly without place in an account of human life and thought. Indeed, Climacus can say that "wherever objective thinking is within its rights, its direct communication is also in order, precisely because it is not supposed to deal with subjectivity."[14] Climacus's view, however, is that we must be diligent to prevent objective thinking and

---

12. Kierkegaard, *Works of Love*, 420–21.
13. Westphal, *Becoming a Self*, 61.
14. Kierkegaard, *Postscript*, 76.

direct communication from being deployed outside of the boundaries that circumscribe their appropriate place. Evans gives a good sense of the nature of direct communication when he writes: "What is communicated directly is essentially intellectual content, and when the recipient of the communication understands the ideas (possibilities), the communication is successful. The recipient only has to grasp the possibilities intellectually . . ."[15]

In *Works of Love* Kierkegaard offers a discussion of knowledge and communication that runs directly parallel to the argument of Climacus in "Possible and Actual Theses by Lessing." He writes: "Knowledge is the infinite art of equivocation, or infinite equivocation; at most it is simply a placing of opposite possibilities in equilibrium. To be able to do this is knowing, and only the one who knows how to communicate opposite possibilities in equilibrium to another, only he communicates knowledge."[16] Kierkegaard and Climacus share the view that direct communication is the passing on of information, results, or objective knowledge—it is a matter of being able to state possibilities and probabilities in a given situation. As Westphal puts it, direct communication is "a social event linking two selves in the act whereby one directly gives to the other what is essential."[17] This is not to say that direct communication does not require imaginative skill or to say that objective knowledge is certain, as is clear from Kierkegaard's words in *Works of Love*, quoted above. It is to say, however, that objective knowledge is such that it *can be communicated directly between one person and another*.[18]

If objective thought correlates with direct communication, then subjective thought correlates with indirect communication.[19] To get at the difference between these it is helpful to attend to Climacus's argument that the objective thinker is engaged in *single reflection* (first reflection) while the subjective thinker is engaged in *double reflection* (second reflection).

15. Evans, *Kierkegaard's "Fragments" and "Postscript,"* 96.
16. Kierkegaard, *Works of Love*, 231.
17. Westphal, *Becoming a Self*, 61.
18. As Mehl notes, according to Climacus (and Kierkegaard, we have seen), "all knowledge about actuality . . . is possibility, is hypothetical; it might be just the truth about things, but it might not be, it is conjectural." See Mehl, *Thinking through Kierkegaard*, 47. And Climacus himself adds that direct communication "does not have to be easy." See Kierkegaard, *Postscript*, 75.
19. Poling points out that Kierkegaard's view is that the communication of the ethico-religious as science and scholarship is both endemic to his culture and completely mistaken. See Poling, "Kierkegaard and Communication," 151.

PART THREE—Between Irigaray and Kierkegaard

Evans explains the difference between single and double reflection by suggesting that the former requires only that the recipient grasp possibilities intellectually. First reflection, for Climacus, is the movement from an external reality, or from a thought, to a concept that captures something of that reality or thought—and direct communication is the passing on of these concepts as knowledge.[20] Moving beyond first reflection and objective knowledge, Evans writes: "When the subject of communication is subjectivity itself . . . the matter is different. Here the aim of the communication is self-understanding. The individual in this case must not only understand the intellectual content (first reflection) but also relate the content to her own existence (second reflection)."[21] Thus, the existential and personal are at stake in second reflection, as Climacus suggests: "[T]o think is one thing and to exist in what has been thought is something else. Existing in relation to thinking is not something that follows by itself any more than it is thoughtlessness."[22] He further clarifies the relation between first and second reflection when he writes: "When a thought has gained its proper expression in the word, which is attained through the first reflection, there comes the second reflection, which bears upon the intrinsic relation of the communication to the communicator and *renders the existing communicator's own relation to the idea.*"[23] Second reflection cannot abide the disinterested nature of first reflection and objective knowledge—second reflection necessarily entails interest and passion.[24]

Evans suggests that the nature of indirect communication requires us to further distinguish between *subjective* understanding and *existential* understanding, which leaves us with three forms of understanding (objective, subjective, and existential).[25] Using the example of Christian knowledge, these three forms of understanding can be explained. *Objective understanding*, which corresponds with first reflection, entails knowledge

---

20. Again, this process is subject to uncertainty—the concept can never fully capture reality.

21. Evans, Kierkegaard's "Fragments" and "Postscript," 96–97.

22. Kierkegaard, *Postscript*, 254 quoted in Evans, Kierkegaard's "Fragments" and "Postscript," 96.

23. Kierkegaard, *Postscript*, 77.

24. In *Works of Love*, Kierkegaard writes: "It is one thing to let ideas strive with ideas; it is one thing to battle and be victorious in dispute. It is something else to be victorious over one's own mind, when one battles in the reality of life." Quoted in Müller, Kierkegaard's Works of Love, 2.

25. In this paragraph and the next we follow Evans's interpretation of *Postscript* as he develops it in Kierkegaard's "Fragments" and "Postscript," 100–105.

of doctrines or historical facts—entails familiarity with the theology and practices of the Christian tradition. *Subjective understanding*, which is the first moment in second reflection, entails reflection on, and awareness of, how Christianity relates to existence (Climacus has subjective understanding since he understands how Christianity relates to existence—but he is not a Christian).[26] Finally, *existential understanding*, which is the second moment in second reflection, entails both knowledge of how Christianity relates to existence (subjective understanding) and a living out of this relation in actuality. "Christianity is not merely understood as a possibility but is known as an actuality."[27] Climacus clarifies the nature of existential understanding when he writes: "The actuality is not the external action but *an interiority in which the individual annuls possibility and identifies himself with what is thought in order to exist in it*. This is action."[28] In the context of Christian faith, existential understanding entails an embrace of Jesus Christ as the prototype (as the embodiment of love) and entails a present interest in becoming in relation to Christ.

Coming back to the question of intersubjective communication, in the context of sexual difference, we note that double reflection implies indirect communication. Climacus writes: "Wherever the subjective is of importance in knowledge, and appropriation is therefore the main point, communication is a work of art; it is double reflected and its first form is the subtlety that the subjective individuals must be held devoutly apart from one another and must not run coagulatingly together in objectivity. This is objectivity's word of farewell to subjectivity."[29] For Climacus, the nature of human existence is such that persons must be held apart from one another in communication. Or, direct communication cannot account for the existential gap that persists between persons. He writes: "[T]he subjective thinker must promptly become aware that the form of communication must artistically possess just as much reflection as he himself, existing in his thinking, possesses. Artistically, please note, for the secret does not consist in his enunciating the double-reflection directly, since such an enunciation is a direct communication."[30] Indirect communication represents an acknowledgment that subjective existence is such that it simply cannot be communicated directly between persons. My pas-

26. Ibid., 102.
27. Ibid.
28. Kierkegaard, *Postscript*, 339. Italics added.
29. Ibid., 79.
30. Ibid., 74.

PART THREE—Between Irigaray and Kierkegaard

sionate and inner existence (my interest in, and pursuit of life) cannot be directly communicated to another person. It is impossible for one person to directly give the other a taste of his or her experience and actuality. Accordingly, Evans argues: "All that can be done directly is to compel the other person to 'take notice' by arousing her attention. Hence the person who wishes to help another existentially is twice removed; he can become the occasion for another's existential development by being the occasion for another's increased subjective understanding."[31]

Here an important link must be made between Kierkegaard's *Works of Love* and Climacus's discussion of indirect communication in the *Postscript*. There Climacus insists that the need to hold subjects apart is also predicated on the existence and nature of God as one to whom each person relates—God as one from whom each person receives his or her being. In his discussion of a hypothetical individual who comes to the conviction that the God-relationship is a secret (and who wishes to communicate this truth to others) Climacus argues that, it is vain "to believe that some other human being needs one's assistance in his God-relationship, as if God were not able to help himself and the person involved. But it is a bit strenuous: in existing to hold on to the thought that one is nothing before God, that all personal effort is only a jest. It is a bit chastening to respect every human being so that one does not dare to meddle directly in his God-relationship, partly because one ought to have enough in dealing with one's own, partly because God is no friend of impertinence."[32] It is apparent that Climacus (like Kierkegaard in *Works of Love*) sees the God-relationship as a possible, and even fundamental, feature of the inner and passionate life of the existentially engaged person. Indeed it is precisely in the context of this discussion of the God-relationship that Climacus will go on to insist that "the subjective individuals must be held devoutly apart from one another and must not run coagulating together in objectivity." For Climacus, the insistence on indirect communication corresponds not only with awareness that the other is at an existential remove from me but also with awareness that the other in his or her subjectivity is decisively and secretly related to God.

31. Evans, *Kierkegaard's "Fragments" and "Postscript,"* 105.

32. Kierkegaard, *Postscript*, 79. In his lectures on communication, Kierkegaard writes: "In regard to the ethical, one person cannot have authority in relation to another because, ethically, God is the master-teacher and every man is an apprentice. If someone were to say to men: You ought to act ethically, it is as if God were heard speaking simultaneously to this important man: Nonsense, my friend, it is you who must do it." Kierkegaard, *Journals and Papers*, Vol. 1, 649/11.

On this same point Climacus writes (words which find an echo in the later *Works of Love*): "Therefore, the subjective thinker, who has comprehended the duplexity of existence in order to be such a thinker, readily perceives that direct communication is a fraud toward God (which possibly defrauds him of the worship of another person in truth), a fraud toward himself (as if he had ceased to be an existing individual), a fraud toward another human being (who possibly attains only a relative God-relationship), a fraud that brings him into contradiction with his entire thought."[33] It is helpful to give a brief explanation of each fraud identified by Climacus:

1. *The fraud toward God.* Since human subjectivity is bound up with the secret and inner God-relationship, and since a person cannot communicate directly concerning this relationship, any attempt to do so will in fact point away from it. In this case the person who might otherwise have been led toward God is led away from the God.

2. *The fraud toward self.* Since the subjective thinker has recognized that his own existence is bound up with the inner and secret relation to God and is defined by passion and decision, it is a fraud against his own existence if he tries to communicate directly (by passing on objective knowledge) concerning this existence and relation. The fraud consists in the fact that there is a lack of integrity between his subjectivity and his mode of communication.

3. *The fraud toward the other.* This third fraud flows obviously from what has already been said, since a failure to communicate in a way that respects subjective existence and the God-relationship cannot put another person in touch with his or her own subjective existence.

To summarize, the nature of human subjectivity, and the secret and inner relation to God, require that communication of existence be undertaken indirectly. It must be undertaken in such a way, we might say, that the other is left to grasp and live (or not) this reality for him or herself.[34]

We have come some distance in articulating an account of communication that corresponds with a Kierkegaardian ethics of sexual difference, and toward answering the question whether and how a man or woman

---

33. Ibid., 75.

34. It is for this reason that we can never guarantee whether or not the other person will actually grasp the truth of subjective existence or live the passionate and secret relationship to God. These three frauds are in some sense repeated in Kierkegaard's discussion in "Love Builds Up," to which we return, below.

might communicate with the other concerning his or her own identity in becoming. To clarify the progress that has been made, in the following paragraphs we will outline the communicative approach of a man who would (i) communicate with a woman concerning his existence in relation to God, (ii) help her appreciate his commitment to a certain path of becoming between actual and ideal, or (iii) share with her concerning his commitment to certain life-projects.

A Kierkegaardian ethics of sexual difference allows that this man might communicate directly with a woman concerning the person and identity of Jesus Christ and concerning the law of love as it finds expression in him. In *Works of Love*, as noted, Kierkegaard assumes the possibility of communicating such knowledge between persons, even if this knowledge is marked by the same uncertainty that marks all other forms of knowledge (including sense perception, speculative thought, and historical knowledge). That communication of objective knowledge might be part of a man's communication with woman concerning his life and existence is also affirmed by Kierkegaard in his lectures on communication, where he draws together the arguments of the *Postscript* and of *Works of Love* by suggesting that ethical-religious (as opposed to merely ethical) communication is "direct-indirect communication"—that is, it is an indirect communication that requires a moment of direct communication.[35] "Ethically, man as such knows about the ethical, but man as such does not know about the religious in the Christian sense. Here there must be the communication of a little knowledge first of all—but then the same relationship as in the ethical enters in. The instruction, the communication, must not be as of a knowledge, but upbringing, practicing, art-instruction."[36] This moment of direct communication between a man and woman can be construed in terms of communication concerning the revelation of God in Christ. Yet communication concerning this objective truth must give way *immediately* to awareness that the communication of lived Christianity is what matters for human life and personality and must give way to a concomitant awareness that this lived reality can only be communicated indirectly.

35. Kierkegaard, *Journals and Papers*, Vol. 1, 653/27.

36. Ibid., 650/13. In saying that man as such knows about the ethical, Kierkegaard is saying that man is by nature an ethical being. In the outline of his lectures on communication, Kierkegaard compares the teaching of the ethical to the training of a young soldier. He writes: "The corporal does not explain to the soldier what it is to drill, etc.; he communicates it to him as an art, he teaches him to use militarily the abilities and the potential competence he already has." (Ibid., 649/5.)

Communication

Here it is helpful to return to Kierkegaard's account of the love command, and of Jesus Christ as the prototype, particularly noting its formal nature. As noted, the love command does not answer, ahead of time, substantive questions concerning an appropriate action or form of life. That is, one cannot determine ahead of time what the love command will look like when translated into the particular circumstances of a person's life and becoming. Furthermore, according to Kierkegaard's account of an ethical intersubjectivity, the rush to judgment concerning the way in which the love command comes to expression in another's life likely represents a refusal of love (a refusal to seek a mitigating explanation, for example) and a refusal to acknowledge the secret, hidden nature of the other's relation to Love, to God.

In terms of a man's communication with a woman concerning his identity in becoming, and concerning his relation to Jesus Christ, Evans offers the reminder that a person must "design his communication in such a way that the recipient is encouraged to apply the content to his own life and situation."[37] All that can be done directly is to compel the other person to "take notice" by arousing her attention. Another interpreter of Climacus puts it as follows:

> One makes actual an ethico-religious situation by recreating just those primitive positive and negative pathos factors that cleanse the receiver of his indifference and make him ready for the ethico-religious possibilities his life harbours. No person develops or sustains an ethico-religious capability without being placed in a position where some thought or mood or emotion or possibility comes alive and present in such a way that that link becomes momentarily firm between subjective need and ethico-religious "shall."[38]

This pedagogically oriented account of communication, when translated into the context of a man relating to a woman, suggests that he is

---

37. Evans, *Kierkegaard's "Fragments" and "Postscript,"* 104. As observed, above, Judge William attempts to encourage his aesthetic friend to embrace a different approach to life. And as Rudd points out, the Judge's writings are not merely abstract philosophical essays (though they are sophisticated arguments). Rather, they are personal letters from the Judge to a friend—he invites this aesthetic friend to consider that his life might be more than it is. The Judge seeks to engage with his friend in such a way that the Aesthete might see his own life-view as despair and might become interested in his self in a way that opens up toward new possibilities of selfhood. See Rudd, "Reason in Ethics," 137–38.

38. Poling, "Kierkegaard and Communication," 156.

PART THREE—Between Irigaray and Kierkegaard

invited to live passionately in relation to God, and to the (sexuate) other, allowing this passionate existence to become the occasion (or not, since there can be no guarantee here) of her subjective and existential understanding of life in Love. In this circumstance, a man and woman do not run coagulatingly together in objective knowledge of Jesus Christ as the prototype (or coagulatingly together in knowledge of the law of love, which is decidedly formal in nature) but acknowledge the existential, epistemological, God-defined gap between them, which prevents direct communication concerning the life each lives in relation to the God who is love, and which prevents direct communication concerning each one's subjective becoming.

Kierkegaard makes an important link between this theory of communication and the ethical vision of *Works of Love* when he explores the difference between the *what* (preoccupation with objective knowledge, direct communication) and the *how* (preoccupation with existence, indirect communication). It is, again, a question of integrity between the content of the communication and the way in which the content is communicated—he argues that the *what* must find expression in a *how* appropriate to it. Employing a specific example, Kierkegaard argues that the Apostle's insistence that "I know nothing except Christ and him crucified" (the *what*) must find expression in words (the *how*) that cannot be merely

> the esthetic, the rhetorical, whether spoken in flowery language or in a simple style, whether with euphonious organ tones or with a scratchy voice, whether drily and unemotionally or with tears in the eyes, etc.—no, the distinction is whether one *speaks* or whether one *acts* by speaking, whether one uses the voice, facial expression, arm-gestures, a single word thrice, perhaps ten times underscored, etc., for emphasis in order to make an impression or whether one uses his life, his existence, every hour of his day, sacrifices, etc., for emphasis. This emphasis is the elevated emphasis which transforms what is spoken into something entirely different, even though a speaker says literally the same thing.[39]

A man's indirect communication with a woman concerning Christian existence and life in Love (in God), requires a faithful living out of the self-sacrificial love that finds expression in Jesus Christ and in his command to "love your neighbor as yourself."[40] According to this maieutic logic, a

39. Kierkegaard, *Journals and Papers*, Vol. 1, 678.
40. We recall the obvious, that self-sacrifice, and self-emptying for the other, stands

man is in no position to bring a woman directly to knowledge of God or to knowledge of the life that he might live in relation to the prototype. He can only persist in his own becoming in relation to the prototype, to Love, and at the same moment endeavour to give expression to this love in relation to the other. Whether and how she grasps this is beyond his ability to control or comprehend—but he is invited to believe that she lives in Love, that she has her being in God, and that she might in her own way comprehend and apprehend the life he lives, in God.

Some will no doubt object (as they have objected to Irigaray's thought) that this emphasis on an existential and epistemic distance between persons (and between man and woman), and the theory of communication corresponding to it, cuts man and woman off from each other and from the possibility of a meaningful encounter. Irigaray's own response to this objection would be to say that man and woman, to this day, have not genuinely communicated with each other, since woman has not been granted a subject position from which to speak. The whole purpose of our argument in this volume, in fact, has been to point toward an alternative account of the relationship between man and woman—toward a Kierkegaardian theory and ethics of sexual difference in which woman attains an existence in her own right and is not defined or appropriated or circumscribed by man, according to the logic of the same. Furthermore, it is not at all obvious that our account of indirect communication (our Kierkegaardian ethics of sexual difference) prevents a man or woman from expressing affection or desire for the other, from truly loving the other according to the command of Christ, or from intending that the other might know and appreciate the passionate and interested life he or she lives. That these possibilities are not subject to straightforward or simplistic description, and that they require both imagination and self-control on the part of man and woman, does not imply that they are not possible or that they do not already take place to some degree. Indeed, in stronger terms, if man and woman are truly to communicate with one another, it will only be as they respect their human nature and identity (i) as subjective (as passionate, interested, and secret), (ii) as dynamic (in a process of becoming that cannot be pinned down), and (iii) as personally and secretly related to the God who creates each, *ex nihilo*, as a distinctive being.

---

at the heart of the vision of love that Kierkegaard develops in *Works of Love*.

PART THREE—Between Irigaray and Kierkegaard

SUMMARY

A Kierkegaardian ethics of sexual difference offers a rich and complex account of the relationship between man and woman, a relationship first of all defined by the gap or interval that persists between persons. This gap is an epistemological gap, since the other in her becoming is beyond my capacity to know—she never "sits still" in becoming, which is to say that her identity as woman can never be pinned down with any certainty. This epistemological gap also takes into account the distinctiveness of the human person, and therefore sexual difference, which is the first or primary aspect of human distinctiveness or particularity. The gap between persons is also an existential gap, by which we mean to say that human existence is a passionate and interested existence and that subjectivity is by definition *individual*—it is not something that can be directly shared between persons. The gap between persons must finally also be conceived in terms of the God-relationship, for the relationship that each person has with God is by definition a secret or confidential relationship—it is a passionate and interested relationship—in which the person is affirmed in her being as loved and loving, as rooted in Love. As with human subjectivity generally, this relationship to Love cannot be communicated directly to another—it can only be lived in such a way that another might reach out (or not) to the God who is Love, by loving.

Intersubjectivity between persons, and between man and woman, is shaped by this epistemological, existential, and God-defined gap. As Kierkegaard would put it, "a separation is placed between two who should be joined in the most intimate and confidential life together."[41] The relationship between man and woman is defined, further, as one in which each respects the other's God-relationship, honors the other's distinctiveness, acknowledges the other's autonomy, affirms the other's self-love, and realizes that the other is mine neither to define nor to possess. Though the pattern of intersubjectivity implied by our Kierkegaardian ethics of sexual difference may strike us as overly concerned with the distance between persons, it is precisely this distance that defines a relationship as ethical and as oriented toward the unity of the human. Thus, the interval between persons is not such that they are utterly cut off from each other. Although communication between persons cannot take the form of a direct passing on of information (an envelope containing a closed truth), according to a master-disciple or student-teacher model, communication remains a real

41. Ibid.

possibility. As we have said, communication that respects the nature of the human must be such that it invites the other to "take notice" by arousing her attention. While there may be a moment of direct communication in the relationship between man and woman—direct communication that centers on the identity of Jesus Christ as prototype and savior—it remains true to say that communication of who I am (in imaginative becoming, between actual and ideal, in relation to the prototype) can only take the form of an invitation to the other that she take notice of the form of my life. There is never a guarantee that she either understands or lives in relation to the prototype as I (trust and pray that I) do. Above all, this communication concerning my identity in God (in Love), must take the form of self-sacrificial service (sustained by the love of God and by love of self) to my neighbor, along with all that this entails, as described in *Works of Love*.

Otherwise put, the gap between persons not only *does not* cut man and woman off from each other, it generates the possibility that their relationship might be one of confidentiality or intimacy—a relationship of genuine sharing in trust and knowledge and faith. As each relates to God, and finds his or her identity in God, it becomes possible for each to relate honestly and confidently to the other—that is, to love the other. It becomes possible for a person to honor the other's difference/distinctiveness, to acknowledge her autonomy, to affirm her self-love, and to realize that she is mine neither to define nor to appropriate nor to possess. God as the middle term represents, and embodies in Jesus Christ, the possibility that man and woman might form a unity through encounter and love. What this unity might look like, we cannot know in advance. We can only reach toward it.

Bibliography

Adorno, Theodor W. "On Kierkegaard's Doctrine of Love." *Studies in Philosophy and Social Science* 8 (1939–40) 413–29.
Agacinsky, Sylviane. *Parity of the Sexes*. Translated by Lisa Walsh. New York: Columbia University Press, 2001.
Ainley, Alison. "The Subject of Ethics: Kierkegaard and Feminist Perspectives on an 'Ethical' Self." *The Oxford Literary Review* 11.1 (1989) 169–88.
Ake, Stacey Elizabeth. "'And yet a braver thence doth spring': The Heuristic Values of *Works of Love*." In *Kierkegaard Studies Yearbook*, edited by Niels Jørgen Capellørn and Hermann Deuser, 93–112. Berlin: de Gruyter, 1998.
Anderson, Ray Sherman. *On Being Human: Essays in Theological Anthropology*. Grand Rapids: Eerdmans, 1982.
Andic, Martin. "Confidence as a Work of Love." In *Kierkegaard on Art and Communication*, edited by George Pattison, 160–84. New York: St. Martin's, 1992.
———. "Is Love of Neighbour the Love of an Individual?" In *Kierkegaard: The Self in Society*, edited by George Pattison and Steven Shakespeare, 112–24. New York: St. Martin's, 1998.
———. "Love's Redoubling and the Eternal Like for Like." In *International Kierkegaard Commentary: Works of Love*, edited by Robert L. Perkins, 9–38. Macon, GA: Mercer University Press, 1999.
Anthony, David. "Le Doeuff and Irigaray on Descartes." *Philosophy Today* 41.3 (1997) 367–82.
Aristotle, *Nicomachean Ethics*. Edited and translated by Terence Irwin. Indianapolis, IN: Hackett, 1999.
Armour, Ellen T. *Deconstruction, Feminist Theology, and the Problem of Difference: Subverting the Race/Gender Divide*. Chicago: University of Chicago Press, 1999.
Barret, Lee C. "The Neighbour's Material and Social Well-Being in Kierkegaard's *Works of Love*: Does it Matter?" In *International Kierkegaard Commentary: Works of Love*, edited by Robert L. Perkins, 137–66. Macon, GA: Mercer University Press, 1999.
Barth, Karl. *Church Dogmatics*, Volumes 1–4. Edited by G. W. Bromiley and T. F. Torrance. Translated by G. W. Bromily et al. Edinburgh: T. & T. Clark, 1956–75.
Bauman, Zygmunt. *Liquid Love*. Cambridge: Polity, 2003.
Beattie, Tina. "Carnal Love and Spiritual Imagination: Can Luce Irigaray and John Paul II Come Together?" In *Sex These Days: Essays on Theology, Sexuality and Society*, edited by Jon Davies and Gerard Loughlin, 160–83. Sheffield, UK: Sheffield Academic Press, 1997.
———. *God's Mother, Eve's Advocate: A Marian Narrative of Women's Salvation*. London: Continuum, 2002.

Bibliography

Bergoffen, Debra. "Irigaray's Couples." In *Returning to Irigaray: Feminist Philosophy, Politics, and the Question of Unity*, edited by Maria C. Cimitile and Elaine P. Miller, 151–72. Albany, NY: New York, 2007.

Berry, Wanda Warren. "Judge William Judging Woman: Existentialism and Essentialism in Kierkegaard's *Either/Or, Part II*." In *International Kierkegaard Commentary: Either/Or, Part II*, edited by Robert L. Perkins, 33–57. Macon, GA: Mercer University Press, 1995.

Bertung, Birgit. "Yes, a Woman Can Exist." In *Feminist Interpretations of Søren Kierkegaard*, edited by Céline Léon and Sylvia Walsh, 51–68. University Park, PA: The Pennsylvania State University Press, 1997.

Boddé, Rene. "A God of Her Own." *Feminist Theology* 19 (1998) 48–62.

Bonhoeffer, Dietrich. *Ethics*. Edited by Eberhard Bethge. New York: MacMillan, 1995.

Bostic, Heidi. "Luce Irigaray and Love." *Cultural Studies* 16.5 (2002) 603–10.

Braidotti, Rosi. "Becoming Woman: or Sexual Difference Revisited." *Theory, Culture and Society* 20.3 (2003) 43–64.

———. "Of Bugs and Women: Irigaray and Deleuze on the Becoming-Woman." In *Engaging with Irigaray, Feminist Philosophy and Modern European Thought*, edited by Carolyn Burke et al., 111–40. New York: Columbia University Press, 1994.

———. "This Essentialism Which is Not One: Coming to Grips with Irigaray." In *Engaging with Irigaray: Feminist Philosophy and Modern European Thought*, edited by Carolyn Burke et al., 57–78. New York: Columbia University Press, 1994.

Bring, Margaret F., and Steven L. Nock. "What Does Covenant Mean for Relationships?" In *Covenant Marriage in Comparative Perspective*, edited by John Witte and Eliza Ellison, 265–93. Grand Rapids: Eerdmans, 2005.

Brown, Alison Leigh. "God, Anxiety, and Female Divinity." In *Kierkegaard in Post/Modernity*, edited by Martin J. Matuštík and Merold Westphal, 66–75. Bloomington, IN: Indiana University Press, 1995.

Brueggemann, Walter. "Of the Same Flesh and Bone (Genesis 2:23a)." *Catholic Biblical Quarterly* 32.4 (1970) 532–42.

Cahoy, William J. "One Species or Two? Kierkegaard's Anthropology and the Feminist Critique of the Concept of Sin." *Modern Theology* 11.4 (1995) 429–54.

Canters, Hanneke, and Grace M. Jantzen. *Forever Fluid: A Reading of Luce Irigaray's Elemental Passions*. Manchester: Manchester University Press, 2005.

Carlisle, Clare. *Kierkegaard's Philosophy of Becoming*. New York: State University of New York Press, 2005.

Chanter, Tina. *Ethics of Eros: Irigaray's Rewriting of the Philosophers*. New York: Routledge, 1995.

Cheah, Pheng. "Of Being-Two." In *Futures of Critical Theory: Dreams of Difference*, edited by Michael Peters et al., 169–86. Oxford: Rowman and Littlefield, 2003.

Cheah, Pheng, and Elizabeth Grosz. "Of Being-Two: Introduction." *Diacritics* 28.1 (1998) 3–18.

Cimitile, Maria. "The Horror of Language: Irigaray and Heidegger." *Philosophy Today* 45.5 (2001) 66–74.

Cimitile, Maria, and Elaine P. Miller. *Returning to Irigaray: Feminist Philosophy, Politics, and the Question of Unity*. Albany, NY: State University of New York Press, 2007.

Colledge, Richard J. "Between Ultra-Essentialism and Post-Essentialism: Kierkegaard as Transitional and Contemporary." *Contretemps* 3 (2002) 54–65.

———. "Kierkegaard's Subjective Ontology: A Metaphysics of the Existing Individual." *International Philosophical Quarterly* 44.1 (2004) 5–23.

Bibliography

Come, Arnold. *Kierkegaard as Theologian: Recovering My Self.* Montreal: McGill-Queens University Press, 1997.

Connell, George B. "Judge William's Theonomous Ethics." In *Foundations of Kierkegaard's Vision of Community: Religion, Ethics, and Politics in Kierkegaard*, edited by George B. Connell and C. Stephen Evans, 56–70. Atlantic Highlands, NJ: Humanities, 1992.

Cutting, Pat. "The Levels of Interpersonal Relationships in Kierkegaard's Two Ages." In *International Kierkegaard Commentary: Two Ages*, edited by Robert L. Perkins, 74–86. Macon, GA: Mercer University Press, 1984.

Daniel, Stephen H. "Postmodernity, Poststructuralism, and the Historiography of Modern Philosophy." *International Philosophical Quarterly* 35.3 (1995) 255–67.

Davenport, John J. "The Meaning of Kierkegaard's Choice Between the Aesthetic and the Ethical." In *Kierkegaard After MacIntyre: Essays on Freedom, Narrative, and Virtue*, edited by John Davenport and Anthony Rudd, 175–212. Chicago: Open Court, 2001.

———. "Towards an Existential Virtue Ethics: Kierkegaard and MacIntyre." In *Kierkegaard After MacIntyre: Essays on Freedom, Narrative, and Virtue*, edited by John Davenport and Anthony Rudd, 265–324. Chicago: Open Court, 2001.

Davenport, John J., and Anthony Rudd, editors. *Kierkegaard After MacIntyre: Essays on Freedom, Narrative, and Virtue.* Chicago: Open Court, 2001.

David, Anthony. "Le Doeuff and Irigaray on Descartes." *Philosophy Today* 41.3 (1997) 367–82.

Davies, W. D., and Dale C. Allison. *A Critical and Exegetical Commentary on The Gospel according to Saint Matthew.* Edinburgh: T. & T. Clark, 1997.

Descartes, Rene. *The Passions of the Soul.* Translated by Stephen Voss. Indianapolis, IN: Hackett, 1989.

De Vries, Roland J. "Sharing Air: Becoming Two in the Spirit." In *Luce Irigaray: Teaching*, edited by Luce Irigaray and Mary Green, 142–55. London: Continuum, 2008.

———. "With Luce Irigaray, toward a Theology of Hospitality." *Esprit Créateur* 52.3 (2012) 52–65.

———. "Wonder between Two: An Irigarayan Reading of Genesis 2:23." *Modern Theology* 24.1 (2008) 51–74

Deutscher, Penelope. "Irigaray Anxiety: Luce Irigaray and Her Ethics for Improper Selves." *Radical Philosophy* 80 (1996) 6–16.

———. "Love Discourses, Sexed Discourses? Luce Irigaray's *Être Deux*." *Continental Philosophy Review* 33.2 (2000) 113–31.

———. *A Politics of Impossible Difference: The Later Work of Luce Irigaray.* Ithaca, NY: Cornell University Press, 2002.

Dunning, Stephen N. *Dialectical Readings: Three Types of Interpretation.* University Park, PA: The Pennsylvania State University Press, 1997.

———. *Kierkegaard's Dialectic of Inwardness: A Structural Analysis of the Theory of Stages.* Princeton: Princeton University Press, 1985.

Dunstan, Gordon. "Marriage Covenant." *Theology* 78 (1975) 244–52.

Dupre, Louis. *Kierkegaard as Theologian: The Dialectic of Christian Existence.* New York: Sheed, 1963.

Duran, Jane. "The Kierkegaardian Feminist." In *Feminist Interpretations of Søren Kierkegaard*, edited by Céline Léon and Sylvia Walsh, 249–65. University Park, PA: The Pennsylvania State University Press, 1997.

Elrod, John. *Being and Existence in Kierkegaard's Pseudonymous Works.* Princeton, NJ: Princeton University Press, 1975.

Bibliography

Euler, Carrie E. "Bullinger's Der Christlich Eestand: Marriage and the Covenant." In *Architect of the Reformation: An Introduction to Heinrich Bullinger*, edited by Bruce Gordon and Emidio Campi, 255–67. Grand Rapids: Baker Academic, 2004.

Evans. C. Stephen. *Kierkegaard's Ethic of Love: Divine Commands and Moral Obligations*. Oxford: Oxford University Press, 2004.

———. *Kierkegaard's "Fragments" and "Postscript": The Religious Philosophy of Johannes Climacus*. Atlantic Highlands NJ: Humanities, 1983.

Ferreira, M. Jamie. "Imagination and the Despair of Sin." In *Kierkegaard Studies Yearbook*, edited by Niels Jørgen Cappelørn et al., 16–34. Berlin: De Gruyter, 1997.

———. *Love's Grateful Striving: A Commentary on Kierkegaard's Works of Love*. Oxford: Oxford University Press, 2001.

———. *Transforming Vision: Imagination and Will in Kierkegaardian Faith*. Oxford: Clarendon, 1991.

Fiddes, Paul S. "The Status of Woman in the Thought of Karl Barth." In *After Eve: Women, Theology and the Christian Tradition*, edited by Janet Martin Soskice, 138–55. London: Marshall Pickering, 1990.

Fielding, Helen. "Questioning Nature: Irigaray, Heidegger and the Potentiality of Matter." *Continental Philosophy Review* 36.1 (2003) 1–26.

Frawley, Matthew. "The Essential Role of the Holy Spirit in Kierkegaard's Biblical Hermeneutic." In *Søren Kierkegaard and the Word(s)*, edited by Poul Houe and Gordon Marino, 93–104. Copenhagen: Reitzel, 2003.

Froese, Karen. "Woman's Eclipse: The Silenced Feminine in Nietzsche and Heidegger." *Philosophy and Social Criticism* 31.2 (2005) 165–84.

Fuss, Diana. "Essentially Speaking: Luce Irigaray's Language of Essence." *Hypatia* 3 (1989) 62–80.

Garside, Christine. "Can a Woman be Good in the Same Way as a Man?" *Dialogue: Canadian Philosophical Review* 10.3 (1971) 534–44.

George, Peter. "Something Anti-social about Works of Love." In *Kierkegaard: The Self in Society*, edited by George Pattison and Steven Shakespeare, 70–81. New York: St. Martin's, 1998.

Gibbs, Robert. "I or You: The Dash of Ethics." In *The New Kierkegaard*, edited by Elsebet Jegstrup, 141–60. Bloomington IN: Indiana University Press, 2004.

Glenn, John D. "The Definition of the Self and the Structure of Kierkegaard's Work." In *International Kierkegaard Commentary: The Sickness Unto Death*, edited by Robert L. Perkins, 5–22. Macon, GA: Mercer University Press, 1987.

González, Darío. "Poetics and the 'Being' of Love." In *Kierkegaard Studies Yearbook*, edited by Niels Jørgen Capelørn and Hermann Deuser, 129–46. Berlin: de Gruyter, 1998.

Gouwens, David. *Kierkegaard as Religious Thinker*. New York: Cambridge University Press, 1996.

———. "Kierkegaard on the Ethical Imagination." *The Journal of Religious Ethics* 10.2 (1982) 204–20.

———. *Kierkegaard's Dialectic of Imagination*. New York: Lang, 1989.

Goux, Jean-Joseph. "Luce Irigaray versus the Utopia of the Neutral Sex." In *Engaging with Irigaray: Feminist Philosophy and Modern European Thought*, edited by Carolyn Burke et al., 175–90. New York: Columbia University Press, 1994.

Green, Ronald M., and Theresa M. Ellis. "Erotic Love in the Religious Existence-Sphere." In *International Kierkegaard Commentary: Works of Love*, edited by Robert L. Perkins, 339–68. Macon, GA: Mercer University Press, 1999.

Bibliography

Grøn, Arne. "The Dialectic of Recognition in *Works of Love*." In *Kierkegaard Studies Yearbook*, edited by Niels Jørgen Cappelørn and Hermann Deuser, 147–57. Berlin: de Gruyter, 1998.

Grosz, Elizabeth. "The Hetero and the Homo: The Sexual Ethics of Luce Irigaray." In *Engaging with Irigaray: Feminist Philosophy and Modern European Thought*, edited by Carolyn Burke et al., 335–50. New York: Columbia University Press, 1994.

———. *Jacques Lacan: A Feminist Introduction*. New York: Routledge, 1990.

———. *Sexual Subversions: Three French Feminists*. St. Leonards, Australia: Allen and Unwin, 1989.

———. *Time Travels: Feminism, Nature, Power*. Durham, NC: Duke University Press, 2005.

Hall, Amy Laura. *Kierkegaard and the Treachery of Love*. Cambridge: Cambridge University Press, 2002.

Hall, Ronald L. *The Human Embrace: The Love of Philosophy and the Philosophy of Love: Kierkegaard, Cavell, Nussbaum*. University Park, PA: The Pennsylvania State University Press, 2000.

Hanna, Alastair, and Gordon D. Marion. *The Cambridge Companion to Kierkegaard*. Cambridge: Cambridge University Press, 1998.

Hegel, G. W. F. *Elements of the Philosophy of Right*. Edited by Allen W. Wood. Translated by H. B. Nisbet. Cambridge: Cambridge University Press, 1991.

———. "Love." In *Early Theological Writings*, translated by T. M. Knox, 302–8. Chicago: University of Chicago Press, 1948.

Hepburn, R. W. *'Wonder' and Other Essays: Eight Studies in Aesthetics and Neighbouring Fields*. Edinburgh: Edinburgh University Press, 1984.

Hirsch, Elizabeth, and Gary A. Olson. "Je-Luce Irigaray: A Meeting with Luce Irigaray." *Jahrbuch für Antike und Christentum* 16.3 (1996) 341–62.

Hogan, Richard M., and John M. Lavoir. *Covenant of Love: Pope John Paul II on Sexuality, Marriage, and Family in the Modern World*. San Francisco: Ignatius, 1992.

Hollywood, Amy. *Sensible Ecstasy: Mysticism, Sexual Difference, and the Demands of History*. Chicago: University of Chicago Press, 2002.

Houe, Poul, and Gordon Marino. *Søren Kierkegaard and the Word(s): Essays on Hermeneutics and Communication*. Copenhagen: Reitzel, 2003.

Howe, Leslie A. "Kierkegaard and the Feminine Self." In *Feminist Interpretations of Søren Kierkegaard*, edited by Céline Léon and Sylvia Walsh, 217–47. University Park, PA: The Pennsylvania State University Press, 1997.

Huntingdon, Patricia J. *Ecstatic Subjects, Utopia, and Recognition: Kristeva, Heidegger, Irigaray*. Albany, NY: State University of New York Press, 1998.

Irigaray, Luce. *An Ethics of Sexual Difference*. Translated by Carolyn Burke and Gillian Gill. New York: Cornell University Press, 1993. (Originally published as *Ethique de la difference sexuelle*. Paris: Les Edition de Minuit, 1984.)

———. "Being Two, How Many Eyes Have We?" *Paragraph* 25.3 (2002) 143–51.

———. *Between East and West: From Singularity to Community*. Translated by Stephen Pluháček. New York: Columbia University Press, 2002. (Originally published as *Entre Orient et Occident*. Paris: Editions Grasset et Fasquelle, 1999.)

———. *Democracy Begins between Two*. Translated by Kirsteen Anderson. London: Athlone, 2000. (Originally published as *La democrazia comincia a due*. Torino: Bollati-Boringhieri, 1994.)

———. *Elemental Passions*. Translated by Joanne Collie and Judith Still. New York: Routledge, 1992. (Originally published as *Passions élémentaires*. Paris: Les Edition de Minuit, 1982.)

Bibliography

———. "From *The Forgetting of Air* to *To Be Two.*" In *Feminist Interpretations of Heidegger*, edited by Nancy J. Holland and Patricia Huntingdon, translated by Heidi Bostic and Stephen P uháček, 309–15. University Park, PA: Pennsylvania State University Press, 2001.

———. *I Love to You: Sketch of a Possible Felicity in History*. Translated by Alison Martin. New York: Routledge, 1996. (Originally published as *J'aime à toi, Esquisse d'une félicité dan l'Histoire*. Paris: Grasset, 1992.)

———. *Key Writings*. New York: Continuum, 2004.

———. "Questions to Emmanuel Levinas: On the Divinity of Love." In *Re-Reading Levinas*, edited by Robert Bernasconi and Simon Critchley, 109–18. Indianapolis, IN: Indiana University Press, 1991.

———. *Sexes and Genealogies*. Translated by Gillian C. Gill. New York: Columbia University Press, 1993. (Originally published as *Sexes et parentés*. Paris: Editions de Minuit, 1987.)

———. *Sharing the World*. New York: Continuum, 2008.

———. *Speculum of Another Woman*. Translated by Gillian C. Gill. Ithaca, NY: Cornell University Press, 1985. (Originally published as *Speculum de l'autre femme*. Paris: Editions de Minuit, 1974.)

———. *The Way of Love*. Translated by Heidi Bostic and Stephen Pluháček. London: Continuum, 2002. (Originally written as *La Voie de l'amour*. Not yet published in French.)

———. *Thinking the Difference: For a Peaceful Revolution*. Translated by Karin Montin. New York: Routledge, 1994. (Originally published as *Le Temps De La Différence: Pour une revolution pacifique*. Paris: Librairie Général Française, 1989.)

———. *This Sex Which is Not One*. Translated by Catherine Porter and Carolyn Burke. Ithaca, NY: Cornell University Press, 1985. (Originally published as *Ce Sexe qui n'en est pas un*. Paris: Editions de Minuit, 1977.)

———. *To Be Two*. Translated by Monique M. Rhodes and Marco F. Cocito-Monoc. New York: Routledge, 2002. (Originally published as *Essere Due*. Torino: Bollati-Boringhieri, 1994.)

———. *To Speak is Never Neutral*. Translated by Gail Schwab. New York: Routledge, 2002. (Originally published as *Parler n'est jamais neutre*. Paris. Les Editions de Minuit, 1985.)

———. "Why Cultivate Difference." *Paragraph* 25.3 (2002) 79–90.

Irigaray, Luce, and Sylvère Lotringer. *Why Different: A Culture of Two Subjects: Interviews with Luce Irigaray*. Translated by Camille Collins et al. New York: Semiotexte(e), 2000.

Johansen, Kjell Eyvind. "The Problem of Knowledge in the Ethics of Kierkegaard's *Works of Love*." In *Kierkegaardiana*, Vol. 17, edited by Joakim Garff et al., 52–65. Copenhagen: Reitzel, 1994.

John Paul II. *The Theology of the Body: Human Love in the Divine Plan*. Boston: Pauline Books and Media, 1997.

Jones, Serene. "Divine Women: Irigaray and Feminist Theologies." *Yale French Studies* 87 (1995) 42–67.

———. *Feminist Theory and Christian Theology: Cartographies of Grace*. Minneapolis, MN: Augsburg Fortress, 2000.

———. "This God Which Is Not One: Irigaray and Barth on the Divine." In *Transfigurations*, edited by C. W. Maggie Kim et al., 109–41. Minneapolis, MN: Fortress, 1993.

Joy, Morny. "Divine Love." *Paragraph* 21.1 (2000) 189–203.
Katz, Claire Elise. "'For Love is as Strong as Death': Taking Another Look at Levinas on Love." *Philosophy Today* 45.5 (2001) 124–32.
Keltner, Stacy. "The Ethics of Air: Technology and the Question of Sexual Difference." *Philosophy Today* 45.5 (2001) 53–65.
Kierkegaard, Søren. *Concluding Unscientific Postscript to Philosophical Fragments.* Edited and Translated by Howard V. Hong and Edna H. Hong. Princeton, NJ: Princeton University Press, 1992.
———. *Eighteen Upbuilding Discourses.* Edited and translated by Howard V. Hong and Edna H. Hong. Princeton, NJ: Princeton University Press, 1990.
———. *Either/Or,* Volumes 1 and 2. Edited and translated by Howard V. Hong and Edna H. Hong. Princeton, NJ: Princeton University Press, 1987.
———. *The Point of View for My Work as An Author: A Report To History.* Edited by Benjamin Nelson and Translated by Walter Lowrie. New York: Harper, 1962.
———. *Practice in Christianity.* Edited and translated by Howard V. Hong and Edna H. Hong. Princeton, NJ: Princeton University Press, 1991.
———. *The Sickness Unto Death.* Edited and translated by Howard V. Hong and Edna H. Hong. Princeton, NJ: Princeton University Press, 1980.
———. *Two Ages: The Age of Revolution and the Present Age: A Literary Review.* Edited and translated by Howard V. Hong and Edna H. Hong. Princeton, NJ: Princeton University Press, 1978.
———. *Upbuilding Discourses in Various Spirits.* Edited and translated by Howard V. Hong and Edna H. Hong. Princeton, NJ: Princeton University Press, 1992.
———. *Works of Love,* Edited and translated by Howard V. Hong and Edna H. Hong. Princeton, NJ: Princeton University Press, 1995.
Kirmmse, Bruce H. *Kierkegaard in Golden Age Denmark.* Bloomington, IN: Indiana University Press, 1990.
La Caze, Marguerite. "The Encounter between Wonder and Generosity." *Hypatia* 17.3 (2002) 1–19.
———. "Love, that Indispensable Supplement: Irigaray and Kant on Love and Respect." *Hypatia* 20.3 (2005) 92–114.
Law, David. "The Place, Role, and Function of the 'Ultimatum' of *Either/Or,* Part Two in Kierkegaard's Pseudonymous Writings." In *International Kierkegaard Commentary: Either/Or, Part II,* edited by Robert L. Perkins, 233–57. Macon, GA: Mercer University Press, 1995.
Lawler, Michael G. "Marriage as Covenant in the Catholic Tradition." In *Covenant Marriage in Comparative Perspective,* edited by John Witte and Eliza Ellison, 70–91. Grand Rapids: Eerdmans, 2005.
Léon, Céline. "The (In-)Appropriateness of Using the Feminine as Paradigm: The Case of Kierkegaard." *Philosophy Today* 44.4 (2000) 339–46.
———. "The No Woman's Land of Kierkegaardian Seduction." In *International Kierkegaard Commentary: Either/Or, Part I,* edited by Robert L. Perkins, 229–50. Macon, GA: Mercer University Press, 1995.
———. "(A) Woman's Place within the Ethical." In *Feminist Interpretations of Søren Kierkegaard,* edited by Céline Léon and Sylvia Walsh, 103–30. University Park, PA: The Pennsylvania State University Press, 1997.
Levinas, Emmanuel. *Totality and Infinity.* Translated by Alphonso Lingis. Pittsburgh, PA: Duquesne University Press, 1969.

Bibliography

Lincoln, Ulrich. "Belief and Hope as Action in Søren Kierkegaard's *Works of Love*." In *Religion in a Pluralistic Age*, edited by Donald A. Crosby and Charley D. Hardwick, 217–30. New York: Lang, 2001.

Løgstrup, Knud Ejler. *The Ethical Demand*. Translated by Theodor I. Jensen. Philadelphia: Fortress, 1971.

Lorraine, Tamsin. "Amatory Cures for Material Dis-Ease: A Kristevian Reading of *The Sickness unto Death*." In *Kierkegaard in Post/Modernity*, edited by Martin J. Matuštík and Merold Westphal, 98–109. Bloomington, IN: Indiana University Press, 1995.

Mackey, Louis. *Kierkegaard: A Kind of Poet*. Philadelphia, PA: University of Pennsylvania Press, 1971.

Mader, Mary Beth. "All Too Familiar: Luce Irigaray's Recent Thought on Sexuation and Generation." *Continental Philosophy Review* 36.4 (2003) 367–90.

Malantschuk, Gregor. *The Controversial Kierkegaard*. Translated by. Howard V. Hong and Edna H. Hong. Waterloo ON: Laurier, 1980.

Marshall, Bruce D. *Trinity and Truth*. Cambridge: Cambridge University Press, 2000.

Martens, Paul. "The Equivocal Judge William: Comparing the Ethical in Kierkegaard's *Stages on Life's Way* and *Either/Or*." In *International Kierkegaard Commentary: Stages on Life's Way*, edited by Robert L. Perkins, 91–112. Macon, GA: Mercer University Press, 2000.

Martin, Alison. "A European Initiative: Irigaray, Marx, and Citizenship." *Hypatia* 19.3 (2004) 20–37.

———. "Introduction: Luce Irigaray and the Culture of Difference." *Theory, Culture and Society* 20.3 (2003) 1–12.

———. "Luce Irigaray and the Adoption of Christianity." *Paragraph* 21.1 (2000) 101–20.

———. *Luce Irigaray and the Question of the Divine*. London: Maney, 2000.

Matthis, Michael. "Kierkegaard and the Problem of the Social Other." *Philosophy Today* 38.4 (1994) 419–39.

McDonald, Dana Noelle. "Moving beyond the Face through Eros: Levinas and Irigaray's Treatment of the Woman as an Alterity." *Philosophy Today* 42 (1998, supplement) 71–75.

Mehl, Peter. *Thinking through Kierkegaard: Existential Identity in a Pluralistic World*. Chicago: University of Illinois Press, 2005.

Miller, Elaine P. "Freedom and the Ethics of the Couple: Irigaray, Hegel, and Schelling." *Philosophy Today* 48.2 (2004) 128–47.

———. *The Vegetative Soul: From Philosophy of Nature to Subjectivity in the Feminine*. Albany, NY: State University of New York Press, 2002.

Mooney, Edward F. "Kierkegaard on Self-Choice and Self-Reception: Judge William's Admonition." In *International Kierkegaard Commentary: Either/Or, Part II*, edited by Robert L. Perkins, 5–32. Macon, GA: Mercer University Press, 1995.

Mortensen, Ellen. *The Feminine and Nihilism: Luce Irigaray with Nietzsche and Heidegger*. Oslo: Scandinavian University Press, 1994.

Müller, Paul. *Kierkegaard's Works of Love: Christian Ethics and Maieutic Ideal*. Edited and translated by C. Stephen Evans and Jan Evans. Copenhagen: Reitzel, 1993.

Murphy, Ann V. "The Enigma of the Natural in Luce Irigaray." *Philosophy Today* 45.5 (2001) 75–82.

O'Donovan, Oliver. *Resurrection and Moral Order: An Outline for Evangelical Ethics*. Grand Rapids: Eerdmans, 1986

Bibliography

Oliver, Kelly. "The Look of Love." *Hypatia* 16.3 (2001) 56–78.
———. "Paternal Election and the Absent Father." In *Feminist Interpretations of Emmanuel Levinas*, edited by Tina Chanter, 224–40. University Park, PA: Pennsylvania State University Press, 2001.
———. "Vision, Recognition, and a Passion for the Elements." In *Returning to Irigaray: Feminist Philosophy, Politics, and the Question of Unity*, edited by Maria C. Cimitile and Elaine P. Miller, 121–36. Albany, NY: State University of New York Press, 2007.
O'Siadhail, Micheal. "Beyond." In *A Fragile City*. Highgreen, UK: Bloodaxe, 1995.
———. "Roofing." In *Poems 1975–1995*. Highgreen, UK: Bloodaxe, 1999.
Pattison, George. *Kierkegaard on Art and Communication*. New York: St. Martins Press, 1992.
Pattison, George, and Steven Shakespeare. *Kierkegaard: The Self in Society*. New York: St. Martin's, 1998.
Perkins, Robert L. "*Either/Or/Or:* Giving the Parson His Due." In *International Kierkegaard Commentary: Either/Or, Part II*, edited by Robert L. Perkins, 207–31. Macon, GA: Mercer University Press, 1995.
Perpich, Diane. "From the Caress to the Word: Transcendence and the Feminine in the Philosophy of Emmanuel Levinas." In *Feminist Interpretations of Emmanuel Levinas*, edited by Tina Chanter, 28–52. University Park, PA: Pennsylvania State University Press, 2001.
———. "Subjectivity and Sexual Difference: New Figures of the Feminine in Irigaray and Caverero." *Continental Philosophy Review* 36.4 (2003) 391–413.
———. "Sensible Subjects: Levinas and Irigaray on Incarnation and Ethics." In *Addressing Levinas*, edited by Eric Sean Nelson et al., 296–309. Evanston, IL: Northwestern University Press, 2005.
Piper, Henry B. "Kierkegaard's Non-Dialectical Dialectic or That Kierkegaard is not Hegelian." *International Philosophical Quarterly* 44.4 (2004) 497–517.
Pippin, Robert B. "What is the Question for which Hegel's Theory of Recognition is the Answer?" *European Journal of Philosophy* 8.2 (2000) 155–72.
Plekon, Michael. "Kierkegaard the Theologian: The Roots of His Theology." In *Works of Love*." In *Foundations of Kierkegaard's Vision of Community: Religion, Ethics, and Politics in Kierkegaard*, edited by George B. Connell and C. Stephen Evans, 2–17. New Jersey: Humanities, 1992.
Poole, Roger. *Kierkegaard: The Indirect Communication*. Charlottesville, VA: University Press of Virginia, 1993.
———. "Reading *Either-Or* for the Very First Time." In *The New Kierkegaard*, edited by Elsebet Jegstrup, 42–59. Bloomington, IN: Indiana University Press, 2004.
Quinn, Philip L. "Kierkegaard's Christian Ethics." In *The Cambridge Companion to Kierkegaard*, edited by Alastair Hannay and Gordon Marino, 349–75. Cambridge: Cambridge University Press, 1998.
Ricoeur, Paul. *Oneself as Another*. Translated by Kathleen Blamey. Chicago: University of Chicago Press, 1992.
Rudd, Anthony. "'Believing All Things': Kierkegaard on Knowledge, Doubt, and Love." In *International Kierkegaard Commentary: Works of Love*, edited by Robert L. Perkins, 121–36. Macon, GA: Mercer University Press, 1999.
———. *Kierkegaard and the Limits of the Ethical*. Oxford: Clarendon, 1993.
———. "Reason in Ethics: MacIntyre and Kierkegaard." In *Kierkegaard After MacIntyre*, edited by John Davenport and Anthony Rudd, 131–49. Chicago: Open Court, 2001.

Bibliography

Rumble, Vanessa. "Love and Difference: The Christian Ideal in Kierkegaard's *Works of Love*." In *The New Kierkegaard*, edited by Elsebet Jegstrup, 161–78. Bloomington, IN: Indiana University Press, 2004.

Russell, Helene Tallon. *Multiplicity and Internal Relationality: Groundwork for a Reconstruction of Selfhood from Kierkegaard and Irigaray*. PhD diss., Claremont Graduate School, 1997.

Salomonsen, Jone. "Love of Same, Love of Other: Reading Feminist Anthropologies with Luce Irigaray and Karl Barth." *Studia Theologica* 57.2 (2003) 103–23.

Sanford, Stella. "Levinas, Feminism and the Feminine." In *The Cambridge Companion to Levinas*, edited by Simon Critchley and Robert Bernasconi, 139–60. Cambridge: Cambridge University Press, 2002.

Sayers, Dorothy L. *Are Women Human?* Grand Rapids: Eerdmans, 1971.

Schwab, Gail. "Sexual Difference as Model: An Ethics for the Global Future." *Diacritics* 28.1 (1998) 76–92.

———. "Women and the Law in Irigarayan Theory." *Metaphilosophy* 27.1–2 (1996) 146–77.

Schor, Naomi. "This Essentialism Which Is Not One: Coming to Grips with Irigaray." In *The Essential Difference*, edited by Naomi Schor and Elizabeth Weed, 40–62. Bloomington, IN: Indiana University Press, 1994.

Schutte, Ofelia. "A Critique of Normative Heterosexuality: Identity, Embodiment, and Sexual Difference in Beauvoir and Irigaray." *Hypatia* 12.1 (1997) 40–62.

Shakespeare, Steven. *Kierkegaard, Language and the Reality of God*. Burlington, VT: Ashgate, 2001.

Siebert, Rudolph J. *Hegel's Concept of Marriage and Family: The Origin of Subjective Freedom*. Washington DC: University Press of America, 1979.

Sikka, Sonia. "The Delightful Other: Portraits of the Feminine in Kierkegaard, Nietzsche, and Levinas." In *Feminist Interpretations of Emmanuel Levinas*, edited by Tina Chanter, 96–118. University Park, PA: The Pennsylvania State University Press, 2001.

Sjöholm, Cecilia, "Crossing Lovers: Luce Irigaray's Elemental Passions." *Hypatia* 15.3 (2000) 92–112.

Soltoft, Pia. "Love and Continuity: The Significance of Intersubjectivity in the Second Part of *Either/Or*." In *Kierkegaard Studies Yearbook*, translated by M. G. Piety and edited by Niels Jørgen Cappelørn et al., 210–27. Berlin: de Gruyter, 1997.

———. "The Presence of the Absent Neighbour in *Works of Love*." In *Kierkegaard Studies Yearbook*, edited by Niels Jørgen Capellørn and Hermann Deuser, 113–28. Berlin, de Gruyter, 1998.

———. "To Let Oneself be Upbuilt." In *Kierkegaard Studies Yearbook*, edited by Niels Jørgen Cappelørn, 19–39. Berlin: De Gruyter, 2000.

Stewart, Jon. "Hegel's Doctrine of Determinate Negation: An Example from 'Sense-Certainty and Perception.'" *Idealistic Studies* 26.1 (1996) 57–78.

———. *The Unity of Hegel's Phenomenology of Spirit: A Systematic Interpretation*. Evanston, IL: Northwestern University Press, 2000.

Stone, Alison. "Feminist Criticisms and Reinterpretations of Hegel." *Bulletin of the Hegel Society of Great Britain* 45–46 (2002) 93–109.

———. "Irigaray and Hölderlin on the Relation between Nature and Culture." *Continental Philosophy Review* 35.4 (2003) 415–32.

———. *Luce Irigaray and the Philosophy of Sexual Difference*. Cambridge: Cambridge University Press, 2006.

———. "Sexing the State: Familial and Political Form in Irigaray and Hegel." *Radical Philosophy* 113 (2002) 24–36.
Taylor, Mark C. *Journeys to Selfhood*. Berkley, CA: University of California Press, 1980.
———. *Kierkegaard's Pseudonymous Authorship*. Princeton, NJ: Princeton University Press, 1975.
Trible, Phyllis. *God and the Rhetoric of Sexuality*. Philadelphia: Fortress, 1978.
Van Leeuwen, Mary Stewart et al. *After Eden: Facing the Challenge of Gender Reconciliation*. Grand Rapids: Eerdmans, 1993.
Vasseleu, Cathryn. *Textures of Light: Vision and Touch in Irigaray, Levinas, and Merleau-Ponty*. New York: Rougledge, 1998.
Walsh, Sylvia I. "Feminine Devotion and Self-Abandonment: Simone de Beauvoir and Søren Kierkegaard: On the Woman in Love." *Philosophy Today* 41 Suppl. (1998) 35–40.
———. *Living Poetically: Kierkegaard's Existential Ethics*. University Park, PA: Pennsylvania State University Press, 1994.
———. "On 'Feminine' and 'Masculine' Forms of Despair." In *Feminist Interpretations of Søren Kierkegaard*, edited by Céline Léon and Sylvia Walsh, 203–16. University Park, PA: The Pennsylvania State University Press, 1997.
———. Review of *Kierkegaard and the Treachery of Love*, by Amy Laura Hall. *The Journal of Religion* 83.4 (2003) 659–60.
———. "The Role of Love in Kierkegaard." In *The Grammar of the Heart: New Essays in Moral Philosophy and Theology*, edited by Richard H. Bell, 234–56. San Francisco: Harper and Row, 1988.
Ward, Graham. "Divinity and Sexuality: Luce Irigaray and Christology." *Modern Theology* 12.2 (1996) 221–37.
———. "The Erotics of Redemption." *Theology and Sexuality* 4.8 (1998) 52–72.
———. "In the Name of the Father and of the Mother." *Journal of Literature and Theology* 8.3 (1994) 311–27.
———. "A Postmodern Version of Paradise." *The Journal for the Study of the Old Testament* 20.65 (1995) 3–12.
———. *Theology and Contemporary Critical Theory*. New York: St. Martin's, 1996.
Watkin, Julia. "Judge William: A Christian?" In *International Kierkegaard Commentary: Either/Or, Part II*, edited by Robert L. Perkins, 113–24. Macon, GA: Mercer University Press, 1995.
Watson, Francis. *Agape, Eros, Gender: Towards a Pauline Sexual Ethic*. Cambridge: Cambridge University Press, 2000.
———. *Text, Church and World: Biblical Interpretation in Theological Perspective*. Grand Rapids: Eerdmans, 1994.
Westermann, Claus. *Genesis 1–11: A Commentary*. Translated by John J. Scullion S.J. Minneapolis, MN: Augsburg, 1974.
Westphal, Kenneth. "The Basic Context and Structure of Hegel's Philosophy of Right." In *The Cambridge Companion to Hegel*, edited by Frederick C. Beiser, 234–69. Cambridge: Cambridge University Press, 1993.
Westphal, Merold. *Becoming a Self: A Reading of Kierkegaard's Concluding Unscientific Postscript*. West Lafayette, IN: Purdue University Press, 1994.
———. "Kierkegaard and Hegel." In *The Cambridge Companion to Kierkegaard*, edited by Alastair Hannay and Gordon Marino, 110–24. Cambridge: Cambridge University Press, 1998.

Bibliography

———. "Kierkegaard's Religiousness C: A Defense." *International Philosophical Quarterly* 44.4 (2004) 535–43.

———. "Kierkegaard's Sociology." In *International Kierkegaard Commentary: Two Ages*, edited by Robert L. Perkins, 133–54. Macon, GA: Mercer University Press, 1984.

———. "Kierkegaard's Teleological Suspension of Religiousness B." In *Foundations of Kierkegaard's Vision of Community*, edited by George B. Connell and C. Stephen Evans, 110–29. New Jersey: Humanities, 1992.

White, Richard. "Elemental Passions and the Nature of Love." *Philosophy Today* 43.1 (1999) 43–48.

Whitford, Margaret. *The Irigaray Reader: Luce Irigaray*. Oxford: Blackwell, 1991.

———. "Irigaray, Utopia, and the Death Drive." In *Engaging with Irigaray: Feminist Philosophy and Modern European Thought*, edited by Carolyn Burke et al., 379–400. New York: Columbia University Press, 1994.

———. *Luce Irigaray: Philosophy in the Feminine*. New York: Routledge, 1991.

Williams, Roger R. *Hegel's Ethics of Recognition*. Berkeley, CA: University of California Press, 1997.

Wirth, Jason. "Empty Community: Kierkegaard on Being with You." In *The New Kierkegaard*, edited by Elsebet Jegstrup, 214–23. Bloomington, IN: Indiana University Press, 2004.

Witte, John. *From Sacrament to Contract: Marriage, Religion, and Law in the Western Tradition*. Louisville, KY: Westminster John Knox, 1997.

Witte, John, and Robert M. Kingdon. *Sex, Marriage, and Family in John Calvin's Geneva*, Vol. 1. Grand Rapids: Eerdmans, 2005.

Wood, Allen. *Hegel's Ethical Thought*. Cambridge: Cambridge University Press, 1991.

———. "Hegel's Ethics." In *The Cambridge Companion to Hegel*, edited by Frederick C. Beiser, 211–33. Cambridge: Cambridge University Press, 1993.

Ziarek, Krzysztof. "A New Economy of Relations." In *Returning to Irigaray: Feminist Philosophy, Politics, and the Question of Unity*, edited by Maria C. Cimitile and Elaine P. Miller, 51–74. Albany, NY: State University of New York Press, 2007.

———. "Proximities: Irigaray and Heidegger on Difference." *Continental Philosophy Review* 33.2 (2000) 133–58.

Index

actual and ideal, 124–27, 145–46, 156–67, 176–80, 184–88, 194, 206, 219
aesthetic, 108, 115, 120–24, 127–31, 134, 144, 215
air, 27–28, 55–66
anti-natural mode of life, 12, 14, 18–19, 23, 63, 151, 162
appropriation and possession, 26, 53, 60, 72–73, 107, 196, 207–8, 218
autonomy, 28, 55, 60–61, 105, 120, 218–19

binary logic, 12, 151–55
bond servant, 72–73, 77, 104, 133
boundaries, 41–42, 49–53, 58, 187, 198

caress, 33, 47–55, 151, 185–89, 195, 198
    risk in, 51, 188
certainty of knowledge, 24, 174–75, 214, 218
child
    and unity of the couple, 6, 8–10, 52, 65, 202
    and relation to the mother, 15–19, 24–25, 45, 160
choosing
    despair, 116–19
    oneself, 115–32
    the natural self, 121, 154, 162
    the social self, 119–22, 161–62

Colledge, Richard, 157–58
collision, 70–71, 75–76
communication in Kierkegaard, 169, 177, 204, 208–19
    fraud in, 213
confidence with God and other, 199, 201, 219
Connell, George, 133
cosmos, bipolarity of, 19–21, 160–62

dash, the, 93–94
despair of finitude and infinitude, 118–20, 125–26, 145, 152–54, 178, 187
Deutscher, Penelope, 17, 26, 35, 39–46, 156–57, 177
diabolic, the, 63
dialogue, 54, 63–65, 205
distinctiveness, 89–95, 102–6, 172–73, 178–79, 183–92, 207, 218–19
divine in Irigaray, 29, 34, 51, 61–62, 157, 193
divine likeness, 74–75, 83–84, 86, 104, 187
domineering person, 90–93, 106, 184, 191
double reflection, 209–11
duty, 8, 85, 103, 106, 127–30, 163

elemental, the, 27–28, 55–59
equality, 26, 74–75, 84–85, 110, 114, 187–88

233

Index

erotic, the, 185–86
   in Irigaray, 48–55
   in Kierkegaard, 82–88, 102–3, 129, 143
ethical, the, 115–31, 132–50, 165, 214
Evans, C. Stephen, 53, 88, 104, 169–70, 179, 209–15

fecundity, 27–33, 51–52, 65–66, 186, 196, 198, 206
fluidity, 21–22, 55, 160, 162
friendship, 70, 75–76, 82–88, 92, 102, 105–7, 143

gap, the, 5, 15, 25, 31–32, 38, 56, 176–78, 200, 206–7, 216–19
genre, sexuate, 12, 14, 40–46, 163, 167
God
   relationship to, 70–81, 86, 88, 94, 103–7, 140–41, 173, 176, 186–87, 199–201, 212–13, 218–19
   adoration of, 77–79, 135, 139

Hegel, G. W. F., 4–12, 32, 61, 153
Holy Spirit, 78, 135, 169

imagination, 124–26, 145, 155–56
indirect communication in Kierkegaard, 208–17
indirection in Irigaray, 203–8
infinite indebtedness, 73–74, 141

Jylland Pastor, 138–41

language use in children, 16–17, 45–47
Levinas, Emmanuel, 48, 51
like for like, 90, 137
love as devotion and sacrifice, 70–71, 76

Mackey, Louis, 128, 131, 134, 137
marriage, 102–3, 114–15, 126–32, 142–43, 152
metaphysical realism, 19–22, 159, 162
middle term, Christ or God as, 69–81, 89, 99, 103–6, 167–70, 201

nature and culture, 6–7, 10–14, 18–24, 27–29, 46, 50, 53, 66, 150–54, 162–63
natural immediacy, 6–14, 54
negative, the, 4–35, 48, 52–53, 65, 153, 175–76
negativity in Climacus, 174
neighbor love, 75–94, 99–107, 136, 143–46, 170–72, 183–87, 191–92, 216, 219

origin, the, 15–19

palms, 50–53, 186, 188
particular. *See* universal and particular
preferential relationships, 82–88, 102–7, 143, 186
presupposing love, 96–106
procreation, 10, 51–52, 103, 106
prototype, Jesus Christ as, 137, 145–46, 165–70, 177–79, 185, 206, 215–19

redeemer, Jesus Christ as, 135–36
redoubling, 80–81, 192
repentance, 120, 137, 161
respiration, 56, 59–63
rhythm(s), 20–22, 46–47, 162–64, 178, 189

same, logic of the, 23, 26, 42–44, 52, 57, 110, 159, 163, 193, 217
Schwab, Gail, 23–24

self-control, 14, 36, 65, 94, 99, 102, 107, 194, 217
self-love, 27–36, 79–88, 99, 102–7, 189–95
  woman's, 31–36
  man's, 31–36
sensate-psychical, 89, 92–97, 144, 183
sensible transcendental, 27–28, 32, 53, 59, 63, 185, 198
sexual difference
  according to Judge William, 108–47
  Irigaray's theory of, 15–22
  transparency of, 41–46, 114, 161
sexuate rights, 24, 34, 50
silence, 35, 53–55, 62–65
small-minded person, 89–93, 106, 184, 191
spiritual, the (in Irigaray), 6–13, 18, 21, 27–28, 51–52, 54, 59–66, 154–55, 190, 197
Stone, Alison, 15, 18, 19–22, 37, 162

touching upon, 54, 188–89
transcendence, horizontal, 24–29, 31–32, 53, 56, 206
two lips, 30–31

unity of the couple, 6–10, 196–202
universal and particular, 13, 24, 30, 74–75, 83–86, 121–30, 134, 141–43, 158–63, 167, 187
upbuilding, 94–102, 106, 137, 139–40, 170

violence, 14, 18–19

Walsh, Sylvia, 115, 117, 192
Wetphal, Merold, 74, 145–46, 174–75, 208–9
whole, the, 5, 7, 10–13, 18, 25, 29, 31, 54, 196–99
wonder, 38–48, 59, 164–67, 178, 205

www.ingramcontent.com/pod-product-compliance
Lightning Source LLC
Chambersburg PA
CBHW050851230426
43667CB00012B/2239